RV THE WORLD

Courtesy of NASA

DAVID RICH

R V

THE

WORLD

DAVID RICH
COPYRIGHT 2009

Preface, Acknowledgement and Caveat

The travelogue portion of this book covers less than three years Rving Europe, a tiny part of the 16 years the author and his wife have RVed the World, and we're not done yet. See our Websites at http://mytripjournal.com/RichWorld.

The author acknowledges his wife, Mary Alexon, as an integral stabilizer in his world travels, whether by RV or sailboat, by public or private transport. Gadzooks, what patience and perseverance.

The precise details of costs must continually be revised upwards, and up and up and up. The expenses and prices reported here were accurate when incurred but necessarily bear no resemblance to current prices in any country on earth, primarily because of the continually sinking U.S. dollar, eradicable inflation and the inevitable passage of time. In addition, cited websites may lamentably cease to exist but will likely be replaced by even better ones, ceding control of the planet to those who Google. Also customs duties and regulations change like topsy; the customs duties we've suffered in various countries may have changed radically, ameliorated by the recent wave of trade treaties, or worsened by protectionism during the recent financial slump.

CONTENTS

CHAPTER THIRTEEN

CHAPTER FOURTEEN

CHAPTER SEVENTEEN

Living on Investments, Taxes and Voting 147

CHAPTER EIGHTEEN

Save a Mint on Airfare 150

CHAPTER TWENTY TWO

You Can Only RV the World if You Hang onto Your Health   165

RV THE WORLD

*For my part, I travel not to go
anywhere, but to go. I travel for
travel's sake. The great affair is to move; to
feel the needs and hitches of our life more
nearly; to come down off this feather-bed of
civilization, and find the globe
granite underfoot and strewn with
cutting flints.* **Robert Louis Stevenson**

CHAPTER ONE
The Monkey on My Back: To See It All

My earliest vivid memory was a photo from an old geography-book: Vesuvius in full-color eruption spewing fluorescent orange magma, burying rich Romans in Pompeii and Herculaneum, striking me between the eyes. *Whoa. I really had to see that in person.* What four-year-old wouldn't?

I could never kick this early memory, which evolved into a recurrent dream of seeing the world, the whole lot of it. I simply had to find the most interesting volcanoes and countries, curiosity spurred by school-teacher parents with a fixation on travel and geography. Call me doomed from the start, bereft of alternatives and required by heritage to see the whole entire world or die trying.

But I found that continuous world travel isn't so tough or dangerous and dying likely isn't on, with the possible exception of touring the hotted-up portions of those countries actively at war. This world travel addiction was aggravated by a stay-at-home aversion, seeking more enchantment than a daily commute past the neighborhood McDonalds Restaurant.

I nagged long-suffering parents to drive down every road, reasoning as a pre-kindergartener that we might stumble across Vesuvius most anywhere. Humoring the four-year-old they drove down lots of roads, mostly dirt with many ending on the edges of deep canyons in Colorado, New Mexico, Utah and Arizona, the Four Corners area where I grew up. They'd brought it on themselves, infecting me with a travel and geography obsession, insisting in return for my see-the-end-of-every-road harassment that I learn context, all the states and capitals, crushed to find Vesuvius nowhere near the Four Corner's Monument.

Umpteen years later I've lived in 147 countries, not a difficult task for a homeless rolling stone. After sixteen years fulltime international travel and decades of sporadic gallivanting, while allegedly working, I've seen three-quarters of the world's countries and 90% of its area in depth. That's enough so far because it leaves places to go next year. With 191 countries in the United Nations and over 200 in the Olympics there are countries left to explore and people to see, new photo opportunities for bombarding myriad inboxes.

The best places on earth are difficult to tally because everyone likes different things. There's no accounting for tastes, or lack thereof. You may like beaches while I rather don't, working and living in Arizona, dodging the sun for decades. Instead I love national parks, mountains and natural wonders, living my first twenty some years in Colorado. If required to list a single wonder from each continent I'd be hard pressed. However, there are eight or ten splendors for each landmass that I can highly recommend, where I hope to return, to see how they've fared in the interim. I found in 2007 Morocco that you can't go back again, to the same country you saw years before. It's disappeared and gone, replaced by a remarkably different place.

Perhaps Europe conjures Paris in springtime, or Viennese pastries, or the Alps, Algarve and Absinthe. The highlights of three years RVing Europe, details later, were the fjords and Lofoten Islands of Norway, the Scottish highlands and lochs, the Picos de Europa in northwest Spain with perhaps the world's best blue cheese, the Greek ruins of Sicily, kitschy Malta, Greek Monasteries, Turkish baths and hospitality, Guinness on tap in Ireland, Scottish lochs, Belgium's Venice-like Brugge and medieval Ghent, most everything in Italy, former Yugoslavia's Marco-Polo-Dalmatian coast and fabulous friends and places in Holland. That's old Europe with years of travel lore omitted.

The undiscovered continent is South America, where we spent two years RVing and which offers more natural wonders than Bayer does aspirin. From the world's highest waterfall, Angel in Venezuela, to the world's largest and most incredible waterfall, Iguaçu bordering Argentina and Brazil, two miles from Paraguay, and most of the world's expanding and clean glaciers in Perito Merino Parque Nacional Glacieres, far south in Argentina's Patagonia, to fantastically photogenic Torres Del Paine in Patagonian Chile, this is South America. Perito Merino includes ethereal Mt. Fitzroy, named after the commander of HMS Beagle, and icebergs bobbing down Lago Argentino, and even further south, Tierra del Fuego, the Beagle Channel and Ushuaia, the world's southernmost city and the jumping-off place for Antarctica. My favorite hike in the entire world is up Roraima tepui in Venezuela where Brazil, Guyana and Venezuela intersect, with more indigenous species than the Galapagos, which are definitely don't-miss islands. The question remains: does South America contain the world's most picturesque country or most perfect volcano?

This barely scratches the surface of South America's nigh inexhaustible wonders, omitting Machu Picchu, the Cordilleras Blanca and Huayhuash in Peru, the death roads of Bolivia, its incredible Uyuni salt flats and colorful lakes, not to mention enchanting Sajama and the border crossing into Chile where twin-volcanic peaks perfectly reflect in alpine lakes, shores pocked with alpaca.

South America would be perfect except for the poverty that encourages disparate desperados in the sprawling urban areas of a few countries, easily made safe if traveled sensibly and with care.

The safest continent is expansive and diverse Asia with its fascinating cultures and cuisines. Asia's incredible jumble of countries laces the continent into an unimaginable potpourri of utter enchantment, very picturesque. But before going I had no interest in Asia until we decided China was must-see. We figured, *Going all that way why not look at the possibilities in the neighborhood?*, so we did and loved it.

We found exotic Thailand with cuisine, temples and people to pine for, tragic Cambodia embellished by Angkor Wat, laidback Laos and beleaguered Myanmar (required to say, *formerly Burma*) with enchanting Bagan (Pagan) and Mandalay where the Mustache Brothers busily 'dissed the military regime. Don't miss surprising Vietnam with short memories of minor wars, cobras in wine and so much more, all indelible. After the first trip I returned to Thailand yearly for routine medical check-ups at my favorite hospital on the planet and for Bangkok's October film festival, always on the way to somewhere in the neighborhood, whether Tibet, Nepal, Pakistan, India, Malaysia, Indonesia or the Stans, former Russian republics.

How about Africa? For some grotesque reason people shy away from Africa. There's little to be shy of outside of two nasty cities, Johannesburg and Nairobi. The rest of Africa, all 56 countries (excluding these two cities that are only dangerous at night), is relatively safe and fairly easy to get about, seeing ultra-close-up. Africa offers gems: the rock-hewn churches of Ethiopia with its wild mountains, ancient tribes and lovely Lalibela; kick-back opportunities in South Africa, especially Cape Town and the south coast with its wine country and wild surf; the easy environs of Namibia with colorful and incredible desert dunes, and Botswana with the phenomenal Okavango Swamp. That's almost all the way up to Victoria Falls on the border between Zimbabwe, innocuous for tourists, and very civilized Zambia with several great game parks. Then it's easy to drive up friendly Malawi via the shores of rift-valley Lake Malawi to the paradise of Tanzania. Vying for the top spot with Mali, Egypt and Morocco, Tanzania offers one of the longest lists of top incredible places in Africa: the Ngorongoro Crater, a perfect subterranean caldera stuffed with Africa's finest big game animals, flamingos and much more, the Serengeti, Mt. Kilimanjaro and Zanzibar.

Go to Morocco before it's too late, before it becomes more Europe-south than it already is. And don't miss incredible Mali: take the Niger River trip to Timbuktu; check out what's likely the world's oldest market aged 1000s of years at D'Jenne and the largest mud mosque, culminating in a few-day hike through the mind-boggling Dogon culture. And there's so much more in Africa, including Tunisia, Egypt and Togo, vast swatches as safe as where you live now.

You can do the same as I did on every continent and better, catering to your own interests, which may include beaches. The best beaches in the world, if that means the whitest sand, most translucent waters, cleanest and most deserted, are the 365 islands of the San Blas, an autonomous refuge in the Panamanian Caribbean, one of the few areas in the Americas fully administered by indigenous, except in the Canadian Arctic. I exclude Africa where corrupt governments and military officials are perfectly indigenous.

There are plenty of ways to travel the world and excluding one, they come up remarkably short of pleasant. My wife, Mary, says I should more diplomatically say, *leave much to be desired*. I always listen to what Mary says, which is an essential key to harmonious international travel, though on occasion she has suggested I'm obliviously hard-of-hearing.

The choices of how to travel the world range from the easiest and most boring **tours**, through the most fattening and shallow **cruises**, to the most back-breaking **back-packing**, to **sailing** with lots of work, tedious problems, iffy weather and inconvenient repairs, and lastly, severely limited **package deals**. When I suggest the best way to see the world you'll laugh like some did when an Arkansas governor moved into a double-wide trailer while his mansion was being renovated, go Huck. The best way to see the world, up-close and intimate, is by RV. Mary agrees.

Sailing around the World: You Must Be Nuts

I started by wanting to sail around the world. People said, *but you live in Arizona. There's no water, except a few ridiculous lakes.* By then everyone knew I'd gone starkers, including Mary, but she gradually and contagiously contracted the insatiable wanderlust encouraged by my parents.

An outlet for itchy feet suddenly appeared when I was teaching at the local law school. A student said, *hey, come on. Help me try out my new sailboat.*

That day one of Arizona's many lakes became a scene of high comedy. By 10 a.m. we finally got the pole up. I later learned it was called the mast. Though we scooted down the lake in half an hour, down wind, it took until sunset to get back, cursing gods whose proper names we didn't know—the gods of tacking, coming about and shifting winds. I was indelibly hooked.

After a few months of intermittent torture on my student-friend's Hobie Cat, including six crazy days down the Mexican coast from Puerto Penasco to Bahia Kino, I finally enrolled—along with Mary—in a learn-to-sail course at the Annapolis Sailing School in San Diego. Then I tackled the advanced sailing course, which theoretically qualified me to bareboat charter.

Between bouts of simulated work I captained seventeen charters in exotic locations worldwide, from Greece, Turkey and Yugoslavia to the world's fair in Vancouver, fantastic off-shore Belize and most of the Bahamas and Caribbean islands. It was my responsibility to find a proper sailing vessel (best price), set up the charter, organize disorganized friends during bouts of personal disorganization and then, once we arrived at the destination, find water, fuel and a likely place to moor or anchor each night. I half-way learned to cruise a dozen different sailboats, while my accompanying friends eagerly split the small, total expense—$300 each for two weeks—for the pleasure of crewing off California, Mexico, Belize, British Columbia, many Caribbean islands, Yugoslavia, Greece and Turkey. Aren't friends fabulous?

The second most glorious day of my life was buying a dream boat to sail around the world: I called her *Grendel*. Mary and I spent years flying on weekends from Phoenix to San Diego, putting every toy aboard from mast steps to radar to a water-maker. After saving every penny on a ten-year plan that took eleven elongated years the big day arrived when I sold everything and sailed *Grendel* out of San Diego harbor.

It quickly became abundantly clear that Dave and Mary sailing around the world was not exactly as it appeared when Michael Douglas and Kathleen Turner sailed into the sunset, living his dream, in *Romancing the Stone.* No, life on *Grendel* was more about *la problema del dia,* the problem of the day, especially for someone who'd flunked grade school shop and was the least mechanically minded in the history of the Montezuma County public school system in Cortez, Colorado. To sail around the world you not only need to know how to sail but also how to fix stuff, all the stuff, including mechanical, electrical and the amount of baksheesh needed to coax replacement parts through foreign customs.

Hollywood had done me a disservice or perhaps like those guys who collect international airports I was a dope. After a year we were still in Mexico, though rather far down the Pacific Coast. As the specter loomed closer, thirty to forty days crossing open ocean to the Marquesas and Tuamotos Islands, I faced up to my terminal ineptness with a multi-meter and a monkey wrench and Mary admitted to hating unending oceans with no horizon. For her, as a compulsive jogger, the deck was too small for laps. We turned north to San Diego where I experienced my most glorious day, selling *Grendel.*

The True Beginning

By no means was this the end of a dream but instead the true beginning. Living on a sailboat relegated us, two non-beach persons, to the coast, while ninety percent of what there is to see is inland. We found sailing the consummate way to spend time fixing stuff in exotic ports, leaving little time for interesting exploration.

We began international RVing in 1994, flying to Germany, buying an RV with the proceeds from *Grendel* and living the next three years in forty countries—summers in the United Kingdom and Ireland, Norway and Scandinavia, with winters in Spain, Portugal and Morocco, Italy where I finally saw Vesuvius not erupting, along with more Greece and Turkey, Israel, Jordan and Egypt, plus all the countries in between. Sixteen years later we're still RVing the world where we can, which is most places.

Pity those who cruise U.S. interstates from retirement to demise. They're missing the world, the other 190 out of the 191 countries in the United Nations, a world they could easily see and experience. Or pity me because I'm forced to travel incessantly, insatiably curious about other places and people, interested in new sights and cultures, cramming the inboxes of friends and relatives with digital pictures, poor, long-suffering souls.

I'm doing what I most like to do: travel, photography, writing books and adventure travel lies, easy for a recovering lawyer. Everyone should do what they most like. Interestingly, I believe that's what we do, whether we admit it or not. If we'd rather stay home and do something as mundane as practice law or take care of an elderly parent, we do so because that's our down-deep druthers. We'd otherwise feel non-productive or guilty. If we'd really rather RV the world we'd all do that instead. As Stephen Dooley, Jr. said, *a man who wants to do something will find a way; a man who doesn't will find an excuse.*

The week before I quit playing Perry Mason several friends confided they envied my plan. The brevity of life had been vividly illustrated to them. They, like me, had always treated life as if it went on forever. One guy's brother had been diagnosed with inoperable cancer, a month before his scheduled retirement. Another's father had prostate cancer, chose the operation and died two weeks after retiring. Mary's boss had dreamed of buying an oceangoing fishing boat but kept putting it off. He needed to add to his retirement kitty. Just before we left he was diagnosed with a brain tumor and died within the year. Do it now, whatever it is you want to do. If you don't do it now the odds are you never will.

On the other hand, why worry? When you're croaked it makes no difference what your dreams and desires were anyway—you won't remember whether you stayed home or RVed the world, perhaps along the way finding the world's most picturesque country and volcano.

Years Rving Europe, Scandinavia, the Middle East, North Africa and More

Life is not the amount of breaths
you take; it's the moments that take
your breath away. <u>Hitch</u>, the movie

My most glorious day appeared on the November calendar in 1994, selling *Grendel* in San Diego. We packed up the detritus, paid $900 to check 14 large boxes on Continental Airlines and flew to Frankfurt, Germany, arriving when the Germans had Germany to themselves because it was too cold for anyone else, in freezing clear December, 1994.

Frankfurt wasn't picked at random. Helen Vander Male had written a book in 1990 entitled *Touring Europe by Motorhome, the Grandest Tour of All*, which we'd run across in a San Diego bookstore while selling *Grendel*. She'd bought an RV from Andy Kurztner at Executive Wohnmobile, a dealer south of the Frankfurt airport and driven around Europe for over a year.

- ## Europe Year One: 1994-1995

After a week checking out the RV dealers in the Wiesbaden/Frankfurt area we bought a used Hobby 500 Camping-car (European for RV), paying $20,000 to Andy Kurztner, the same dealer used by Helen Vander Male. *Grendel II* was eighteen feet of German craftsmanship on a Fiat diesel chassis that got 23 miles per gallon; 10 kilometers per liter in European speak. We paid $716 to AIG Europe for a year's RV insurance covering 34 European countries and saved $2800 in German VAT by immediately exporting the RV from Germany. Today I'd crank up the internet, check out the RV classified ads in English, German and Spanish newspapers in Europe and find target RVs online, easily done many places in the world from Chile and Argentina to Australia, New Zealand and South Africa.

We spent almost three years driving this excellent German RV around old Europe, Eastern Europe, parts of north Africa, Scandinavia and via ferry from Athens to Cyprus and Haifa, around a patch of the Middle East, principally Jordan and Israel, and back to the UK, living for extended periods in forty countries.

These weren't virgin territories, Europe or RVing Europe. I'd bought a Volkswagen Campervan at the factory in Wiedenbruck, Germany in June, 1969, a present to myself for actually graduating from law school. I drove it around for three months, behind the iron curtain through East Germany to Denmark, Holland, Belgium, France, Spain, Italy, Yugoslavia, Austria and back to Germany to ship the VW Van to Phoenix from Bremerhaven. These three months constituted the longest of five trips to Europe between the 1970s and 1994, including two sailing the Greek Islands (1984) and the Yugoslavian coast (1989), with ground excursions tacked on at the end.

Three years RVing Europe made for an astounding trip. We met loads of friendly people and saw a big chunk of the world in depth, living in every country in Europe except Romania and Switzerland, which we'd visited on previous occasions; plus Egypt, Morocco, Israel, Jordan, Cyprus and Turkey. A weighty tome would be insufficient to convey the richness of this near three-year meander and how much we learned about wildcat RVing. The journals filled five minutely written notebooks.

During years in Europe we spent a winter in Spain and Portugal, another in Spain and Morocco and the third in Egypt, Israel and Jordan. Seeing all of Europe presented logistical problems, where to go to avoid freezing in the winter. There's little choice because 95% of Europe is north of San Francisco and South Korea. Go south.

Having fled frigid Germany on a meager budget of $1300 a month we headed for sunny Spain, rambling through jolly Christmas throngs in Strasbourg, France and 600 year old vineyards for free wine-tasting, knocking a corner off the top hatch going under a too-low metal gate in Sete, France. We were learning, not only to watch the RV's height but never to park so close to traffic that the tailwind from 18-wheelers caused the RV to rock and roll all night long. Here's a summary of our years in Europe and environs, and a few later escapades:

Sunny Spain and Portugal: December 1994-February 1995: Meeting RVing friends from all over Europe and discovering sunny climes in amazing detail.	*Bonny Belgium and France*: April 1995: Belgium's ancient cities and the canaled city of Brugge, criss-crossing France the first of five times in three years.	*Happy Holland*: May 1995: Joining 50th year anniversary celebrations of VE Day and uncovering untouristed Dutch treasures.
A Real Summer in the UK, Scotland and Ireland: June through August 1995: English Cliffs and pasties, Scottish brogues, lochs and mountains; Irish hospitality and Guinness.	*Italy*: Sicilian Mafia and Greek Ruins, and back to *Spain*: September to December 1995: Italian and Sicilian mountains, Gelato, Cappuccino, Chianti and quaint Hill Towns.	*Moroccan Winter*; December 1995 to February 1996: Goats climbing trees down the Atlantic coast to the Sahara and up through the Atlas through Marrakech, pure Morocco.
Nostalgic Spain and Portugal: March 1996: Back meeting friends RVing Europe south for the winter, and new discoveries of castles, ruins and similar gems.	*Too Soon North to Denmark* April 1996: Across new parts of France to Denmark April and May 1996: Loire Valley and Alps through Holland and Germany to freeze in Denmark.	*Extremely Fabulous Norway*: June to July 1996: Most striking geography on earth with excellent fjords and the amazing Caribbean-like Lofoten Islands north of the Arctic Circle.
Sweden and Finland: July 1996: Reindeer everywhere, laundry in icy lakes, tons of Skeeters and jovial new friends.	*Rough in Russia, Balmy in the Baltics*: August 1996, St. Petersburg during the Olympics and down through fascinating Estonia, Latvia and Lithuania.	*Surfing Poland and the Czech Republic*: September 1996: Polish castles and characters to Gothic Prague and with an old friend from the US and Spain.
The Serbian Incident: September 3-4, 1996: Black market hustling of hostages who dig up dough in Sofia, Bulgaria to spring the RV.	*Happiness is Bulgaria*: September 1996: Ancient cities, turreted orthodox churches, monasteries and local characters.	*Greek Home Weeks*: September to October 1996 touring the Peloponnese and Greek Heartland on the way to Crete

The Cretan Connection: October to November blanketing ancient Crete, towns on precipitous slopes to the Sumerian Gorge.	_Cyprus Gripes Us_: A less than idyllic week on Cyprus, loving the mountains and antiquities, escaping to Israel.	_Adventuring Israel_ and How: November 1996 to February 1997: Visits by Helicopters, the Dead Sea, Negev Desert and intrigues.
Jordan and Egypt: February 1997: Side trips from Israel, a few weeks in Jordan for Petra, Jerash and Wadi Rum	Is _Petra_ the most fabulous archeological site on the Planet?	_Egypt_: We dislike tours because of stifling, boring tour guides and itineraries.
Rhodes for February to March 1997, seeing it all while waiting for the scary ferry to Marmaris, Turkey.	_Turkey's Turquoise Coast_: Antiquities and adventures on the coast with an aborted attempt on Cappadocia in a blizzard.	_Springtime in Turkey and Greece_: Home Sweet Home to Meteora with Mary's Greek forebears and the Ferry to Venice
The European End Game and bottom line expenses of $11 a day for depreciation, total cost of $50 a day.	Rolling Stones: Off Again in June 1997 with a year in _Mexico_ on the way to _South America_, then Hurricane Mitch.	Changing Plans after Hurricane Mitch wiped out bridges and roads in Honduras and Guatemala: _Off to Alaska_ for 1998-99.
Years in Australia and New Zealand: November 1999 to May 2001, seeing it all with two RVs, from the great wilds of OZ to fabulous hiking on South Island, NZ.	_An RV-less Year_ from 2001-2 in China and Southeast Asia, exploring Thai temples, Chinese parks, the Mekong in Laos, Angkor Wat and Bagan in Myanmar.	_The South American Connection_: 2002 and 2003 driving from Columbia to Brazil and Venezuela to Chile, including by ship to Antarctica from Ushuaia.
Beginning Africa and Central Asia: Three lengthy trips 2004 through 2007 scouting Africa from the south to Egypt and the west coast from Morocco to Cameroon, then the Stans.	_A Few Highlights_: camping with kangaroos, Mt. Cook out the back window, camping atop Mt. Vesuvius, lunar eclipse in Alice Springs, Tasmania, Lake Titicaca in Bolivia and Peru, Parks in Chile and Argentina.	

Those wishing to see precisely how to RV the world instead of accompanying *Grendel II* through Europe, North Africa and the Middle East should skip to Chapter Nine entitled *How abut RVing the World,* beginning on page 91.

• **Sunny Spain**

We arrived at Camping Rosaleda in Fuengirola, Spain, 18 miles (30 km) west of Malaga, on Christmas Eve, 1994. A month's parking, electric and hot showers cost $200. The budget was tight but because monthly rates at RV parks were a third to half the daily charge we could relax and thaw out while day-tripping the southwest quadrant of Spain. Meanwhile we met dozens of RVers from Scandinavia, Holland and the UK, who spent every winter in Fuengirola. We made fast friends with RVing neighbors from Holland and Norway, later visiting fantabulous hosts Margit and Berger in Drammen, Norway, and Yanni in rural Holland. The only American we met the first year was Charles, who taught four months of the year at a university in Prague and otherwise scooted around Europe in his VW Camper bus with feisty German Shepard Bulyar.

As a crusty retired customs agent Berger offered an invaluable tip: buy lots of your favorite tipple, inexpensive in Spain, better still in duty free Ceuta, Spanish North Africa, to take elsewhere in Europe and especially to Scandinavia. Gin in Ceuta was two dollars a bottle; in Norway, $42. With the strong Euro and Norway the most expensive country on earth these prices may have doubled.

During the month in Fuengirola we took daytrips, savoring the many picturesque whitewashed hill-towns of southwestern Spain, from Mijas 3 ½ miles above Fuengirola, over an hour's energetic climb to quaint cobblestone streets and great views over the Spanish coast, to Ronda a few hours west by RV, split by a 1000 foot deep gorge on a high plateau. A favorite getaway was El Torcal with acres of natural stone sculpture; there we learned to never park where an icy wind would blow into the vents and to carefully level the RV, not only to avoid sleeping on our ears but to prevent terminal damage to the RV's refrigerator.

After a month and fond goodbyes to new friends we explored Gibraltar in early 1995, biking around the rock and climbing to the top of Gibraltar amongst inquisitive Barbary apes. The RV's first oil change was a shocker, costing $95. We later learned this was about twice what it'd cost in most of Europe, though perhaps an average price in the early 21st Century. The most interesting experience on the way out of Spain was stumbling onto the dedication of a whitewashed church it'd taken a dozen years to build in the Guadalquivir swamp at El Bocio, people streaming from all over Spain for a colorful parade along non-existent streets and we were the only tourists in town.

• **Portrait of Portugal 1995**

Lovely little Portugal's Algarve was uncompromisingly scenic, crashing surf against towering orange cliffs, great overnight parking on barragems, dams overlooking vast lakes, and alongside scenic rivers where it was easy to camp for free and which the locals cleverly called free-camping.

We gradually learned the rudiments of safe and carefree free-camping: always avoid private property and buy the best atlases and maps available because they accurately pinpoint the best places to park free overnight. We also learned the price of extensive magazine subscriptions: mail forwarding was costing between $57 and $90 a month. Sixteen years of express mail delivery by DHL, FedEx or Airborne averaged only 72 hours to most anywhere in the world.

In Monte Rosso we first met long-term British friends Bernie and Liz, later using their second address in Northhampton to re-register the RV. We explored Southern Portugal with Liz and Bernie, artists into country music and square dancing, learning to play the hilarious English card game of *Bullshit* and taking in the raucous carnival and excellent baths at Loule. That summer we visited with Liz and Bernie in Northamptonshire.

In Moncarapacho we met Joan, a retired philosophy professor and artist from Ulster, busily helping restore the Roman mosaics at Estoi and trying to persuade the Portuguese to stop shooting local birds. We visited her sprawling house several times that year and upon return from Morocco the next winter, keeping up a lively correspondence. Mostly we were relieved at being able to stay within a puny monthly budget, spending an average of $200 a week, staying in campgrounds only once a week to wash clothes, fill water and clean the RV. An early Portuguese highlight was Cabo Sao Vicente, the furthest southwest point with crashing surf 200 feet up high cliffs, forming continuous waterfalls next to Henry the Navigator's fort with a monument commemorating the sailor's essential Compass Rose, where we shed a tear for *Grendel I*.

- ## Spain to Bonny Belgium

Portugal was a land of copasetic people and piri-piri chicken, spicy and nice, but we were soon back in northwestern Spain hiking the spectacular mountains of the Picos de Europa, reminiscent of Switzerland. We took the Fuente De cable car up a mountain to slog over glaciers next to waterfalls, down ravines 2000 feet deep and a second long hike along a precipitous ravine from Puente Poncebos high over the Rio Cares along canals carved from solid granite, incidentally sampling what may have been the best blue cheese on the planet.

By the time we rolled back into France we'd found laundromats were practically nonexistent and when we could find them, for example in Hendaye, France, it might cost $16 for two self-serve loads. In St. Jean de Luc, after arguing whether to spend $25 out of a tightening budget, we bought a 200-page road atlas of France, showing every canal, river, abbey and freeway RV parking. Mary was completely correct and I learned to never scrimp on maps and atlases.

At Mont-Saint-Michel, a rocky islet near the northwest corner of France designated a UNESCO World Heritage site in 1979, we sat with other RVers watching the sunset as the tide receded from the medieval walls and towers encircling the hilltop village/island where an ancient abbey crowned the summit. Another highlight was the striking town of Eretrat with natural stone arches next to a great river where we found excellent chocolate crepes near a plaque commemorating the WWII entrance by General Dwight David Eisenhower. During this fiftieth anniversary year after VE Day we met returning allied troops everywhere, awed by the unending line of German bunkers on the French coast.

Belgium was a happy surprise. Brugge was laced with extensive canals, a medieval city with free RV parking on the south end of town at Minnewater Park. Ghent was another medieval city with gilded guild houses, towers, cathedral and an old university where fifty students staged a friendly water fight in front of the RV's picture window. The genial Belgians were a welcome contrast to the predominantly dour French who remained diffident with those who spoke little of their musical language and that little bit with an incomprehensible accent. In Antwerp we met local diamond merchants,

Hassidic Jews with dreadlocks, and passed an entertaining evening at a city park, apparently the rendezvous for Antwerp gays. Meanwhile we listened to the BBC and VOA every morning; in Dinant we were informed about the Oklahoma City bombing.

In three months we'd found no place to refill German propane bottles though we'd scoured hard-to-find propane factories in the industrial areas of large cities. Almost out of propane we were forced to buy a Camping Gaz system to which we were directed by a neighborly Belgian who jumped in the RV to help us find the closest store. The cost of propane refills had ranged wildly, from nine dollars in Spain, $17 in Germany and $24 in France. Propane bottles in a unified EU are perhaps similarly threaded and more easily fillable; with the strong Euro they must be far more expensive.

The Herald Tribune Newspaper, published only in Europe by the Washington Post and New York Times, was an essential source of stock market and mutual fund information in pre-internet Europe. We bought it every Monday for mutual fund quotes, happy our funds were growing heartily during our first year in Europe.

- ## Happy Holland

May was Holland, the whole month. In Den Haag we met a Dutch lady who'd biked 1000 kilometers on a pilgrimage from Bayonne to Santiago do Campostelo and was shocked when we *said* we'd occasionally spent the night in public parks. We stuttered and backtracked, assuring her we weren't really that uncultured. May 5 marked the 50th year celebration of VE Day at Kuekenhof gardens amidst two square miles of tulips, windmills, fountains and sculpture pocked with a hundred Canadian veterans from WWII, returning to the scene of battles and lauded as heroes by the Dutch. Holland shone because 90% spoke fluent English, taught from earliest grade school.

The best Dutch overnighting was in the Het Triske parkland a few kilometers north of Amsterdam: 17 kilometers of canals, wind surfing, a water park, bicycle paths like all over Holland and a nude beach made palatable by 90 degree weather. We biked to Amsterdam and rode around the city. In the far north of Holland, well off the tourist trail, we enjoyed Esinga Planetarium in Franaker; a mechanical solar system built over seven years by an eccentric astronomer. The system was geared 20,000 million to one among sun, moons and planets rigged by an intricate pulley system in the ceiling of a sprawling house. Bourlange, near the German border, was a strikingly restored fortress town in the form of a five-pointed star bordered by canals and armored in the 10th Century. At Westerbork 102,000 Jews had been interned during WWII; 600 survived. Throughout Europe we enjoyed constant American oldies music on six FM stations.

Wiltz, Luxembourg was traumatic because we were yelled at by a gas station attendant for attempting to fill the RV's water tank after buying dozens of dollars of diesel. Luxembourg seemed the most rigid country in Europe, and expensive after a five liter oil change cost $90. The budget was working out to a third for fuel and oil changes, a third for food and occasionally eating out and the other third for fun such as admissions, beer and ice cream, the journal concluding we were *seeing lots cheaply and having a good time, relaxed, indulgent and wildly decadent.* In northern Europe we found weekly ATM withdrawals were rapidly spent on groceries and fuel during the first couple of days, leaving a pittance for the balance of the week and severely limiting site admissions.

The daily routine was up at 7 a.m., do exercises and run a few miles, breakfast of coffee with crepes and fruit, yogurt or cereal while listening to the BBC, sightsee the next twenty to fifty miles until about 3 p.m., broken by a huge lunch of sumptuous raw vegetables, finding a good overnight parking spot for a few hours repose before making dinner and relaxing over a game of gin rummy, then reading and writing.

• A Real Summer in the UK, Scotland and Ireland

The radio said it'd been raining for months in England but we still rolled aboard a P&O ferry in Zeebrugge, Belgium to Felixstowe in the UK, paying $203 for a roundtrip ticket; Calais-Dover would have cost almost $400. Two years later we took the Chunnel back to the UK for $115. It was initially tough to drive on the wrong side of the road but only for a few hours. We were happy to roll into Cambridge with its fantastic old stone colleges, attending Eventide at King's College and Cathedral, parking overnight in a lay-by next to a cricket field where players dressed in purest white cavorted through an inexplicable ritual.

The next morning we were forced to call the Royal Auto Club for a jump start. AAA membership in the United States provided free service. The night before I'd forgotten to disconnect a wire I'd placed between the starting and house batteries in order to charge the latter while driving; hence the necessity of a jump start. This disconnection ritual was necessitated by a wiring a defect in the RV, one I never solved, requiring constant nightly precaution.

The 34 used-book stores in Hay on Wye were an English highlight, simply because it was the single town allowed to sell secondhand books, though they could also be found in the occasional thrift shop. We scoured bargain bins for hours, exchanging a bag of previously read books for 25 used books and adding five travel guides for 12£. Because Mary read nearly a book a day we were ecstatic to add to the stash. A few weeks later we spent a relaxed day with Bernie and Liz in Aylesbury.

Admissions to historical sites were hefty in the UK, requiring that we save the expense for special entries, such as Warwick castle for $26, now likely closer to $40, scrambling around the labyrinth of ruins fortified since 915 C.E., dungeons, gardens and towers in welcome sun on the languorous River Avon. But our passion was hiking and climbing mountains, which began in Wales with Mt. Snowden, 3 ½ miles up one of five converging trails to a surprise on top where hundreds of people milled around after disembarking a tram.

On July 10 we boarded a ferry to Northern Ireland, beginning a love affair with Guinness *for your health,* touted on ancient billboards. Guinness was intertwined with the Irish welfare system, which was funded with taxes on Guinness that were in turn spent on Guinness by welfare recipients and non-welfare recipients like myself. The stuff exported to the States, which I'd tasted and rejected years before, had been a pale shadow of Guinness on tap in the old country.

The Giant's Causeway provided hours of hiking drama through hexagonal basalt cylinders 20 feet long, stacked 500 feet high.

Northern Ireland was in its usual turmoil, Orangemen building bonfires in Londonderry to commemorate a 307 year old battle won by Protestants over Catholics in 1688, making for interesting views from the city walls. For the first time we paid $1 a liter for diesel; the further north in Europe the more expensive the fuel. Also the bike rack fell off while driving at full speed, the belated result of backing into a tree in France. But with a trusty rechargeable drill and a few rivets I was able to jerry-rig the rack back onto the RV and somehow straighten Mary's handlebars while chatting with a 70-year old Sheepherder who'd never been to a town 45 miles away; the furthest he'd ventured from his place of birth was 35 miles.

Often it'd take an hour to find suitable overnight parking, off road, away from private property, on a scenic lake, river, canal or trailhead for early morning hiking. Meanwhile we continued the frustration of meeting the one year deadline for reregistering the RV, having tried in Portugal and by letter to Florida, and then in Ireland. Without a local address it continued impossible and the year wisped away. Absent-minded, I'd again forgotten to disconnect the starting and house batteries in Rock of Cashel, Ireland. Upon seeing the RV's raised hood three carloads of locals screeched to a stop, helping push the RV, hollering and laughing like they were actually having fun. In Killarney we finally bought a duvet for $32 (19 Punt), salvaging innumerable frigid nights.

Highlights in the Republic of and Northern Ireland included not only Guinness on tap but many friendly red-haired locals asking whether we knew a cousin in Pittsburg, a two-hour Gaelic wedding with 40 costumed O'Neills on the Hill of Tara

and a fascinating hour spent at the Linen Hall Library in Belfast examining the most complete collection of posters, videos, buttons, books, paraphernalia, newspapers and dissertations on *The Troubles.*

After a month driving most roads in the Irelands we rolled out of bed at 2:30 a.m. to board the ferry back to Stranraer, Scotland. Within the week we took the bikes on a pedestrian ferry to Arran Island for a 33 mile ride around, up and down, in five hours meeting heaps of colorful locals. Back on the mainland we missed Jimmy Carter's appearance in Luss by one day, parking on Loch Lommand and climbing 925 meter (3000 foot) Beinn Lorain with views over five lochs. After braving two weeks of mostly rain in southern England we'd earned what the Scots assured us was the best weather they'd had in 26 years, 80 degrees and no rain our whole month in Scotland. At Ft. Williams we parked overnight near the trailhead for Ben Nevis, the highest mountain in Scotland, not a major expedition at 3300 feet. The strategic parking gave us the jump on hundreds of hikers the next morning, enjoying dramatic views of lochs, snow, rivers, waterfalls and forests studded with meadows. We stopped at nearby Lake Gary for a hokey photo of a bagpiper marching next to misty lochs.

Scotland was the favorite country to this point, particularly in the far north watching Europeans slap Scotland's vicious midges as they put up tents in front of the RV's bug-proof picture-window. We met a French lady who'd been bitten by midges so severely that she looked like a terminal case of measles; she literally had to scurry back to France for refuge. Mary continued our gourmet ways, cooking up dinners such as Thai noodles with garlic, ginger, molasses, lemon juice and red peppers with carrots, celery, zucchini and sprouts, stir-fried.

The Cairngorm Mountains formed Scotland's 2nd and 4th highest peaks, supplying excellent hiking with views over sailboats on lochs, idyllic until a bus driver in the parking lot backed into the RV. The poor guy, who hadn't had an accident in 48 years and was retiring the next week, withered under Mary's volcanic scolding. Though it took months it worked out in the end, a new bike rack from the factory in Belgium paid for by Shearings Coach Lines. It was actually a super deal because I'd half-trashed the bike rack on several backing-without-looking occasions.

Near Balmoral castle, the Queen's hideaway, Bill Gates paid for the London Times, a promotion for Windows 95. Our favorite town in Scotland was St. Andrews of golf course fame, punctuated with 15 high spires poking from ruins surrounding an old castle and cathedral, the most photogenic in the country.

After Hadrian's Wall and old Roman Fort Chester we explored Lindisforne Priory on Holy Island, accessible 12 hours a day at low tide, fascinating ruins of the oldest abbey and castle in the UK. England forced the RV onto the steepest short roads, outside the long steep roads in Jordan, often between a 15% and 25% grade.

In Lincoln, back in England, we finally registered the RV at a spare address loaned by Bernie and Liz when we'd visited them a few weeks previous at a country swing festival: 5 Junction Road, Kingsley, Northhampton, requiring the purchase of local insurance costing $141 for six months and $225 in road tax, but we got 75% of both back when we left the UK on September 13. The registrar issued a *Q* license plate, about which we hadn't a clue. The locals said it was a special plate and it surely was, signifying, as we learned two years later, that the vehicle's year of manufacture couldn't be verified, costing dearly on resale.

• Italy: Sicilian Mafia and Greek Ruins

Disembarking the ferry back to Belgium we sped to free parking on the south end of favorite city Brugge, along with 20 other European RVs, a few days later picking up a new bike rack for $315 with insurance proceeds. Re-entering France we'd crossed 17 national borders and hadn't been able to obtain a single stamp in our passports. A recurring problem was finding ATMs that'd cough out cash on a Visa debit card; using the MasterCard credit card meant mailing a check back to the U.S. as soon as possible. We also found it politic to only fill with fuel at gas stations offering water, the easiest and often only way to find drinking water. The highlight of France, this time out of five times across in three years, was Laon with two miles of walls surrounding a hilltop city with a fancy 11th Century cathedral spiked with gargoyles and cows carved in stone.

The rainy French weather forced a decision to skip Switzerland and its *expensive* $30 driving permit, instead heading for what we hoped was sunny Italy. Good move because Italy was brilliantly sunny and we loved the great gelato and cappuccinos. I admired the well-dressed ladies and cringed from the wild Italian drivers. Stumbling onto a marathon in Pavia Mary suffered nostalgia for running and we made double-sure to pursue the habit every morning, far short of a marathon. We found tranquil parking on a canal ten kilometers south of Venice, walking around the city for five hours.

By the end of September Italian campgrounds were closed or closing, requiring further practice in free-camping. We drove through San Marino, surprised its patron saint was Abraham Lincoln. In Florence a German RVer warned we shouldn't park on city streets or we'd be burgled. His radio had been stolen. We parked anyway and were burgled, the likely youthful culprits taking the rechargeable drill, which worked only on 110 volt and not on Europe's 220 volt. They'd taken my laptop computer out of the cupboard and left it upside down on the table. We continued to skip many sites to save the often exorbitant cost of admissions, practicing extreme frugality on a sparse budget.

Italy was Mary's favorite, while mine would be Norway yet to come. In Italy we particularly liked the hill towns such as San Gimignano's striking Gothic architecture accented by fourteen towers, Orvieto's four square miles atop a high mesa and Duomo with colorful murals of hell, Assisi's steep hill with a half-mile long fortress on a ridge hosting millions of tourists and sobbing women, and particularly tiny Civita with 15 inhabitants, reachable only by a two mile hike and footbridge over a deep precipice.

On October 9th we overnighted high on the side of Vesuvius overlooking the Isle of Capri and the Bay of Naples, watching city lights glisten under a full moon. To avoid further burglary we walked ancient Heraculum in shifts, for a relatively measly $8 examining well-preserved homes, baths, murals, mosaics, columns and amphora frozen in 79 C.E. by an eruption of Vesuvius. We'd explored Pompeii on a previous trip. On Capri, originally reconnoitered in 1969, I took a mask and snorkel to dive the Blue Grotto on my own, tourist boat captains glaring malevolently. We stayed at the Seven Hills Campground on the north side of Rome, practically a zoo with Emu, red deer and a caged baby tiger.

Mary warily accompanied the RV on the ferry to Sicily, antsy about the mafia.

During a ten-day drive around Sicily we waited in line with locals to fill water containers at springs from Macari to Prizzi and Corleone, enjoying topless beaches in the balmy weather around Trapani, snorkeling coral reefs and buying supplies from trucks toting vegetables, clothes and kitchen wares. Sicilian highlights were the rainbow of mosaics in gold covering the ceiling of the Monreale cathedral, a south Palermo suburb, 30 rooms of perfectly preserved mosaics uncovered from a mud-covered villa at Via Romana Casale and the fine Greek ruins at Syracuse, Ragusa and Agrigento, the last made more compelling by a wedding party from Rome celebrating with the bride and groom posing for photos in a classic Bugatti Roadster next to a perfect Greek temple.

We learned more about the RV's dimensions in Altofonte where the carabinieri had to stop and clear a mile of traffic behind the RV so I could back away from an arch half its height. The sides of the RV almost scraped the walls, requiring precision backing. When we gained the main square the locals provided a hearty standing ovation amidst copious smiles and waves. The day after overnighting on the side of Mt. Etna, near a 2000 meter red cone formed during a 1953 eruption, we took the ferry back to Italy. I drove remembering a 1969 trip when I'd seen most of Italy from Naples north, having difficulty believing only half of Italian cars were severely dented; why not all? When we returned in 2006 we found Italian driving etiquette had radically improved.

The last Italian highlight was Cinque Terra, five miniature villages at the base of steep hills terraced in grapes on the northwest coast, accessible only by hiking or train. We scrambled down steeply cascading terraces of wine grapes to Manarola and along the beach to Corniglia and Vernazza, the next day driving to Montorossa de Marc and taking the train through a tunnel to Vernazza with its quaint horseshoe-shaped harbor, hiking out.

Back in Spain we thought Charles might be at his favorite campground in Mojocar and he was, making an early home week before a happy return to the familiar digs at Fuengirola for $207 a month. It was great knowing where to find everything we wanted, from newspapers and coffee to bakery, post office and drugstore, enjoying excited reunions with Margit and Berger, and Yannie. We made fast new friends with 72-year old American Eileen on her third solo trip through Europe in a VW Camperbus, worried about her houseboat in Sausalito, and Chris and John from the UK.

CHAPTER THREE
Europe Year Two: The Adventure Continues

Boring was two weeks sitting in Fuengirola's campground, though we kept busy planning a winter in Morocco. We booked the ferry from Algeciras to Ceuta for $314 roundtrip but we were already worrying where to spend a third winter. We'd seen all there was to see in Europe's only palatable winter climes of Spain and Portugal. Greece and Turkey were too cold, as we'd find out in spades the next year, the Canary Islands too small, Tunisia too far for a ferry, Egypt requiring an expensive carnet de passage and prohibiting diesel engines across the Sinai, on and on.

Moroccan Winter 1995-6

We suffered teeth cleanings by a pathetic Norwegian dentist in Fuengirola and bid fond goodbyes to fellow RVers, leaving for Morocco on December 20, 1995. The ferry sailed from Algeciras, across the bay from Gibraltar, to Ceuta, the duty free port of Spanish Morocco. Everything was inexpensive in Ceuta. Diesel was $1.25 a gallon, half the price in Spain. The border guard asked if I'd been to Morocco before and I admitted having spent a few weeks 26 years previous, watching the moon landing in 1969 Tangiers, the year the border guard was born.

In Morocco Mary quickly learned the most important Arabic word was *emshe, go away.* Most Moroccans were impoverished, necessarily hustling for tours or begging, having no notion of Western personal space. They'd flock around the RV wherever we stopped, displaying wares or begging for Dirham, the local currency, which Mary detested. This single bad aspect of Morocco had fortunately changed upon return in 2007. In a single decade Morocco seemingly became a southern extension of Europe.

On Christmas Eve we drove into Mehdiya Plage, a suburb of Kinitra where our new Brit friends Chris and John had suggested we look up Gordon Stromberg, a British ex-pat they'd met two years previous. I opened the RV door and here came a thin mustached chap strolling down the sidewalk with a German Shepard. I asked, *Are you Gordon?* Nonplussed, he admitted he was, immediately issuing an invitation to Christmas Eve dinner with his informally adopted Muslim family that included three rambunctious kids. Gordon had retired from Citibank and Thomas Cooke, lonely and happy for company. We were used to eating between 5 and 6 p.m., finally settling into the Christmas Eve banquet at 8 p.m., lasting until 10:30 pm with desert at midnight. Naturally we had to stay for Christmas dinner the next day; it took three days to escape.

Mary was worried about free camping in Morocco but we survived with no bother at Mohammedia, a beach where fisherman employed huge black inner tubes to troll the raging Atlantic. Down the Atlantic coast we saw plows drawn by a camel/donkey team and goats grazing in trees, sheparded by kids who threw rocks at anyone failing to tip them when taking photos of their tree-climbing goats.

New Year's Eve dawned at Essaoira, Morocco's most charming coastal town in both 1996 and 2007, jam-packed with art galleries, colorful pottery, intricate wood carvings, veiled women and tourists from France and Germany. Camping Gaz cost a dollar to refill, versus $24 in France. Moroccan beer, because it was a Muslim country, cost 2 ½ times as much as Spanish beer, and every Moroccan town's single beer depot was securely hidden.

Tagazoute camping ten miles north of Agadir was full of a hundred RVs, primarily from France, Italy and Germany. There we met Dutch Peter and Paula headed to Mauritania, hoping to drive all the way to South Africa with a pop-top tent on the cab of their four-wheel-drive Toyota. We were terminally envious, trying to think up ways to tag along. The dilemma was solved when a German lady pointed out five ball bearings underneath *Grendel II*; the main drive-train bearing had shattered. A British couple kindly pulled the RV into Agadir for repairs, using a short tow rope that left me a nervous wreck; cars and buses continually pulling out without warning as we toiled up and down hills, taking an hour for nine miles of towing. The Fiat garage replaced the bearing in a single day for $100 while we sat around listening to the *Eagles* on the garage speakers as German hippies and veiled Muslim women trudged past.

At Agadir's excellent souq, amongst colorful stacks of spices, we bought roasted sugared peanuts, tomatoes, cukes, carrots, cauliflower, apples, oranges, olives, fennel, bread, bananas, pears, zucchini, green peppers, leaks, lemons and eggs for a total of $5.

At Tifnite Plage we stuck the RV in the sand but were helpfully pushed out by two Italians, two locals and a Canadian named Saul. We spent hours with Saul, exchanging travelers' lies.

On a narrow road to Guelmin we suffered a flat tire. Two Germans in a Unimoc stopped to help; it took an hour to change the tire by digging out the sand underneath, a technique revisited in similar circumstances in 2007 Senegal. There were no tires in Morocco the RV's size except an old Michelin retread that looked iffy. Accordingly we drove 125 miles north to Agadir in the rain, where there were also no properly-sized tires. The closest tire that fit was hundreds of miles away in Casablanca; it'd take a full day to ship and would cost $190. We drove back to Guelmin and paid $50 for the retread.

In Ouarzazate, Morocco's movie capital, we watched a German movie being shot, then headed 100 miles south to Zagora over a wild pass to Adgz in the palm-tree strewn

Draa River Valley. I'd always hankered for a camel safari into the Sahara, signing up for a full day's ride and overnight in the desert, paying a $30 deposit and arranging to meet the camel boss at 8 a.m. No one arrived until 9 a.m. We took a jeep to the camels and found complete disorganization; no preparations for lunch or dinner. Mary raged, forcing the return of the deposit and I settled for a photo of the camels on the Zagora billboard, *52 Days to Timbuktu.*

At the Zagora campground we chatted with Germans from Berlin, the wife a former soviet technician for Aeroflot in East Berlin. After a trip to San Diego she'd returned amazed that Americans weren't the scurrilous criminals she'd been raised to believe and we found this East German quite a non-ogress herself.

In Tinehir, picturesquely situated below the snow-capped Atlas, we met Kamal, adamantly a Berber and not an Arab. He taught English at a private school and insisted on showcasing the real Tinehir. We spent half a day following Kamal with his long flowing djellebah through an old Jewish quarter abandoned in 1948, past the women's market and along a palmary to meet a rug-weaving family, who carded wool, spun and dyed the thread and loomed Berber rugs, handling the complete process in-house, from baa to bath.

Marrakech's ten miles of city walls were pocked with 200 towers surrounding a 220 foot Mosque covered with gold that had been paid for as penance by a sultan's wife who ate three grapes during Ramadan. The great square was filled with snakes and snake charmers, monkey performers, water sellers in red costumes wearing spangled hats, street performers, acrobats, fortune tellers, jugglers and a fully clad belly dancer, each surrounded by large groups, and behind the square lurked miles of colorful souqs where we became happily lost.

Outside Marrakech on January 31, 1996 the retread literally exploded, summoning ten kids fascinated while I dug a hole through boulders to fit on the spare, providing the kids with an hour's entertainment. To Mary's great unease we blithely continued driving around Morocco without a spare tire. The blowout had knocked a side out of the compartment next to the refrigerator, temporarily repaired with a plastic bag and *fixed* a week later by taping a plastic box inside.

Nostalgic Spain and Portugal

Back in Ceuta, taking Berger's advice, I bought sixteen 750 milliliter bottles of gin for $2 each. We arrived in Fuengirola for a three-hour welcome-back party thrown by Eileen, Margit and Berger, Yanni, Dutch Jack and Jane, Scots Pat and Don, and several Finns who gifted a map of Scandinavia; Finns perpetually occupied a third of the campground. Discussing where to go the next winter, Dennis, a professor at the London School of Economics, and his wife Ann, suggested Israel, spinning stories of Kibbutzim and Petra. First thing the next morning we bought a new tire for $104.

Campground life rapidly palled. We'd planned to leave in two weeks but the rains began and we were delayed until March 2. Upon escape we parked the first night at our old favorite, El Torcal, making sure we were turned so the wind wouldn't roar through the refrigerator vents. The next morning we took a long hike around stacked granite pancakes, spiky pointy rocks and deep crevasses.

After Cordoba's yellow and red-striped mosque we were excited to head back to Portugal and Monte Gordo where the usual 40 RVs were free-camped on the waterfront, including Bernie and Liz. Saying hello took two hours. Here's an envelope we later received from these artists extraordinaire.

We escorted them around the Roman ruins and mosaics Joan was helping rcstore at Estoi, also visiting Joan on several occasions and returning to old favorites such as the market and baths in Loule, all between bouts of rain that made Mary exclaim she was homesick for sunny Phoenix. Later that day she told friends we'd be in Europe another 1 ½ years. On the bright side the rains had carpeted Portugal with yellow, red and purple flowers.

After a few weeks we left the south coast to explore Evora's Capella do Ossas built from the femurs and skull of 4000 cadavers, the 100 foot high and five mile long aqueduct at Estremoz and our favorite, Tamar, where a river with waterfalls ran through it past a Knights Templar castle with a medieval monastery overlooking town. We met Dennis and Ann and other Fuengirola acquaintances at the Tamar campground, Dennis reiterating his advice to winter in Israel, which we began to seriously consider after finding out about a convenient ferry from Athens to Rhodes to Cyprus to Haifa.

33

Back in Spain I half-remembered Toledo from a trip 27 years previous. We enjoyed Segovia's long Roman Aqueduct and many-spired cathedral on a sheer cliff surrounded by snow-capped peaks. In Segovia the *USA Today* map showed cold and rainy weather blanketing Europe so we headed for the Spanish Mediterranean between Valencia and Barcelona, slowing down and taking it easy for two lazy weeks, but not slowing down nearly long enough.

Too Soon North to Denmark 1996

Just to be on the safe side the shopping list for duty free Andorra included tires, nineteen additional bottles of gin and a second bottle of camping gaz. A scheduled rendezvous with stateside friends in Brussels gave us eleven days to cross France, where we knew it would be easy to free camp courtesy of the detailed French atlas. Replacing worn front tires cost $88 each, after which the Andorran traffic was a bumper to bumper madhouse because the Pyrenees were packed with skiers. The crush likely assisted French customs in overlooking 35 hidden bottles of gin, safe for a summer in Scandinavia and the long meander to and fro.

The best day crossing France was near Millau where we followed the crystal clear Tarn River along steep green hills through cutesy villages in brilliant sunshine. French freeways offered sprawling picnic areas or Aires every 40 kilometers (25 miles) allowing free overnight RV parking, shown on most maps and the detailed atlas. We traversed France, land of expensive everything, in ten days, spending less than $200 because we'd stocked up in Spain. With the formation of the EU France and Spain have become equally pricey.

The Brussels Atomium was impressive thirty years after the 1956 World's Fair: a hundred meters (325 feet) high with nine globes representing atoms, our German Hobby

RV proudly in front: Shortly after we started downtown to meet stateside friends, an absent-minded 52-year-old woman swung from the outside lane without looking, forcing the RV onto the sidewalk where she sideswiped it anyway. The lady was hysterical and Mary little better. The lady left her purse with Mary, frantically returning to the nearby Trade Mart building to salvage whatever she'd forgotten that had indirectly caused the *accident*. In her absence I took the opportunity to write out a statement for her signature, in which she admitted complete and sole responsibility for all damage to the RV, which was minor: a crunch to the left rear fender, in the process knocking Mary's bike off the bike rack and further trashing the accident-prone rack. We were able to meet our friends in downtown Brussels on time, having lots to chat about during the next four hours.

We met with the distracted lady's insurance adjuster in Wetteren, Belgium for a $1000 settlement; her signed statement worked wonders. We also had a phantom water leak repaired for $128, leaving ample money to replace the back bumper and again, the bike rack, finding a large county park for convenient overnighting. Driving into Holland we stopped by Yanni's place in rural Emerlo for tea and molasses cookies, picking up our mail and leaving twenty paperback novels for her son who was always on the look out for English language books.

Happiness was Denmark at the end of April; for the first time in 1 1/2 years we were able to get the passports stamped. Danish roads offered great picnic areas with free heated bathrooms well off road for overnight parking, which might have been forbidden but who can read Danish? However, we were never hassled. Similar to the Dutch 90% of Danes spoke fluent English, though disconcertingly the national dish was a hotdog gooped with catsup, mustard, horseradish sauce, onions, pickles and bacon bits.

The Danish map showed a snaky trail covering every nook of the miniature country, the Daisy or Queen Margerite's Trail, which we followed faithfully past excellent castles, snug under the Irish duvet on windy 42 degree mornings, typical in May. We'd obviously driven north way too fast. Denmark is at the latitude of Newfoundland and Labrador.

Medieval Ribe, Denmark's oldest old town, was surrounded by farms liberally fertilized, bringing tears to the eyes and gorge to the throat, suggesting something rotten in Denmark. Still, the country was perfectly manicured, with hedges, blond thatched roofs and flowers everywhere, mostly tulips and daffodils edged with purple and lavender ground cover. At Sondervig we visited the Elvis Presley museum with its giant guitar-

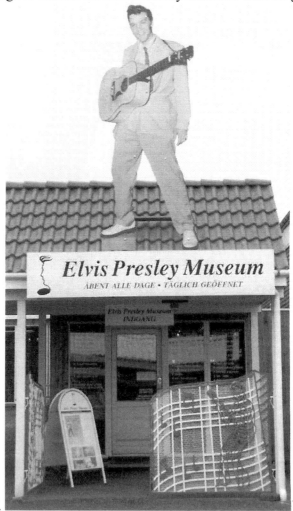

playing statue on the roof. Weirdly, the strongest English language shortwave radio station was Radio Jordan in Amman. We unpacked down-filled parkas for early morning driving and reminisced about the Caribbean, Phoenix with 80-degree nights and even Florida.

To celebrate my birthday I opted for Legoland in Billund, where the sun fortuitously appeared. For $17 each we marveled at miniature Scandinavian towns,

Disneyland's Frontierland and Pirateland, the White House and Mt. Rushmore, as we slurped ice cream. That night we huddled and read in down jackets. On a truncated budget we were too cheap to use the propane furnace; refilling Camping Gaz cost $24 and only lasted a week. The cordial Danes, spurred by the *USA* in big letters on the RV's front bumper, made up for the chilly weather. After three weeks in Denmark we'd relished four sunny, slightly warm days.

Mail had been ordered for delivery to a huge campground in Copenhagen. Upon arrival we found the campground wouldn't open for a week and was packed with trailers and carnival rides, hosting the biggest flea market in Denmark. The friendly camp manager said, *don't worry about it,* adding, *you can stay for free.* We plugged into electric that fired up the *heater* and hooked up to water we hoped wouldn't freeze before the mail arrived. The free campground let us save enough money to see Copenhagen in style. We biked downtown daily, a mere four miles away, watching freezing tourists provide photos ops when climbing onto the lap of the harbor mermaid. My highlight was the Carlsberg Brewery tour led by a comedian in a very short skirt; I was forced to avoid wasting non-beer-drinker Mary's three free beers at the end of the tour, biking back tipsy. We wound up our Danish tour wearing gloves, down jackets and wool hats as we stalked Helsingor, Hamlet's castle, preferring Fredricksborg Castle hulking across three islands.

Onto Sweden

We took the ferry, the next year replaced by a bridge, to Sweden for $78. The first impression of Sweden was *Why so many Chevy vans,* which we'd seen nowhere else in Europe. We found out that Swedish auto dealers in the mid-eighties had gotten bargains on fleets of Chevy Vans and these cheesy breadboxes had caught on, hence the plethora. Like Denmark, Sweden had built fancy picnic areas with heated bathrooms every ten miles along major roads, making it easy to free camp.

Sweden was the only country where people tried to steal the bikes off the back of the RV, twice, including during 6 ½ days of rain we suffered the first week on a loop through southern Sweden. Mary summed Sweden up as *green, pretty and boring.* The boredom was compensated for by her cooking, bolstered by the three boxes of almost a hundred spices we'd shipped over.

When the rain stopped we biked a stretch of the Gota Canal, 58 locks stretching 110 miles from Soderkoping to Stockholm, watching sailboats negotiate crowded locks. Stockholm was an architectural dream, over a hundred buildings turreted in gold and marble stretching across fourteen islands with fifty bridges. The Royal Palace stood in the old town of Gamla Stan, hosting a striking changing of the guard on horseback. The guards, naturally in blue and yellow, wore silver pike-tipped helmets. For 45 minutes they marched to the cadence of trumpets strung with vivid quilting while horses clomped in time.

Camping prices were exorbitant so we parked at the ferry terminal on the water, $9 for 26 hours, putting the laptop and other valuables in a locker so we could bike the city together; Stockholm was notorious for theft from vehicles, the worst in Europe. The security guards at the ferry terminal were the second Swedes who tried stealing the bicycles, foiled by an ever alert Mary as I snoozed the night away. Uppsala, the burial place of Swedish kings in a cathedral with 400 foot high towers was a highlight because the campground offered washers half price, $6 for two tiny loads taking 2 ½ hours. The weather finally turned permanently sunny in June, still light at 11 p.m., requiring a sleep mask for Mary.

Extremely Fabulous Norway

Voila, we'd sailed through the final hurdle, Norwegian customs without confiscation of the rapidly depleting gin, over-nighting in Oslo next to the ferry terminal. Oslo highlights were the Vigelands Sculpture Park with 200 awesome stacks of fat naked people, one 200 feet high containing 180 figures, and the Viking museum with ancient longboats on a splurge of $6 each.

Margit and Berger wined and dined us in near-by Drammen with high views over the fjord, where we were further excited by an oil change for $34. They escorted us up the mile long Spiralen tunnel to a mountain top where we hiked through an open air museum past old houses and along a nature trail. Their breakfast smorgasbord consisted of two types of herring, salami, salmon, yoghurt, cukes and hard boiled eggs, four breads, two jams, four cheeses; cream, sweet butterscotch colored, Jarlberg and yellow gouda; honey, butter, juices, milk, tea and coffee, where we sat and grazed. After two idyllic days we rushed away to avoid obesity. Two tiny tomatoes, a small carton of milk, bread, dab of sugar and four mushrooms cost fourteen dollars at a cut-rate supermarket.

Our first favorite fjord was Lysefjorden, driving steeply down 3000 foot cliffs to the bottom along 28 switchbacks, accosted by a fjord pony on the way back up.

This stocky miniature palomino wouldn't let the RV pass until we fed him a cookie. We overnighted on a ledge above the narrow fjord in the non-vertiginous RV.

Norway offered too many 3000 foot waterfalls to count, a great place to run each morning along fjords, lakes and rivers. The City of Bergen provided RV parking on a bay 1 ½ miles north of town center for $13, packed with German, English, Austrian and Dutch RVs. We biked to town and took the funicular to the top of the mountain 3000 feet over Bergen, riding up with cute kindergartners who commuted daily to a school on top.

We chatted with a French sailor off a submarine playing war games with a Dutch sub; he proudly brandished a fancy Norwegian knife he was convinced would kill boar, which he hunted by hand in France, having bagged one the year before. Bergen's sunny weather was lucky, a Brit griping he'd waited out five days of rain to see finally see the city and mountain.

The obligatory $45 fjord cruise sailed up Naeroyfjorden to Sognefjorden, down Aurlandsfjorden to Ausland and Flam, and back to Gudvangen; Norway was a mountainous land littered with tunnels three to ten miles long. We climbed the RV 4000 steep feet out of Aurland, naturally overheating, blocking the narrow road and being cursed by an irate Norwegian who appropriately called me a *foreign born idiot*. The RV skirted alpine lakes with blue ice to Laerdal where we found a festival of food, baked goods and trolls, shooting stalls, a girl's accordion band, BBQ, horseback rides and loads of gorgeous lupines in a rainbow of colors. A twelve minute ferry to leave Laerdal cost $25 and the disembarkation toll road, $18.

The RV suffered a flat while sitting at lunch, tire obviously ruined, but we received copious help, advice and offers of extra jacks from fellow RVers. I asked the friendly German loaning a jack how he liked Norway and said he loved it except, *too many Germans,* who seemed to own most of the RVs in Norway. The long fjords perfectly reflected snow-capped mountains above crystal-clear waters in colors from gray, pale green, lime green, turquoise, dark green, light blue and dark blue, each translucent lake bed providing a double reflection and phenomenal photos,

and a new tire cost $122. Ravenous goats on a river surrounded by Matterhorn-like high peaks (named Eggemea) tried to munch the RV's hood, forcing our relocation 100 meters away.

At the Briksdalbreen glacier trailhead we paid $4.50 to overnight with fifteen other RVs. The next morning's hike proved it a great glacier, a hundred colorful waterfalls pouring from blue ice holes, providing the cover photo for local tourist brochures. At Gerianger Fjord, the most famous in Norway, we parked next to a five hundred foot waterfall, enjoying Greek lemon chicken soup, dinner with a view. The Flydalsjuvet was featured on international Norwegian tourist brochures, showing the Fjord surrounded by jagged granite mountains where a single rock, the Flydalsjuvet, jutted high over the fjord, tiny cruise ships and quaint town far below, providing a perch for tourists and a favorite photo opportunity. Mary shrank from the edge.

Charming Alesund, situated on a long peninsula split by a river dotted with sailboats and old wooden vessels, provided RV parking in the center for $12 including hot showers at an adjoining marina with self-serve laundry for $3 a load. Alesund's old wooden buildings were turreted and ornate, painted in pastels. A hike up 498 steps above the city provided a panorama of the long town stretched next to teal waters sprinkled with islands. It was never dark when we were awake, the sun setting at midnight and up at 3 a.m., the same latitude as Mt. McKinley and we weren't halfway north, suffering dramatic overnight parking spots for six weeks running.

Trondheim's Nordal Cathedral starred the tomb of St. Olaf, buried in 1020 after converting Norway to Christianity. The city was torn up, preparing for its 1000 year celebration in 1997, obviously founded in 997. We found lettuce sold in flower pots; twist off the heads to harvest leaves. Berger was proved correct; gin was $42 for a bottle that cost $2 in Ceuta; good thing I stocked up. Margit and Berger had presented a fabulous going away present: a comprehensive guidebook with detailed maps of Norway that pinpointed perfect parking on lakes, rivers and fjords.

On the ferry from Holm to Vendsud we met a lady who'd managed the Monastery Bar in Phoenix, reminiscing about mutual drunks we'd known. We found a scenic overnight at one end of Vefenfjorden with the sun shining on the Seven Sisters' Peaks 30 miles away at the other end. The RV almost became too familiar with a moose and kid on the road near Gutvik, just before we crossed the Arctic Circle. We stopped at the Polareirkelen Center, surrounded by pink granite memorials and mobbed with 50 RVing Germans buying reindeer skins, Norwegian sweaters and midnight sun postcards, halfway up Norway's 2672 kilometers (1657 miles):

It was an additional 830 miles to the frigid Norwegian border with Russia.

At Ulvavag we caught the first view of my favorite scenery on the planet, the Lofoten Islands twenty miles across the Arctic Ocean, snow-capped and breathtaking with dazzling sunlight on the peaks, sun all night long. We endured a shockingly scenic drive to Skutnik among triangular granite peaks 2000 feet vertical from sea level, green spikes tipped with snow. The ferry took three RVs and 25 cars to the Lofeten Islands, costing $55 and taking two hours to Svolvear, the capital. We sailed via Skrova, a rocky fishing village accessible only by boat, surrounded by overwhelming mountains on the neighboring islands across sea green water lapping on white sand beaches, looking like the Caribbean. Though it seemed incredibly inviting, diving, even in the middle of summer, should be discouraged, except for Germans or those with antifreeze for blood. Otherwise, tutus would be shrunk.

Near Svolvear we overnighted next to red fishing huts on stilts, the ocean bed visible through perfectly clear water, the land covered with yellow, purple and white flowers. Far above the Arctic Circle the beaches were strewn with sunbathers in weather that could only be called gorgeous. The string of rocky Gibraltar-like islands ended south in Reine and A (actual name of the village), often covered in a weird fog where we saw a man with a bike and trailer pulling a kid reading a comic book in the drizzle under a plastic roof. The weather was ultra-strange with sun for an hour, then cloudy, more sun, then drizzle, again cloudy, then sun, hourly. After umpteen years of continuous travel Norway is world number one for scenery, topped by the Lofeten Islands. Number two is Roraima Tepui that sits at the intersection of Guyana, Brazil and Venezuela.

Sweden and Finland: Reindeer and Skeeters

After six incredible weeks we left Norway for Sweden, used to rinsing clothes in ice water. We'd learned to soak the laundry in a bucket as we drove, the RV's motion washing it clean, leaving the only chore to rinse and hang dry, thanks to John Steinbeck in *Travels with Charlie.* A thirty mile-long lake began at Bjorkliden, surrounded by snow-streaked mountains in a national park packed with Scandinavians in tents and trailers; German-free. Isolated Kiruna sat at the south end of the lake, a large mining town in the middle of nowhere with heaters on parking meters to keep engines warm in winter, and perhaps summer too. We overnighted 15 miles out of town at the entrance to a large hunting estate; at 8 p.m. a French RV stopped and we chatted with Patrice and Makalay for hours over coffee, brandy and beer, until 11 p.m. when they left to drive further. We corresponded for years, unfortunately never able to accept invitations to visit their home in Normandy.

Beginning at Junosuando we found herds of caribou, the locals laughing when we took photos of common old reindeer. Several friendly reindeer followed Mary on a morning run along the Tornealven River, which we crossed into Finland. The adult reindeer were molting but the babies were cute with splayed hooves, big eyes like velvet paintings and tiny velvety horns. They were owned like cattle, rounded up by snowmobile each winter for slaughter. I enjoyed an excellent reindeer burger smothered with mushrooms topped with lettuce, tomatoes, leeks and ketchup, far better than the local specialty of pork and fish in a fried turnover.

Finland was lakes; the tourist office bragged it had 187,888, 18 times as many as Minnesota. With a surface area of 10% water Finland was also umpteen trillion mosquitoes. We had difficulty keeping mosquitoes out of the RV, preferring them outside where they drove the reindeer nuts as they jerked, twitched and suffered. The mosquitoes didn't often bite us but they buzzed like crazy, interrupting sleep, hibernating in the RV during the daytime, avoiding detection and destruction. We found parking away from trees and stagnant ponds difficult in Finland, but we finally lost mosquitoes completely a few degrees south.

Roveniemi is five miles south of the Arctic Circle on which sits the Santa Claus Post Office, a kitschy tourist magnet. We arranged with FinnTours in Roveniemi, co-owned with a Russian agency, to fly from Helsinki to St. Petersburg, four days and three nights for $666; two weeks budget blown in four days, why not? RVs couldn't enter Russia without proof of prepaid accommodation during each night of temporary residency, basically impossible to achieve, which we later confirmed.

Upon arrival in Helsinki we booked the ferry for Tallinn, Estonia for $151, scheduled the day after return from St. Petersburg. At the ticket office we met an American couple who'd shipped an RV from Texas and had spent six weeks unsuccessfully trying to arrange prepaid camping accommodation in Russia, the primary condition for a Russian visa. They'd almost given up RVing Russia after driving around Europe for ten months. During three years RVing Europe and environs we met only two other American couples, in Sicily and a week later in Estonia.

Rough in Russia, Balmy in the Baltics

Aeroflot flew to St. Petersburg on July 31 along with several obvious members of the Russian mafia and a German businessman forced to upgrade to business class because he was flying on a business visa. The plane was shabby and nothing worked; the seats fell forward, the cabin attendants were unattractive, fair enough, but nasty; the free champagne tasted like kerosene, all on a too-long forty minute flight. A Lech Walesa look-alike drove us from the airport hell-bent for the Muscova Hotel, past drab apartment blocks, police speed traps and flocks of kiosks. The Muscova Hotel was a concrete monstrosity, passably decent inside, ignoring the occasional roach and the evening posse of mosquitoes. We collapsed in the room, happy to survive the hotdog Aeroflot landing. The television offered eight channels including one in English that provided continuous coverage of the Summer Olympics.

The Muscova sat on the south end of Nevsky Prospect near the Nevsky River, three miles from city center. Snazzily-dressed blonde ladies in mini-skirts strolled the main boulevard; if they'd been brunettes I'd have thought we were in Rome. Then we witnessed a wedding that showcased the bride in a see-through mini-skirt. Sad old ladies sat begging for near-worthless rubles at 5100 to the dollar. Stores were unsigned, anonymous doors hiding who knew what?

The city was sprinkled with marvelous onion-turreted churches; the jewel was the Blood of the Savior Cathedral with gold-onion domes atop flashy ceramics and mosaics, similar to St. Basil's in Moscow. For $8 we browsed the Hermitage for hours, exhausted hiking three floors, each covering two square blocks, benumbed by Greek sculpture, Egyptian tombs, French paintings, Mongolian artifacts and Roman antiquities.

Russian pork burritos were a $1 and thus became a twice daily snack. The Metro was always packed, offering directions only in Cyrillic, failing to match our map. However, subway attendants were helpful and friendly, at least three four, as were the locals. Most signs outside the Metro were in Russian and English

The weather was hot and humid, sunbathers strewn outside St. Peter and Paul's Fortress in the middle of the river where the czars were buried. We ignored peeling paint and torn up roads, while Italian tourists lustily applauded a freelance Russian opera singer accompanied on accordion. A highlight was the tombs of famous Russian composers from Borodin and Mussorgsky to Rimsky-Korsakov at Nevsky Monastery, practically next door to the Muscova. We were tempted to kiss the ground upon landing in Helsinki, all the same happy with the intriguing side trip to St. Petersburg.

The ferry to Tallinn was huge; seven stories high, carrying tons of trucks and three RVs, taking three hours. We relished diesel for 38 cents a liter, the cheapest in nineteen months, enough to kindle a love affair with Estonia. Tallinn was built on a steep hill overlooking the old town and Gulf of Finland, stuffed with fanciful Orthodox Church towers sporting onion turrets of copper and a rainbow of ceramic, sandwiching the usual

McDonalds Restaurant. Because supermarket prices were half that in Finland the Finns ferried over to buy cheap liquor on raucous weekend cruises.

The guidebook warned; *don't leave vehicles unattended*, so we sauntered around town in shifts, avoiding guarded parking for $9 an hour. We found an immaculate campground nine miles south of town for $8 at a Best Western Hotel, meeting Finns who'd wintered in Fuengirola and a Texas couple, Jeff and Dee, in an RV with British plates. We chatted with the Texans until midnight. Jeff had retired as an engineer after years in Egypt; they were duplicating a trip from twenty years ago to the Lofoten Islands and Nordcapp, off to St. Petersburg for five days: we discussed finding propane in Europe, water in Italy, BBC and VOA frequencies, and unsafe countries in South America and touring Australia, which they disliked and we later loved.

Estonia's Parnu was a lively beach town with stylish walking streets, eighteen parks on lakes, colorful wooden buildings, orthodox churches and low prices. Mary celebrated her 47th birthday in balmy August weather, pleading a migraine and sending me out for pizzas, mushroom with onions and Mexican with jalapeños and pepperoni, chocolate ice cream for desert. The migraine may have been caused by the bikinied platinum blondes on the beach and in miniskirts sashaying down Parnu's walking streets, several at whom I may have inadvertently glanced.

Latvia required the purchase of five days insurance, uncovered by the European insurance card. The only alternative was to cash Mary's hidden $20 bill. She was direly upset at spending her secret stash for a measly $6 of insurance. (Now we travel with $1000 hidden away.) I passed an hour in Riga withdrawing local money and finding a forex to procure two $20 bills, doubling Mary's security blanket for a well-spent $5 commission. The great Riga market filled five dirigible hangers built by Germans in WWII, offering unbelievable prices after Scandinavia, where I'd felt compelled to give up beer. Latvian beer was between 55 and 71 cents, versus $5 in Scandinavia. Happy days were here again.

We drove a dirt road to save ten minutes on a short-cut to see a Latvian palace, later requiring hours to clean the inside of the RV. Near the Lithuanian border we befriended Visalya at a Texaco station selling diesel for 35 cents a liter; he'd been born in the Ukraine, served eight months in the French Foreign Legion and yearned to move to San Francisco to teach languages. We also met thirteen Finns in an RV; parents, grandparents and nine kids returning from a whirlwind trip to visit cousins in Hungary, the only other European country with a language similar to Finnish.

Lithuanian border guards failed to require the purchase of local insurance thus preserving Mary's new stash of two 20-dollar bills though our European insurance policy provided no coverage in Lithuania. When given a choice we almost always forego vehicle insurance, having found collection in foreign countries ranges between impossible and out of the question; the only solution was to drive ultra-carefully. Trakai was the most attractive part of Lithuania, surrounded by lakes flecked with sailboats around a four-turreted castle next door to a sprawling 24 acre campground where we stayed two nights to sightsee close-by Vilnius. The feisty manager had opened the campground in 1992, one year after the Soviets were kicked out of Lithuania.

The local English-language newspaper, *The Baltic Times*, was enlightening about government corruption and ineptitude, failing banks, the fledgling stock market and illegal immigrants transiting to Scandinavia; 58 had been apprehended the day before, from Sri Lanka, Pakistan, India and Bangladesh. Vilnius displayed Coke ads featuring Lithuanian players in the NBA who'd just won bronze at the Olympics, a dozen onion-spired churches and perfect weather. We saw five separate Lithuanian wedding parties, each slavishly following the apparent tradition of requiring the groom to carry the bride, often hefty, across a long bridge, grunting and stumbling for memorable photos.

Surfing Poland and the Czech Republic

While waiting to cross into Poland we watched customs dismantle a car smuggling thousands of Lithuanian cigarettes in hidden compartments. Small Polish grocery stores restricted customer entry to behind a long counter where those who spoke no Polish could point at their selection. At the first campground we were the only Americans who'd stayed in over a year. An oil change costing $47 took three hours that included finding an oil filter and oil, neither provided, and a bus service station where the RV would fit, an impossibility without assistance by 21-year-old Dan who spoke some English and had a morning to kill.

The Poles were exceedingly bad drivers, inattentive and in a perpetual rush. We saw accidents every day during a three week stay, requiring concentration on the rear view mirror, always looking for cars passing and merging. The weather turned rainy after a sunny month, but we were able to counter the resulting chill by filling both German propane bottles, ten liters for $2.25, the best price in Europe. Everyone was ultra-friendly from the Baltics south through Poland, people waving, relieved to recently escape Soviet domination and curious about the USA letters on the RV. They were likely wondering what people from the land of Hollywood looked like; we were sorry to disappoint them. Overnight parking was difficult to find with fields up to fences but restaurants, bars and gas stations happily begged the RV to park for free.

We temporarily exited Poland to visit Charles in Prague where he'd recommended a campground on an island in the middle of the Vitava River, which bisected the city. Prague is the best city in Europe for medieval architecture and pickpockets, the latter discovered years later by friends visiting at our suggestion. The city harbors 1400 ornate gothic buildings protected by UNESCO,

including the striking National Museum, Wenceslas Square, Tyn Church, Royal Palace, Gunpowder Tower, Hus Monument, Clock Tower and Charles Bridge lined with statuary. Prague was the only major European city undestroyed or badly damaged during WWII.

The first day in Prague we walked eight hours nonstop, gawking. On day two, led by Charles and his big German Shepard Bulyar we explored the Castle side of the river, finding half the people were afraid of Bulyar and the other half were compelled to pet. Charles gave a six hour tour, talking nonstop, through the Royal Palace Drabovsky, St. Vitus Cathedral, Prague Castle and St.George's Cathedral, along with a million other tourists. Charles Bridge was hopping with jazz bands and puppeteers.

Back in Poland we stayed at Campground Krakow. The city showcased St. Mary's Cathedral on the largest Renaissance Square in Europe. The square was thronged with costumed singers and bands dressed in red, hats embellished with peacock feathers and homemade statues of straw and flowers. August was vacation month in Europe, not a good time to sightsee anywhere, tourist horse carts clogging the thoroughfares from the fire-spouting dragon statue and along the old city walls around the ancient square.

From Krakow we meandered to Oswieam, aka Auschwitz, spending hours over exhibits of shoes, hair, brushes, suitcases and photos of inmates, most surviving two months of hard labor before demise. The tourists were somber with many crying, the original entrance arch still shouting, *Arbeit Macht Frei;* quite horrible. We parked overnight in a close-by gravel pit, our universal refuge in many countries, always quiet with no one else about.

Hungary to Serbia

After Slovakia's scenic mountains we detoured to Austria to find a genius who could repair the hot water heater. Finally getting through on the phone to a Vienna RV-repair shop the man assured me he could schedule the RV for repair in only two weeks.

When I choked he kindly asked the problem, which I described; the hot water heater flamed up and refused to stay lit. He said, *go to a gas station and blow the pilot out with compressed air because it's likely clogged with dust or a bug.* I did and the problem was fixed for $2.30 in phone calls.

The Hungarian border was lined with Austrians reviewing rather plump and unattractive hookers on the highway, similar to the parade alongside many Italian roads. We followed the twisty Danube 105 kilometers to Budapest and the best stocked supermarket we'd found in months, two long aisles for every commodity from coffee and chocolate to pasta, stocking up encouraged by very low prices. We grabbed the *meal deal* at Burger King for $1.33, mostly to forget the terrible rush hour traffic up steep hills with the RV overheating; Burger King managed to pivot our moods 180 degrees.

At a campground near Castle hill we chatted with a Norwegian couple who said we'd seen far more of Norway than they had, feedback we've gotten in countries all over the world. The bus driver refused to sell us a ticket to town, requiring that we ride free, saving 67 cents. The Budapest Hilton Hotel had been incorporated into a 11th Century monastery on Castle Hill, blending in for great views over Parliament in Pest on the other side of the Danube. St. Matthias was a smaller version of St. Stephens in Vienna, sitting smack in the middle of Castle Hill with a magnificent tile roof, admission to the ornate inside 28 cents. Outside we were serenaded by a twenty piece band in Hungarian folk costumes. Across the bridge in Pest we walked for hours, checking bookstores for Yugoslavian visa information.

CHAPTER FOUR
Year Two in Europe Becomes Even More Interesting

Mandatory insurance cost $60 on the Serbian border and as usual at border crossings we'd spent the last of the currency from the country we were exiting, requiring a return to Hungary and the closest ATM nine miles away in Szeged. We withdrew Hungarian Forints for exchange into Deutch Marks at a terrible rate; German currency was de rigueur in Serbia. Back through the Serbian border we found a neat well-kept country. Patient locals offered frequent directions because our maps were woefully inadequate until we could exit east into Bulgaria. Serbian towns were snarled by horse carts, tractors, cars, trucks, bicycles, 18-wheelers and our solitary RV. We saw no other tourists in the country and one other RV in four days, happy to arrive in Nis and turn east toward Sofia, Bulgaria.

The Serbian Surprise: September 3-4, 1996

The next morning the RV would turn over but not start, killing the battery in four extended tries. I'd barely propped the hood up when an ancient Yellow Mercedes flashed by, did a double take and screeched to a halt, beginning two days of non-stop adventure.

Instead of helping push the RV the occupants of the Mercedes, who we came to know well, towed the RV three miles to an Aute Servis garage, which employed staff reminiscent of an Appalachian hillbilly village: a 65-year-old head mechanic with wispy white hair and blue, blue eyes dressed in ancient nylon pants, who looked like Sid Caesar; a 30-something porker with sad eyes and crew cut, stomach spilling over his pants, who performed most of the manual labor; a 40-year old nonstop smoker wearing an ancient jogging suit smeared with oil, the ostensible boss man, vaguely reminiscent of Richard Wagner; an indeterminately-aged chap with a hatchet nose, half asleep, roused from his bed in a cottage next to the filthy garage.

The four-man crew pushed the RV inside the garage over a six-foot deep oil pit that hadn't been cleaned since the Renaissance, sole decoration a faded pin-up of Vladimir Ilyich Lenin on the wall over two snoring sows and a dozen pecking chickens. Shooing the animals away, ineffectively, the crew went to work with ardor, pronouncing the fuel pump defective. No one spoke English; the only common language was my largely forgotten German.

The fuel pump was transported to Nis and back but the RV still wouldn't start. The diesel injectors were removed and after many comings and goings *new* injectors were somehow located. The work began at 10 am and finished by 2 pm when the RV was pronounced copasetic. During these four hours we were served coffee in filthy cups around a ramshackle table, formerly a cable spool. Richard produced a Serbian newspaper in Cyrillic with photos showing a US missile attack on Iraq, apparently to punish Saddam Hussein for attacking a Kurdish village in Northern Iraq. People had died but no Americans were killed. At 2 p.m. Richard fired up the RV for a triumphant test drive and it was perfect, really.

The bill was formally presented, for 1750 DM, $1166 for four hours, itemized at $533 for four injectors, $233 for a fuel pump that looked new and $400 labor for four guys sometimes toiling while most of the community looked on. I extracted the money belt and dumped our last 170DM on the table. Richard went berserk in a nonviolent fashion, frothing. The colorful crew discussed options in German: take out the fuel pump and injectors and ship the RV to Bulgaria by truck. They'd suddenly accept $800, discounting labor to $34. Our 170DM, about $120, left a gap. Whereupon I accompanied Richard to Nis to see whether money could somehow be advanced on a credit card, knowing full well there was no possibility because of the U.S. embargo. This two hour adventure featured the yellow Mercedes peeling out of various bank parking lots and Richard chatting with assorted street scum and other wheeler dealers. After two hours Richard was more sullen than ever.

I suggested we go to Sofia, Bulgaria to find money, whereupon Richard retrieved his passport from a Nis suburb, the Mercedes broke down and we were towed back to the garage. Richard countered that a piston must first be removed from the engine to ensure our continued presence during the night. I had a good laugh and Richard cringed. We drove the RV to a nearby restaurant with bus parking and enjoyed an excellent dinner with the three mechanics, while I bought drinks around. Richard refused to eat or drink so I quaffed his beer, chatting jovially with Sid.

Richard demanded 150DM, $100 for driving me to Sofia and I chortled. The loyal crew guarded the RV in shifts through the night while Mary slept little. At 6 a.m. I piled into a decrepit white car with Richard and the driver, a Danny DeVito look-a-like with oak cask arms, east to the Bulgarian border lickety split. It was raining in sheets and the border wouldn't open until 8:30 a.m. We stood under a leaky parapet for 1 ½ hours while gypsies queued up to cross.

I paid $44 for two visas, for Richard and me, and Richard found us a ride to Sofia in a new Mercedes with two friends who looked like Tweedledee and obese twin brother, Tweedledum. During the ride to Sofia the Tweedles drank 1½ liters of Pepsi and chain smoked in a car tightly closed up in the driving rain. The Tweedles let Richard and I off on the outskirts of Sofia where I proudly paid for a taxi to city center.

It took two hours to find a bank willing to advance cash on MasterCard and exchange $1433 of Bulgarian Lev for 2000 Deutch Mark with a $102 commission. I told Richard I was only able to get a maximum of $800; the MasterCard limit was $16,100. Then I paid $10 for a taxi back to the Serbian border. Though still raining in sheets a Bulgarian cop made the cab stop half a mile from the border, resulting in our further drenching.

Danny sped us back to Mary and the lonesome RV by 2 pm. On the way we saw an 18-wheeler aftermath that had destroyed two little cars, one Jugo cut in two and another under the rig, blood and auto parts everywhere. I paid Richard the grand total of $500 (750DM) for transport to the border, parts and labor and we left happy in the like-new RV, giddy. We parked in a quiet spot ten miles from the Bulgarian border, thinking *been there, done that*, crossing back into Bulgaria at 10 a.m. the next day, ending this particular adventure until the next one.

Happiness was Bulgaria

Taking the RV over the Bulgarian border promoted a scam, officials charging a border tax of $44 on top of visas for $90, $3 for health insurance I sensed was uncollectible, $5 for a nonexistent veterinarian inspection and $40 for travel permits. It was great to escape the drama of Serbia and revisit Bulgaria after a trip there twenty seven years previous. The Bulgarians were extremely nice, the same as people everywhere, excluding a single lady in Luxembourg; we've found that only governments differ, not their unfortunate subjects.

The most important Bulgarian date was 1885 when they were liberated from the Turks with Russian assistance, making the Russians and Bulgarians old allies. Hram Pametnik Siska, a replica of a Russian Orthodox Church built during the liberation year of 1885, was dazzling, probably why I vividly remembered it from the 1972 trip, huge golden onion domes atop four smaller ones, tall brightly colored ceramic spire in front, admission 100 Lev. With 230 lev to the $1 this worked out to 42 cents.

Quaint Veliko Tornovo had been the capital of Bulgaria from the 12th to 14th Centuries, where I was happy to find gin at $1.05 a bottle. Spending $15 a day was difficult because fuel was a dollar a gallon and food was bargain-basement priced. A half pound of the world's best feta, Bulgarian according to Greek Mary and her family, cost 42 cents.

The Veliko Fortress was huge, a mile around on a narrow mesa-like peninsula with fully restored walls. A boy who spoke English volunteered to find me a variety of Bulgarian car stickers, returning with five flashy ones and refusing money, happy to practice his English. Here's a photo of the stickers we ended up with on the back of our European RV:

In Targoviste we looked for sugar in an ancient country store but couldn't find it. We took a cup full from the RV and showed it to the lady, who tasted it and wheeled out a fifty gallon barrel, selling a kilo for basically nothing.

A ruin listed in the guidebook had gone missing so we asked two policemen where it might be; they jumped in their police car and led the RV two miles to extensive Byzantium ruins from 800-1200 AD, completely devoid of tourists, perhaps because no one could find it. There was no admission charge and no restrictions. We wandered through old churches, along walls, into baths and atop foundations covering 50 acres for an unsupervised hour.

Back on the highway some genius had cut blocks out of the roadway, 10 to 20 foot chunks half the width of the road, holes that would blow the tires of any vehicle traveling over ten miles an hour, too fast to thread among gaping voids. The guidebook warned of thieves in Varna so we took turns sightseeing two square blocks of ancient Roman baths. During a moment of my inattention someone removed chairs from the bike rack in seconds, probably aiming to next try the locked-on bikes.

Camping Europa on the extremely blue Black Sea offered views over a broad bay to Burgas and its striking lighthouse, where we relaxed after the interesting Serbian adventure, catching up on chores, which included removing oily handprints from the RV. Kilos of celery, apples and peaches were 20 cents each in Ajtos, where we met George at his hopping restaurant bar; he kindly exchanged 3100 Lev for 20 Deutch Marks and presented us a bonus bag of huge walnuts we'd seen people knocking out of trees, very tasty after drying in the sun for a single day.

A Bulgarian highlight was the fabulous Rila Monastery 15 miles up a scenic road along a burbling river. The ancient monastery encircled a richly decorated clock tower covered with colorful murals in the center of a broad courtyard surrounded by a four story building with carved wooden balconies, 14 chapels and elderly women sweeping the cobblestones with crude straw brooms.

Greek Home Weeks

The return to Greece, an oft-visited country for us, was particularly happy because my child support obligation had ended, adding 60% to the monthly budget for a new grand total of $2000 a month. We could never kick impulse shopping the day we withdrew weekly money, which meant we stocked up on spanakopita at a dollar a slice, feta, olives and spent $3 for Domestica red wine, a favorite since the first Greek trip in 1972, wine I bought by the case in Phoenix for $6 a bottle. Greek prices, relatively inexpensive in 1996, exploded upon Greece's entry into the EU, and Bulgaria's membership has with certainty driven prices comparatively sky high. Diesel was 70 cents a liter in Greece and 30 cents in Bulgaria; by 2006 diesel was two dollars a liter EU-wide.

Hiking up the Aoos River gorge to a remote abandoned monastery at Stomion was exhilarating. After lunch I climbed a rope into a second story window, finding wide views over the gorge and audio tapes strewn on the floor. A liberated tape revealed Gregorian chants.

At Perama we explored an enormous cave that filled a large hill shaped like a loaf of bread, parking overnight on Lake Ioannina next door to the cave, opposite its namesake city bristling with castles and ancient churches on a peninsula jutting into the lake. The ferries for Venice and Corfu left from Igoumenitsa, a few miles away where we opted for Corfu, a resort island 36 by 17 miles (58 by 27 kilometers); one hour, $44. Corfu Town was dominated by two fortresses, one British and the other ancient Venetian. The island was one large tourist resort but we found isolated parking on a cliff 20 feet from the ocean, calling Camping Dionysis in Dasias, also on Corfu, to confirm its address and order mail. Corfu, excluding its pricey resorts, was picturesque towns, colorful fishing boats and loads of British tourists, meaning signs in English.

Poseidon Travel in Corfu Town quoted the ferry from Athens to Israel via Rhodes and Cyprus for 3 ½ days at $600 each way with private cabin; we thought about buying the tickets but dithered. According to Lawrence Durrell the best beach in the world was at Mirtiotisa on Corfu but we were too lazy to look for it.

Back on the mainland at Nafpaktos we paid $9 for the Peloponnese ferry, which took 15 minutes. The BBC reported the U.S. embargo of Serbia had been lifted the day before, on October 2, 1996, rendering credit cards again operable. The active monastery high up a cliff at Mega Spileo cost $1.60 for the exploration of a cutesy chapel, ornate cave with statuary and a museum with old parchment books stacked amongst gold and silver icons where Mary was required to don an ugly monastical skirt to enter. Peloponnese roadsides were littered with shrines of miniature blue and white Greek churches.

Olympia was a must-visit with ancient ruins of 25 buildings, stadium and temple of Zeus, while at Andritsena four teenage boys bravely flashed the RV, chagrined as we laughed uproariously and gestured *how tiny* with thumbs and forefingers an inch apart. We watched a woman walking a tortoise on a leash near the lofty hill town of Karitena, its unusual bridge pictured on the 5000 drachma note. In town we were collared by George, mentioned in *Let's Go Greece*, for his unbiased opinions on the wonderfulness of religion, the Turks and their 400-year occupation of Greece, dwelling at length on the uniqueness of the picturesque bridge.

The guidebooks raved about Tega and other sites where we found nothing worth seeing. We concluded flowery guidebook descriptions should be distrusted and Mary added, *travel writers* such as me. But we found Nafplio utterly charming: eclectic ancient architecture, a three-block long Saturday market, a fortress on an island 300 meters offshore, cute churches and taverns and most impressively a fortress 1000 meters long that could be accessed only by 999 steps, sprawling over a cliff high overhead and pocked with old cisterns and remnants of high walls.

Old Corinth's extensive ruins sat below the vastest fortress in Greece, Akrokorinthos. It covered the top of a mountain affording great overnight views above the Bay of Corinth. Next morning we meandered Akrokorinthos' towers, cisterns, ruins, church and a wall three kilometers (two miles) long. The mountain-top ruins had been inhabited since the Stone Age, which at the pace of onsite workers would take until the next Stone Age to restore.

King Agamemnon's huge beehive tomb and slightly lesser beehive for Queen Clyremistra made Mycenae by itself worth the trip to Greece. Though neither may be authentic tombs they were thronged with tourists in a sweltering hot sun. A Volkswagen camper with California plates pulled next to the RV for the night. It'd been shipped from San Francisco by Dave, a Brit, for a six month trip including Nordcapp. Mary screaming in the shower the next morning meant the water heater had balked again.

The architecture on the middle finger of the Peloponnese was towers and more towers built by rebel descendants of the Spartans, striking designs above the clear blue Aegean. We found the best photos were taken outside archeological sites, justifying continuing refusal to pay most admissions. The newspaper showed a major storm headed toward Greece from Italy and it began to sprinkle. Based on a story in the same newspaper we briefly considered staying in Crete for the winter because Israel was heating up with spats between Benjamin Netanyahu and the Palestinians, a yahoo crimping our plans.

Sparta was relaxing after we finally arrived. The steep road to Sparta had been highly scenic and twisty, precipitous vertical views next to copious wild blackberries and kumquats we'd freely picked. The Byzantine ruins at nearby Mistras' nine churches, small palaces and fortress were awesome, completely covering a 1000 foot cliff; we gladly paid $5 to spend a morning's exploration, Greece's best bargain. A Tripoli garage kindly changed the oil for $25, charging only for the oil. We were $100 ahead of the monthly budget, cutting back to pay for the ferry to Israel, assuming we went, living on feta, olives, fruit and vegetables, not to mention beer, coke, wine and gin, the tough and the frugal. Mary blamed a recurrent bad stomach on the water while nothing fazed mine; I doted on roadside food. Meanwhile Mary had a blast chatting up Greeks about her Papou and Mamou, grandfather and grandmother, always great fun.

The Cretan Connection

We suffered the usual clogged traffic through Athens to the port of Piraeus, boarding the Minos line ferry, *Nikos Katzanzakis* for Crete, a large Greek island 160 miles (260 kilometers) long and between eight and 37 miles (13 and 60 kilometers) wide. At 4:00 p.m. I backed the RV up two long ramps to the ferry's second level and the ship left promptly at 7:30 p.m. The long trip to Iraklion took 11 hours, costing $225 with private cabin for a good nights' sleep. We chatted with Germans who bragged how great the U.S. and Germany were compared to primitive Greece, which they visited three weeks every year.

I promptly got lost in pre-dawn Iraklion but a scooter driver guided the RV to the proper road and we rushed west to Hania (aka Khania) to organize a hike down the Samaria Gorge before it closed on November 1, the reason for the slightly early trip to Crete. Hania was an attractive town with a pleasant waterfront, dozens of inexpensive tavernas and restaurants, and an old Venetian lighthouse at the end of the spit. It was also crowded with U.S. servicemen from a close-by base who spoke an idiom we'd nearly forgotten, fun for eavesdropping. We stayed at Camping Hania four kilometers west of town and 100 meters from a horseshoe-shaped beach surrounded by sheer rock cliffs: ours was the only RV.

Campground Germans told us they'd hiked the Samaria Gorge uphill with full packs; 99% hike it downhill and so would we. The Samaria Gorge bus ride, hike, boat ride and bus back took 13 hours roundtrip for a nominal $22 each including admissions; we left the campground on bikes at 6:30 a.m. and were back at 7:30 p.m., five minutes before it rained at the end of this unremittingly sunny day. The bus ride to the gorge entrance, 36 kilometers (22 miles) above Hania at 5000 feet of altitude, took 1 ½ hours up sharply climbing switchbacks barely wide enough for the bus to swing around, necessarily taking the whole road and more. After hiking 2 ½ steep miles down the gorge we became concerned about a white-haired man sitting on a rock, huffing and puffing, asking him if he was hiking up. He was hiking down and we found out the next day he'd suffered a heart attack and died before he could be carried out. Samaria highlights were the sparkling yellow stream perhaps enhanced by sulfur-bearing rocks, old churches and village and the spot where the vertical canyon walls narrowed to ten feet, a kilometer before the end of the hiking part at Agia Romeli. The ferry to Hora Sfakion for the bus back to Hania hugged a rugged picturesque coast, making for a tremendously scenic day.

Mary consulted an English-speaking doctor in Hania who diagnosed her stiff and sore hand problem as carpel tunnel syndrome from years of weight lifting, prescribing an anti-inflammatory that cost $10 and illustrating exercises she faithfully followed for two years, completely curing the problem. The office visit with unlimited follow-ups cost $25.

Beginning a month's drive around Crete we found steep terraced hills covered with olive trees and flowers from red geraniums to star jasmine, bananas and palm trees. A scenic hike high above Piso Moni Preveli beach passed an old monastery vertical over the Libyan Sea where a river cascaded down steep hills and turned 90 degrees, providing a 30-mile view of the jagged coastline far below. Southern Crete was uniformly spectacular with deep gorges, high peaks and small whitewashed villages seemingly pasted halfway up.

A serpentine road led to Agni Galini stacked on four levels above a tiny harbor where a tractor was trying to pull a tour boat off grounding. Most of the town's residents were shouting advice; the scene was unchanged an hour later when we meandered back through town. In Iraklion we finally bought ferry tickets for Israel, paying $1530 return on a prepaid MasterCard, hoping Israel would be an adventure short of another seven days' war and toasty warm for the winter.

The Lasithiou plateau above Iraklion was 23 kilometers (14 miles) in circumference and surrounded by mountain peaks where Zeus was born in a cave at Dikteo Andro. Steep switchbacks led to grand views rimmed with elderly windmills and quaint villages stuffed with octogenarian women in black selling honey, apples and walnuts. Off the plateau bordering the sea in Elounda we found scenic overnight parking with picture perfect views of town and island from a causeway leading to the near-island of Spinatonga, mercifully devoid of traffic.

On Election Day 1996 we were unable to vote because Florida insisted our sole permanent American address was a mail forwarding service, which was perfectly true, this anomaly preventing our voting for 12 years. On the furthest east end of Crete at Kato Zakros we found a perfect little town a single block long on a beach below sheer cliffs pocked with caves that sandwiched the town. There we hiked four miles up steep Dead's Gorge to Ano Zakros along caves and a verdant river with deep swirling pools, voting the hike superior to Samaria Gorge. During the month on Crete we took turns reading *The Odyssey,* great fun as we visited many of the starring locations on Crete.

After discovering Troy and Mycenae the amateur archeologist Heinrich Schliemann barely missed uncovering Knossos, which was likely destroyed in the cataclysmic eruption of Thera that formed Santorini. We spent happy hours poking around restored red columns and frescoes, leaving upon the onslaught of tour buses. The next day we returned to see the museum because it was free on Sundays, saving $13 for a celebration of the month on Crete. The Knossos Museum ranked among the top in Europe, showcasing artistry from the 19th-17th centuries B.C.E., including delicate gold sculpture, seals of fantastically horned-bulls, frescoes, double axes, colorful ceramics, statuary, weapons, house models, amphora, crystal and sheer poke-around pleasure.

After visiting the tomb of Nikos Katzanzakis, famous for *Zorba the Greek* and other fiery works, I backed the RV onto the ferry for Athens and we reminisced about Crete's succulent tomatoes and squash, donkeys with wooden saddles, drivers parking in the middle of the road to gossip the same as in Ireland, quaint villages with rickety windmills, the crystalline Aegean, old women in black with matching mustaches, hotdog drivers, precipitous canyons and the blessed absence of tourists out of season.

CHAPTER FIVE
A Dab of the Middle East: Cyprus, Israel, Jordan and Egypt

All wars are civil wars, because all men are brothers....Each one owes infinitely more to the human race than to the particular country in which he was born. Francois de Salignac de la Mothe-Fenelon (1651-1715), French writer and Archbishop of Cambray

Cyprus Gripes Us

Back in Piraeus at 6 a.m. we enjoyed five hours of pandemonium during the loading of the ferry to Israel, which no longer runs. On board we were befriended by a German Jew, Enrique, a ringer for my father. Enrique had fled to Chile in 1939 where he'd lived twenty years, later teaching solar engineering at Oxford. He was off to Tel Aviv as a visiting professor at the University. The next morning the ship sounded a *muster station drill* to man the lifeboats but no passengers showed up because no one had been briefed or had a clue what was going on. At noon we dropped anchor off Rhodes.

The next morning we drove *Grendel II* off the ferry in Cyprus, planning to stay two weeks before reboarding for Israel, taking two hours to clear customs, paying $90 for two week's RV insurance and $50 for something else. Driving on the British side of the road took less time getting used to than the summer before in the UK. Spotting an ATM we stopped to withdraw 210 Cypriot pounds, costing $462. We *never* carry travelers' checks, which are difficult to cash in every country, while ATMs dispense local currency everywhere except Myanmar. It was nice having signs in English but the countryside was amongst the ugliest we'd seen, white soil like chalk. Then the RV's 12 volt system burned out. We'd smelled smoke an hour before but couldn't find the source. With no electrical we searched out candles when the sun set at 5 p.m.

Mary was sapped by Cyprus after a single day but we soldiered on to Hala Sultan Tekke, the 4th most holy Muslim site. In 647 C.E Mohammed's aunt broke her neck falling off a donkey and the faithful built a commemorative mosque alias tomb, quite ugly next to a half dry salt lake crowded with flamingoes. In Larnaca we found a propane plant to fill both 5 kilo German bottles for $4.40, a bargain making Cyprus look a speck better. Scenic Cape Greko sat on the furthest east point of Greek Cypriot territory, seemingly a good overnight spot a 100 meters from raucous breakers, where we read by candlelight. Next morning the RV was covered with salt. However, inquisitive Mary, after I'd given up, had found charred wires under a settee. We bought a few feet of wire for 77 cents, substituting new for charred and fixing the 12 volt electrical system. Her dogged diagnosis won Mary a humongous ice cream cone.

Guarded parking in the capital of Nicosia was $1.55 for a half day, allowing lots of time to wander the old town and check out the Green Line fence crowded with gawking tourists, a UN soldier in a guard post and beyond that no man's land with Turkish flags. The biggest shock was a happy one, diesel for 24 cents a liter, 90 cents a gallon, lowest in the world until visits to Venezuela in 2003 and Turkmenistan in 2008.

High in the Troodos Mountains we saw an electrifying sign, *camping permitted,* a first in two years. We pulled into a sprawling picnic area with water, trash containers and restrooms, deserted in the middle of a cool forest with good hiking on the Kaledonia trail, steep along a sparkling stream with waterfalls, polished wooden bridges and pines shrouded in vines. We felt we'd earned it because the mountain road was a windy single lane above vertical drop offs. The lofty Kykko Monastery was overlaid in chromatic mosaics and bright frescoes with an interior of glistening gold. This was Makarios' old church, his adjacent tomb gilded with two Cypriot guards and panoramic views over steep gorges.

We overnighted on a cliff 50 feet above the sea near the Baths of Aphrodite, a romantic pool of crystal clear water formed by a spring emerging from the side of a grotto surrounded by ancient trees. The museum at the Leda Swan house next to the Temple of Aphrodite was crowded with school kids sneaking off to smoke cigarettes. The best ruin was at Kourian, a Roman villa high on a cliff overlooking three peninsulas jutting into the sea, offering flocks of mosaics, old arches and a House of Gladiators next to a reconstructed stadium. A week had been enough to see Cyprus. We reboarded the ferry to Israel at 6 p.m., receiving a small cabin with a porthole. We were affectionately remembered by the Burmese crew, who shared their potato chips.

Adventuring Israel and How

Grendel II was the 2nd vehicle off the ferry at Haifa, ahead of a German RV. It took 2 ½ hrs to clear customs and passport control while I spent $400 for three months' RV insurance. The delay was caused by Israeli security literally dismantling cars, from windshield wipers and doors to floors, trunks and wheels, including the red Saab ahead of us, owned by a graduate student entering Israel to study at a local university. But security didn't even peek inside the two RVs.

Our first stop was to stock up on groceries at a shopping center in Haifa north, where we were evacuated for a bomb scare. Upon exit Mary's daypack was searched and we heard an explosion: they'd blown up a left-behind package, standard operating procedure that welcomed us to Israel.

In November of 1996 Israel was commercially a 1st world country with 3rd world litter and extremely kind people; by May 2007 when I next returned Israel was completely 1st world, without litter and exponentially more expensive. We parked overnight on cliffs with a view of Lebanon, during daylight adjoining a continuous parade of people walking, jogging and pushing baby carriages. Soldiers sat with Uzis in jeeps sprouting four mounted machine guns at the Lebanese border where a sign read: Beirut 120km (75 miles north) and Jerusalem 240km (150 miles south).

At the trailhead for a hike to the Crusader Castle at Monfort we joined dozens of locals, one in every group carrying an Uzi, the gun of choice. I had to settle for a t-shirt with the picture of an Uzi on front. Happily, diesel was only 38 cents a liter, half the price of gasoline.

Soldiers in a jeep with the regulation four machineguns stopped by the RV one evening at 9 p.m., suggesting it was too dangerous to overnight where we'd parked. I asked if they were dangerous and they denied it. *Where do we go*, I asked, peering into the dark; they said a kilometer up the road. I drove two kilometers for a quieter night, guessing we must have been too close to a hidden Israeli army base. At massive Crusader Castle Godim we bought a year's entry pass to all 43 Israeli National Parks for $38, a deal which saved hundreds of dollars in admission fees.

Zefat aka Safed was a mystical town built on three levels with views of Mt. Meron topping 1208 meters or 4000 feet, where the Messiah was rumored to be coming back. Zefat's old Jewish quarter was clogged with ancient synagogues from a mystical branch of Judaism and the Arab quarter was full of artisans. Lunch began Mary's love affair with falafels, $2 for a full meal.

The furthest northern point in Israel was Qiryat Shemona, its entrance guarded by three decorative tanks painted rustic red, electric blue and painful yellow,

where we turned east onto the Golon Heights past ruins at Caesarea Philippi, formerly in Syria. The Golan's best castle was Nimrod's with unending nooks and crannies, towers, keeps, cisterns, lookouts, walls and views of a valley below, home to hyraxes, cousins of elephants that looked like tail-less elephant rats. Mt. Harmon sat behind the castle, forming the border between Syria and Lebanon. Upon exiting we found thirty Israeli army soldiers, kids sitting around the patio with Uzis, waving friendly goodbyes as we exited.

The abandoned city of Kuneitra sat on the Syrian border, roadside signs warning of mines as we wound off the Golan among continuous army and UN vehicles, through Syrian towns refusing Israeli citizenship at Buqata, Elrom and Masadah. We were off to Gammla, an extensive ancient site on a long ridge below a steep cliff with rivers on both sides far below, when a tank rumbled toward the RV. I rather immediately drove onto the shoulder of the road, waving as the tank snarled by. The Romans had invaded Gammla in 67 C.E. and were repulsed; the next day 9000 Jews jumped off 1000-foot cliffs to escape inevitable captivity.

It took several hours to hike around Kursi's old monastery and little chapel decked with extensive mosaics where demons had traditionally been cast into 400 pigs that apparently found demons uncomfortable, running into Lake Kinneret aka the Sea of Galilee, and drowning. We found a close-by campground at Susito beach, full facilities but no one around to charge admission. Because Israel was miniscule we could daytrip anywhere in the northern half of the country and return to this exquisite free camping spot, ending up there for a week, off and on. Tiberias sat across the often choppy pear-shaped lake, which measured 13 by seven miles or 21 by 11 kilometers and 686 feet or 209 meters below sea level. The Golan Heights towered above and behind the campground where we reveled in unlimited fresh water for convenient hand laundry.

- ## Visited by Helicopters

A hike around Qarne Hittim, the Horns of Hittite where the Crusaders met their final demise high above Tiberias in 1197, provided grand views over the Golan, Lake Kinneret, Syria and Jordan. We waited until the last Israeli tour group left before leveling the RV, difficult on the steep hill but close enough to preserve the refrigerator. There was peace and quiet until 8:30 p.m. when two helicopters flew by, one coming back to land with an extremely noisy whish. The pilot jumped out bristling while I was quite relaxed after a gin and tonic. He asked *where from* in patchy English. Upon hearing Arizona he took a second to figure out that was somewhere in the U.S. He seemed quite relieved and said it was fine to park the rest of the night. He threw a scarf around his neck and took off in a swish rapidly diminishing in volume, leaving a shakily quiet night.

Zippori was an ancient Jewish, Arab, Roman and Byzantine site with an aqueduct 33 feet deep, walkable through carved rock, a 4000 seat Roman amphitheater, old Jewish houses, a Muslim cemetery, a Crusader fortress with a watchtower on top, artifacts, extensive mosaics of the Nile River with Roman and Greek motifs and a broad Roman road with antediluvian cart tracks, the sprawling site taking two hours to skim. Driving through Nazareth was a bad move, an ugly Arab town without traffic lights, rendering driving a free for all. But we found a large shopping center on the outskirts to stock up with fruit and veg, and Mary called her family to say, *Happy Thanksgiving*, collect; we'd accidentally figured out what day it was, having lost track years previous.

Forests became a refuge for quiet overnight parking away from noisy helicopters and jeeps with machine guns. Megiddo, or Armageddon, another free entry with the National Parks' pass, exhibited well preserved mosaics of the Nile River and 20 layers of civilizations from the Chalcolithic in 2500 B.C.E. through the Crusaders in the 1170-80s C.E., plus a 100 meter (325 foot) deep cistern with an aqueduct to a spring outside the walls. We climbed out of the rift valley onto a high ridge holding the Crusaders' last refuge, Castle Belvoir with massive black basalt walls, a broad moat, secret passages and a Sculpture Park with a bird's-eye view over Syria and Jordan, the green Jordan River valley far below. Saladin, the commander of the Crusaders' opposition, was so impressed with Belvoir's tenacity that after a 1 ½ yr siege, instead of chopping off Crusader heads, he shooed them home.

The extensive Roman ruins at Bet She' an were the best in Israel and the most extensive we'd found outside of Italy, until a month later when we were stunned by the incredibly preserved Roman ruins at Jerash north of Amman, Jordan. Tourists overran Bet She' an, filling the large amphitheater and blocks of baths, snaking along the hundreds of Roman columns, through old temples and around 21 layers of civilizations crammed into a square mile. At the exit we called Enrique to arrange a tour of Tel Aviv University the next day, heading toward Caesarea to park on the beach. Little remained of ancient Caesarea, though a massive amphitheater had been reconstructed and used for such as a recent Eric Clapton concert, sitting next to an old harbor, odd minaret and a headless red statue of an anonymous Roman general. The only impressive remains were the kilometer long aqueduct next to good overnight parking on the beach. Dinner was falafels from a convenient mix while listening to the BBC describing demonstrations ten miles east on the West Bank.

Tel Aviv University's manicured campus was crowded with modern buildings and students sprawled on extensive lawns in bright sunny weather. Enrique gave an exhaustive tour of the campus ranging from views atop the highest building, soldiers brandishing Uzis mere specks below, to the law school library that stocked U.S. reports and State statutes, causing a slight shudder at the sight of the complete Arizona Revised Statutes. The tour finished with the three-story Diaspora Museum, Enrique warning us as we left to watch out for the hookers near our intended overnight parking on north Tel Aviv beach. Indeed, they were out in droves accompanied by more droves of men checking them out.

Next day's traffic to Jerusalem was impacted and tedious so we bailed out to an old Crusader Castle and Convent ruins at En Hemed with a spring in the middle where a movie crew was shooting a religious film. We skirted Jerusalem's old city to the Mount of Olives and excellent views of the Dome of the Rock, its solid gold half circle dominating the old city. Entrepreneurs had engaged two schlocky camels for gathering shekels from the crush of tourists; I was able to scrape most of my inadvertently acquired camel dung off of one shoe. After the obligatory tour of significant churches from Mary Magdalene's to the Church of All Nations' colorful mosaics next to the Garden of Gethsemane we threaded the RV though regrettable traffic to the Mt. Hertzl Military Cemetery, which offered a large lot, water tap and bathrooms for convenient overnight parking; unceasing highway traffic provided a soothing rumble for a good night's sleep.

Jaffa Gate parking, near the Citadel and David's Tower, provided safe haven for the RV while we explored old Jerusalem. We walked the extensive walls no longer open to the public, through a junky Armenian quarter and persnickety Jewish section out the Dung Gate by the Wailing Wall where Jews were separated by sex, wailing and bobbing. Palestinian security checked a long line of tourists into an Arab quarter no longer open to non-Muslims, around the Dome of the Rock and Al Aqsa Mosques, like being back in Morocco but with less litter. We walked the Via Dolorosa and several stations of the cross to the Lion's Gate and back by St. Anne's, amongst religious tours and turbaned Arabs, through the Chapel of Flagellation, Damascus Gate and fascinating souqs sectioned by clothes, veggies, spices, glass, meat, pastries, leather, plastic junk, jewelry and Biblical tinsel, similar to Marrakech except the very last part.

The Church of the Holy Sepulcher was falling down and dowdy because the dozen occupying Christian sects refused to cooperate on its upkeep, each greedy for control; there tourists kissed everything in sight with no consideration for germs or disease. The colorful religious costumes, overwhelmed women and tombs of absent deities created a spectacle deluxe. We were relieved to bask overnight in the relative tranquility of Mt. Hertzl Military Cemetery.

An Israeli highlight was the 3000 Bet Guvrin caves carved in rock five to six stories in depth. Large living areas had been hewn among pigeon caves or columbariums and decorated with bright murals in a corking labyrinth surrounded by Roman and Jewish ruins and connected to bell-shaped caves fifty feet deep that encircled the perimeter. In an Ashqelon supermarket I watched a persistent sportsman attempting to score furry toys with a dangly three-fingered skyhook game. On the way out he snagged Mary in the parking lot and gave her a multi-colored bunny with suction cup for bonding with a window and she was thrilled, displaying the increasingly motley bunny inside Grendel II and successor RVs for a decade. To avoid the Gaza Strip we swerved southwest to Beersheba Tel, gabbing with a math professor and wife from Tuscaloosa, Alabama on sabbatical in Israel for seven months; he'd taught in Oslo and like us, loved Norway.

Near Bedouins in tents with hunkered-down camels we overnighted in the stark desert next to Tel Arad, inhabited from 4000 B.C.E., a mostly-restored Canaanite city. The ancient city was as impressive as the 77-year-old cyclist from Arad Town who stopped by to gab, proud of a daughter in Phoenix. The next day in Arad, a city settled by Russian emigrants, we bought a Nature Reserve card at the national headquarters. The card was good for one year, a measly $44 we should have spent at Gammla, saving the cost of that admission. The Nature Reserve Headquarters showed a comprehensive slide show of the Negev desert, providing copious clues for nifty free overnight camping.

East of Arad 22 kilometers (13 miles) sat the Roman Ramp entrance onto Masada where 967 Jews, after a two year siege, jumped off the vertical mesa rather than be captured by Romans. A Replica War Machine and Ramp built for a Universal Studios Film was overwhelmed by hundreds of kids from tour buses on the Sabbath, hiking up the steep trail to the top, past zealots buried in a mass grave 1900 years after their last jump. Deep cisterns held water sufficient for eight years, connected to extensive ruins including an old synagogue, Herod's Palace and a Byzantine church with panoramic views of the Dead Sea and Jordan.

- **The Dead Sea**

The RV practically slid down a steep winding road to scenic overnight parking on the Dead Sea, ten feet from embankments encrusted with salt. We sat in front of a perfect reflection of red rock cliffs at the lowest place on earth, 1300 feet below sea level, balmy in December. While concocting dinner we decided Israel had the best fruits and vegetables we'd found during the trip; succulent avocados, celery, radish and fennel, with that realization celebrating the first day of our third year in Europe and Asia with croissants dripped with chocolate. At the base of Masada we met an Israeli soldier named Menachem, querying why he sported an M16 instead of an Uzi, ending up chatting for an hour about his RVing plans upon discharge from the Army. We gave Menachem the Vander Male book on RVing Europe and a ride to En Gedi, dropping him at the bus stop for Jerusalem.

En Gedi was the best Dead Sea spot for RVs, offering a gargantuan free-camping lot next to the most popular Dead Sea swimming beach, free cold showers with warm ones for $1.50 and 25 cent bathrooms. The alternative was pay camping next door for $19 but why spend that much extra for hot showers and electric? We had our hiking hearts set on climbing Masada but the snake path up was closed during the construction of a new cable car system, relegating hiking to elsewhere the next five days. We tried to hike up Nahal Arugot gorge, carved from solid rock and sprinkled with springs along a river, but after a dab of sprinkles when we were halfway up the rangers closed it for fear of a flash flood; foiled again, though we had crept near a herd of ibex and flushed many less than elephantine hyraxes.

We splurged $13 for an afternoon at the Dead Sea spa where a group of American women modestly wore clothes over their swimsuits. Participants covered themselves with black mud and let it dry before washing off in hot sulphur pools, floating on the Dead Sea, repeating until bored stiff and the price of admission had been fully amortized. We drove north into the West Bank through a jolly checkpoint of Palestinian soldiers to 10,000 year old Jericho from 8000 B.C.E. After paying a $4 admission we found nothing save nondescript mud brick foundations. Neighboring Hisham's Palace, included in the admission, had been destroyed by an earthquake four years after completion in 700 C.E., finally justifying the $4 outlay with its brilliant decorations, mosaics and two columns.

Little remained at Qurum, where the Dead Sea Scrolls had been discovered. The museum was packed with Bible enthusiasts but we preferred the surrounding cliffs with excellent tourist-free hiking to high caves with spectacular views over rock climbers below and an ibex silhouetted on a high peak above.

Finally we hiked the snake trail up Masada, little more exciting than hiking miniature Squaw Peak in Phoenix, the name of which was recently changed to something else, both about 1200 vertical feet. Few tourists bothered climbing, most taking the new cable car where we passed throngs of Japanese queuing to ride back down. With the Masada hike accomplished we headed south into the Negev desert, lamenting the schism between religious (10%) and nonreligious Jews (90%). The police were forced to bust businesses open on the Sabbath, as a practical matter because the secular were taking business from the religious who were piously required to close. In addition the large secular majority resented the religious exemption from military service, and so much more.

• The Negev Desert

The ancient Nabataean towns of Mamshit and Horvot Avedot, 400 B.C.E. to 200 C.E., straddled the tail end of the Nabataean Spice route from Yemen through Saudi Arabia and Jordan, the former Nabataean capital at nearby Petra in Jordan. We strolled the extensive ruins of Byzantine churches converted from *pagan* temples, studded with vivid frescoes, stables, baths and watchtowers, a restored fortress, multiple Roman burial caves, arches, columns and fancy villas. The trailhead into En Yorqe'am, theoretically harboring a Crusader castle, began at a nearby camel ranch; though we never found the castle the seasonal springs were ethereal, cascading along steps cut 100 feet vertical into solid rock. Ben Gurion's tomb sat high on cliffs over Zin Canyon, a botanical garden of plants from all over the world next to the En Avedat nature reserve. The Reserve covered a dramatic desert canyon carved from solid stone bisected by running water from a spring birthing two 30-foot waterfalls, which we fled when three busloads of school kids raucoused up the canyon.

Overnight parking three miles north of Mizpe Ramon was too close to a firing range; though the tanks were over a mile away explosions occasionally shook the RV to its roots. The locals called Makhtest Ramon the Israeli grand canyon, an impressive crater 40 kilometers (25 miles) long by nine kilometers (5 ½ miles) wide and 400 meters (1300 ft) deep; but it was no Grand Canyon. Hikes near an inexpensive $6 campground without electric at the crater's east end were stark with cliffs streaked a bright greenish-blue by copper oxide along white limestone canyon walls where observant Jews were silhouetted, bobbing on the mesa top above. Chunks of sandstone the size of houses had fallen into the canyon where a spring had burbled up near the Roman fortress at Har Sararonim. An ammonite wall guarded the crater's exit, formerly crowded with fossils of titanic snails that had mostly been purloined.

Next morning we rolled into duty free Eilat at the bottom of the Negev, one of the most interestingly-situated towns in the world. This resort city sits at the head of the Gulf of Aqaba on the Red Sea and on the border with Jordan, five miles either direction from the borders with Saudi Arabia and Egypt. We checked into the only campground, five miles south of town and practically on the Egyptian border, to order mail we'd forgone for two months. Across the road sat the Coral Nature Reserve on the Red Sea, a mile south of a Club Med. Exploring town we found two German RVs, one Swede and two Dutch RVs free-camped on the beach next to the fence with Jordan, along with twenty trailers and thirty tents for whom the city had defensively provided garbage bins and water next door to fancy high rise hotels. Mary was excited about washing sheets after two months.

At the campground we met chatterbox, 30-year old Marisol, who'd worked two years in the Galapagos, having earned the necessary marine biology degree, spoke four languages, sired of a Spanish mom and Polish father; she'd taught English in Japan for a year, worked in Goa, India and had come to Eilat to learn scuba while working as a masseuse. A trail behind the campground led to a peak with high views over Egypt, Jordan, Saudi Arabia and Israel, after two hours exiting behind the Club Med near the Texas Ranch, a hokey amusement park constructed as wild-west frontier town.

We snorkeled daily across the road from the campground at the Coral Reserve on the Red Sea, free with the Nature Reserve pass. Mary was excited over eel, needlefish, the many fluorescent tropical fish, huge groupers, parrot fish and healthy coral, their attraction enhanced because exiting the water took a Herculean effort in the often gale-force winds. The Reserve's hot showers enabled RV free-camping for an aggregate month around Eilat. Instead of the usual three days the mail took a week to arrive, an anomaly inexplicable by Christmas holidays in Israel. When it finally showed up the price tag was $113 for a huge box that included way too many magazines.

Fixing a sensitive amalgam and filling another tooth took a short 25 minute dental appointment and cost $45, encouraging appointments for cleanings quoted at $33. Leaving the campground we parked on Eilat's north beach with other free-campers, which was an engaging experience. First we talked to the around-the-world Canadian biker we'd met on the ferry to Israel. He was in the middle of a four year ride, a benefit for AIDS; he'd hated Egypt and was off for Syria and Jordan, where we'd be following in two days. A dotty Israeli lady living in a tent wore a bikini bursting at the seams, outspokenly instructing the German RV we'd accompanied on the ferry to Haifa to immediately, if not sooner, buy chemicals to ameliorate its stinky toilet that drew mosquitoes and flies; fair enough, but I'd been lassoed into translating the conversation into German, rather rustily. Campers gathered stacks of wood for a beach bonfire on New Year's Eve and the city sponsored extravagant fireworks at midnight, at which we awoke from a sound sleep; the extravaganza must have cost a million dollars.

CHAPTER SIX
Jordan and Egypt

Crossing the Israeli-Jordanian border took two tedious hours, mostly on the Jordan side, costing $30 to exit Israel, $50 for a month of Jordanian vehicle insurance, $10 to clear the RV's registration, whatever that meant, and $45 for entrance visas exchanged for a $30 receipt. The traffic in Jordan was 80% 18 -wheelers along spectacular canyons and rock formations as we dropped off the plateau by Mt. Mabrak into Wadi Musa and Petra, parking overnight next to the police station at the entrance to spectacular Petra. Admission for two days cost $75 for two, which we happily paid for perhaps the most impressive archeological site on the planet; however, exiting tourists looked truly beat up.

- **Petra: the most fabulous archeological site on the Planet?**

This was my take on Petra during a visit ten years later in 2007: I've often puzzled over which is the world's most fabulous archeological site. Of course, superlatives such as most fabulous, best and crème de la crème may depend entirely on taste, or lack thereof. But still, without arguing definitions I throw out the gauntlet to begin the debate. For me the best of the ancient best is Petra in Jordan, hands down the most photogenic, colorful and extensive on the planet, its Treasury first stumbled upon from the depths of a narrow chasm, the opening scene for *Raider's of the Lost*

Naturally there are those who prefer the grossly eroded antiquities of Egypt (admittedly Karnak in Luxor isn't too shabby), or the-jungle-snarled temples of Cambodian Angkor Wat (among 295 temples Banteay Srei is the most exquisite), or the rapidly-slipping-off-the-hillside Peruvian Machu Picchu (decent location) or bewitching

Bagan in Myanmar with 4,022 grandiose and lesser temples, pagodas and chedis. But none of these, or other potential candidates for the best of the archeological best, offer the psychedelic labyrinth of rainbowed sandstone from which Petra was born. Indeed, Egyptian stone is monotonously beige, Angkor mostly obtuse gray granite, Machu Picchu grass-covered and weathered, and who goes to Bagan? An informed voter should first visit each and every potential candidate.

Petra was carved from miles of living stone by the wily Nabataeans who controlled the spice trade among China, India, Greece and Egypt for 400 years from 300 B.C.E. The site was embellished by the Romans with stadiums, columns, baths and temples after conquering the less-wily spice-traders in 106 C.E. Yet the grandeur and location of Petra was unknown in the West until rediscovered by Swiss gallivanter, Johann Ludwig Burckhardt, in 1812.

Petra sits on a modest plateau a hundred miles south of the Dead Sea. Its location is skewered by Wadi Mūsā, Arabic for the Valley of Moses where tradition says a rock was struck and water gushed. The locals would dearly love a repetition to fix a severe water shortage. The signs in a local hotel said, *Fine of 10 JD for washing of clothes; water too expensive.* A $14 fine would add frosting to the insult of having to wash clothes by hand.

The so-called *Rose City* of Petra is actually a *Rainbow City.* Its hundred meter (325 feet) vertical cliffs are swirled in shades of magenta, pale blue, pink, tangerine and gold, whirled together with pinwheels of alternating white sandstone to form the fingerprints of antiquity, jammed with elaborately carved temples towering out of vertical rock faces, a World Heritage site since 1985.

This is how it unfolded: First, a ticket office selling passes for one to three days, from 21JD ($30) to 31JD ($43.50). Without pushing the average athlete to exhaustion it takes a minimum of two days to see the highlights, requiring purchase of at least the 25JD ticket for $35. Once through the gate expensive horses were vigorously offered to tote those not yet tired a few hundred meters (yards) to the entrance gorge, graced by the first of many souvenir shops. At least skip the horses until the less energetic trip out.

To this point the trail followed a dry river bed, hikers' spirits rising in the saunter past temples that were all tombs, caves and carved stone blocks that would do any archeological site proud. How could this be topped? It immediately was by the gorge itself. The cliffs thundered a hundred meters straight up, with patches only two meters wide, which in the morning rush may result in a sudden bottleneck of way too many tourists. The sun seldom shines on the canyon floor between these high walls, sheer relief from the often-sweltering Jordanian desert.

Snaking through the slot-chasm of gorgeous sandstone the suspense palpably rose, on my entrance embellished by the leader of a Japanese tour-group who linked her minions in single-file, ordered their eyes closed and set them marching in set cadence toward the expected surprise. Hilarity was watching seventeen Japanese with eyes tightly clinched, marching the bunny-hop, blinking awake on leader-command, shrieking in unison, *Look at the Treasury*; with no ability to speak Japanese this was merely my language-hindered assumption.

The Petra experience ballooned when the Treasury loomed a hundred feet (30 meters) overhead, six massive Doric columns on the lower level supporting a temple façade of more columns, massive cupola and temple tops stacked above that, carved from the solid rock surrounding it. Not only the color changed with the day's subtle altering of light but the thinning of tourists removed the atmosphere of feverishness; by early afternoon camels sprawled docilely in front of the Treasury for perfectly composed shots, untrammeled by the presence of pesky other tourists.

From the entrance of Petra to its furthest famous edifice, the Monastery, was six kilometers, almost four miles. This distance was interrupted a hundred times by temples and tombs covering miles of cliffs in every direction, down seemingly deserted wadis and up mandatory steps to the shirt-drenching High Place of traditional Nabataean sacrifice, offering expansive views over the enormous complex. On the way there was a huge Roman coliseum carved from red sandstone, temples and ruins, all chockablock with the brilliant stone that makes Petra unique, interspersed with a hundred more temples and decorously carved caves.

The climb to the Monastery may unnerve the average couch potato, for whom saddled mules can be readily hired. The Monastery was so massive that viewing it from a close-by hill rendered humans standing in front almost too small to notice, and mules miniscule. The journey to and fro, from the Treasury to the Monastery, revealed the grandeur of Petra, the swirl of color peppering the miles of canyons like a Joseph's coat of many colors.

Petra is Greek for rock; appropriately, because Petra indeed rocks.

In a preliminary internet vote published May 7, 2007 the world's top ten archeological sites were the Acropolis in Greece, the ancient Mayan city of Chichen Itza in Mexico, the Coliseum in Rome, the Eiffel tower in Paris, the Great Wall of China, the Incan ruins of Machu Picchu, Petra in Jordan, the statues on Easter Island, Britain's

Stonehenge and the Taj Mahal in India. Egypt refused to participate because that might lower what it considers its obviously number one status. The final vote ridiculously substituted the Christ Statue above Rio for one of the above.

Back in 1997, thanks to the early Muslim call to prayer, we woke at 5:15 a.m. to hike Petra, on the long hike out as beat as the tourists we'd seen the day before. We overnighted overlooking Petra in *Grendel II* above the ruins of Al-Wu'ayra fort, camels and donkeys parading below us under a full moon.

Jordan's steep roads, dropping into wadis and climbing out near vertically, routinely overheated the RV, requiring timeouts of an hour. Karak was the largest Crusader Castle in Jordan, half a mile long built on seven levels with secret passages, dominating the city with admission only $1.50 each. We were across from En Gedi ten miles from the Red Sea with only way to get back via Eilat, the long way we'd driven into Jordan.

Jerash may be the most extensive Roman Provincial City in the world: a mile with hundreds of columns, two colossal amphitheaters, a sprawling oval forum, triumphal arches and Byzantium churches, taking two hours to tromp around. On the way out of Jordan we stopped by Wadi Rum where Lawrence of Arabia hid out and it was a ringer for Monument Valley, if Arizona had camels. Ten kilometers before Aqaba the RV endured a flat tire better than I did; it took half hour to change it on the edge of a freeway swirling with 18-wheelers.

Back in Israel: Home Sweet Negev

At the border the Israelis checked the RV chassis for bombs and we scurried to overnight at our favorite out-of-the way spot in the Negev's Hidden Valley. Next morning we found the flat tire had been ruined, spending $75 for a new one, commiserating at Coral Beach by snorkeling for the first time with no wind. Mary called a sister in Phoenix who couldn't understand why we'd gone to Jordan, wherever that was, and had never heard of Petra.

German neighbors at the Eilat free campground described a car ferry from Rhodes to Marmaris they said would cost $213, save 1000 kilometers of driving to Turkey and a week of cold weather along the way. While we pondered this possibility the Egyptian consul in Eilat confirmed that diesel vehicles were prohibited from crossing the Sinai and a travel agent found an eight day tour of Egypt for $745 each; we nattered on for days whether to spend the money, finally shelling out, belatedly realizing we hadn't a voucher in sight; what were we thinking?

Eilat was hopping during our lengthy stay in the general area: two sets of people offered to buy the RV, including one who practically coerced our appearance at his shop, introduced his wife and failed to blink when we said it would cost the $20,000 we'd paid two years previous. The Dow-Jones Industrial average was up to 6850 on January 20, 1997, raising worries of a crash. In hindsight the Dow doubled every eight years until the big crash in 2008, even with the tech meltdown of 2000 that spun out while we were in Australia. Airborne sent word our mail was in Tel Aviv but couldn't be delivered to Eilat. How had they managed the month before? I mentioned the 72 hour guarantee world-wide, pointing out the bus to Eilat only took five hours; the mail again took a full week and would have remained forever undelivered had we not found it in an industrial suburb of Eilat. Teeth cleanings were the best and most vicious ever, a relief after the worthless cleanings in Fuengirola the winter before.

Fond goodbyes were said to friends at the grocery store, a Russian clerk who loved our National Geographic World Atlas, the pharmacist at SuperPharm who'd worked in New Jersey for 20 years, the clerk at the used bookstore, Marisol and a half dozen others. We left for Tel Aviv, already nostalgic for the overnight parking at Hidden Valley, that night tucking into the big free lot at En Boqeq on the Dead Sea. The Dan Panorama Hotel in Tel Aviv said RV parking would cost $37 for eight days and another couple inquired about purchase of the RV; Mary suggested we ship it to the U.S. for $1500 to avoid the bother of selling it in the U.K.

Egypt: Why We Hate Tours

Next morning the tour receipt, our only paperwork, was suspiciously regarded by the Tel Aviv bus driver. But he let us aboard and the hectic day began. Along with an Argentinean, two Israelis, two Dutch and a Croatian we paid an exit tax of $54 at the Egyptian border in the no-man's land between Israel and the Gaza strip. Israeli border guards insisted we must have illegally sold the RV, noted in my passport, in the Gaza Strip. Fortunately the bus driver confirmed that *Grendel II* was safely in Tel Aviv. Finally released to cross the border we waited interminably for an Egyptian bus; then five buses arrived and we hadn't a clue which to board, if any. A bus driver volunteered he'd been instructed to carry two more people to Cairo. Assuming they were us we boarded. The buses dithered two hours before leaving with a full police escort in front and behind the five-bus caravan, sirens wailing and lights blazing five noisy hours across the Sinai and Suez Canal into Cairo. By then we'd dieted for eight hours.

Cairo's 16 million inhabitants were gorging the roads in the worst melee we'd seen, far worse than Italy, passing in a hair-breath against oncoming traffic and turning three lanes into five. We had no idea which of the hundreds of Cairo hotels might be ours and Mary was certain doom was nigh. Suddenly the bus was flagged down and the CIT tour representative for Cairo appeared, bundled us into a beat-up car and dodged through suicidal traffic amongst merging buses, trucks, cars, bikes and motorcycles while explaining the luxury eight-day itinerary in detail. Wondering how he found the bus we arrived at the Atlas Hotel, shaken but exhilarated, a supposedly four star hotel that might rate two stars elsewhere. It took us five minutes to cross the first street, cars taking right-of-way over pedestrians with a vengeance. When I returned in 2007 Cairo traffic had improved enormously.

Egypt's main highlight was its downtown Cairo Museum, the second floor filled with Tutankhamen's fabulous golden treasure, which was mind-boggling for a minor child king out of 3000 years of far more important kings. Tourists snapped photos non-stop; now photos are prohibited. The Museum would have taken a week to see properly. By 2007 it'd become shabby, unmaintained in anticipation of moving to new facility near the Great Pyramid of Giza.

After the Pyramids we lunched at a cookie-cutter KFC/Pizza Hut the length of a football field away from the missing nose of the Sphinx. Mary bought silver cartouches for her sisters, spelling out their names in hieroglyphics, $10 each. That evening we boarded a train with sleeping car for Aswan, organized similar to a keystone cops comedy. A new guide couldn't identify his clients in the lobby of the Hilton Hotel but somehow finally delivered our vouchers for the train, Nile Cruise and the ever present envelope for tips containing the names of contacts and cab driver in Aswan. We barely made the train, a nice French reconditioned sleeper. A steward delivering the world's tiniest bar of soap had to be pushed out of the compartment; he'd have waited all night for a tip. A horrific dinner was served late, micro-waved spaghetti with chicken, Mary's moldy. We arrived in Aswan two hours late because the train ran over a man on the tracks. The townspeople carried him by our compartment window while he bled copiously from a mangled arm and face.

We were delivered to a Five Star Sheraton Hotel Ship on the Nile, one of four Sheratons rafted up; 200 other fancy hotel boats ranged the shoreline. In the souk we bought a t-shirt everyone hated: *9 of 10 men who try Camels prefer women, $3*. We were assigned to an English-speaking group of 16 people and shuttled off to a felucca cruise for two hours around Elephantine Island. The felucca skipped listed itinerary stops at the botanical gardens on Lord Kitchener Island and the Mausoleum, our main interests, but the little sailing expedition was still droll with copious wind and sun and feluccas dodging each other, though the guide was exceptionally pedantic. After 12 minutes we despised him.

The English-speaking group was railroaded to the Unfinished Obelisk, where it should have been reburied, our time wasted in a cold wind. The only interesting sight was a funeral procession with the body wrapped in a red plaid sheet on a board. After the boring High Dam we chanced on quite phenomenal Philae Island with its series of 14 temples relocated to Philae when threatened by rising dam water. The temples took ten years to move and reconstruct by sluggish Egyptians. The supremely boring tour guide told lame jokes and repeated trivia four times for emphasis. We vowed to never again take a tour.

Sailing down the Nile we tromped to the first-class ruins at Kom Ombo, a far more enjoyable experience in January 2007 during a two day felucca trip up the Nile on the predictably happy *Bob Marley*.

The Sheraton Captain's cocktail party at 7:30 p.m. featured two miniscule non-alcoholic drinks as an excuse to introduce the hotel staff and siphon tips. Each language group met immediately after this heady party to discuss the appropriate amount to tip. The tour guide suggested a $100 daily tip for him; we tipped $5 for the staff and nothing for the guide.

After an another boring day drifting down the Nile on the top deck in the sun we refused to accompany the group or guide to the Valley of the Kings in Luxor. The longsuffering tour coordinator found a local guide, quite a nice guy with a sense of humor, navigating our group of two through three tombs for the best photos, categorically prohibited when I visited in 2007. Hatshepsut Temple, alliterated by guides as hotchickensoup, commemorated the only female king of Egypt; her son obliterated all her monuments after she died, except for the Temple.

At the Karnak and Luxor temple complexes we melded with an English-speaking group from another hotel boat, cleverly avoiding our stuffy assigned guide. Karnak was the second highlight of Egypt, the most extensive complex visited, with a sacred lake reflecting well in photos, major obelisks and hundreds of colorful columns covering a square mile. Back in Cairo we happily lost the hated tour guide and were taken by another guide to Memphis and Saqarra, bang-up sites with pyramids 5000 years old, which meant worn to the nub. The Egyptian tour experience may explain why we tour no more.

Israel and Away

The bus back to Israel suffered five hours of cacophonous police escort, arriving at the Dan Panorama Hotel in Tel Aviv at 4 p.m. The parking attendant suggested we owed $120; that we'd been misquoted the hotel guest price. After interminable argument he literally threw up his hands, saying *gift*, which we accepted in amazement. This made up for the onerous $54 Israeli exit tax we'd paid. We relaxed for three days at our favorite free-camping spot on Lake Kinneret, happy to be back running, breakfast with the BBC on the trusty shortwave and home-cooked coffee.

In Haifa on February 13 while waiting for the ferry back to Cyprus and Rhodes we met a 21-year-old Brit named Matt from Northhampton; he'd spent four months on a kibbutz for an archeological dig at Tiberius before being kicked out for Christian proselytizing. Matt was flat-broke, his fare back paid by the Church of Scotland. We fed him three peanut butter and jelly sandwiches, coke and potato chips, avoiding his gung-ho religiousness, cringing when the Israelis blew up his unattended daypack. We also met a Swiss couple who'd driven a zebra-striped Toyota four-wheel drive from South Africa up the east coast of Africa. He built power plants, thus far in China, Indonesia, Texas, Ohio and South Africa; they traveled six months after completing each job, the next one on the Polish/German border, then to India.

On the ferry we befriended a Russian Army major age 34, wife Inna who ran a music school in Moscow and 8 ½ yr old terrorist son Roma. Dad had been a UN peacekeeper in the Middle East, close to the Suez Canal after five years in Afghanistan; we'd been drawn to inquire about the Sears' top-box on his car, which he'd bought in Los Angeles. At Cyprus the ferry required the offloading of the RV to put on 18-wheelers, taking all day to negotiate. We arrived on Rhodes, 540 square miles (1400 square kilometers), at noon. The first chore was checking the ferry to Marmaris, Turkey; it was dry-docked for painting and might be ready in ten days; price $280 for an hour's float.

• Rhodes

Happiness was two weeks on the resort island of Rhodes, back in Greece with feta and olives. Near Lindos, the site of Mary's scooter accident a few years previous in 1994, someone stole the milk off the step overnight, first time on the trip; we'd left it out every night for two years. The Valley of the Butterflies I'd biked to in 1972 provided a scenic walk along a stream past two waterfalls to a monastery, sunny after a day of sprinkles. In town we met John and Sherral, who we recognized from the Haifa ferry, Canadians from Ft. McMurray, Alberta, also off to Turkey on the Marmaris ferry. They were headed to the Ukraine for two months, visiting relatives on a year's sabbatical that Canadian teachers receive every five years. Back in Lindos we hiked around Rhodes' best archeological site, a charming whitewashed town strung along a 300 degree enclosed bay. With cherry trees in bloom the castle high above town supplied crackling views.

Scary Ferry to Turkey

The ferry was delayed a few more days allowing the detailed exploration of every road and town on Rhodes. We gave Swiss backpackers, who were catching the ferry to Israel, our Israeli National Park and Nature Reserve cards while we sat flummoxed by the tiny ferry to Marmaris. The ferry's open deck was miniscule, taking a miracle to back onto without a catastrophe, encouraged by half a dozen volunteer directors. Two hour later we paid Turkish port taxes of $10 and $20 visa charges, fronting fees for Americans from Atlanta. Dave was a physiotherapist and Carol a TV producer; they'd sold a house to travel for six months and were moving to Alaska upon return. As I began to drive off the ferry a line came loose, the ferry launched itself from the dock and the RV came within a whisker of settling to the bottom of the ocean. I was saved only by burning rubber to gain purchase on the dock.

Turkey's Turquoise Coast

Dave and Carol found the closest ATM, reimbursing the money we'd advanced. Meanwhile Mary chatted with Norm and Paulie in a 6.6 meter (22 foot) Autotrail RV, Brits who insisted we park together overnight because we were both headed west along the 120 kilometer (75 mile) long Datca Peninsula. Marmaris had grown what seemed 100-fold since a visit in 1972; 25 years before it had been a quaint fishing village but by 1997 it was a modern town with horrific traffic. Chatting with Norm and Paulie over drinks we found them terminally boring; however, they offered tidbits of helpful information after traveling Europe for 40 years, fulltime the last four. Most amazingly the Autotrail's extra three feet of length seemed to double the inside space. Ditching Norm and Paulie was easy; Norm's muffler rattled loose and Marmaris was the closest place to have it fixed. We waved a sorrowful goodbye as they u-turned back toward Marmaris.

Datca town was surrounded by hundreds of beehives and thousands of fruit and nut trees, sitting pretty on a large bay fifty miles west of Marmaris. For 67 cents we bought the Turkish Daily News, an excellent English-language newspaper. As we'd found on two previous visits the Turks, including near Datca, were incredibly friendly. We stopped at a spring to fill water, noticing a hose leading 50 yards to a wooden shack. Two extremely shy girls in scarves appeared and we said hi in Turkish, nearly exhausting our limited vocabulary. One girl offered chai, tea, and Mary followed her while I finished filling the RV, bringing half a German dark chocolate bar. I took off my shoes at the door. The floor was covered with cushions and Mary was exhibiting extremely abnormal behavior, holding a three month old baby. A plump toddler played among the cushions next to his mother while grandmother had to be propped up on the settee, Mary whispering that she'd already fallen over twice. The toddler spent 20 minutes nibbling a square of chocolate, giving us ample time to observe: the *house* had no electric, only a propane stove and boom box with mattresses and blankets stacked in the back. We could only speculate how many lived in the 9x12 foot room. They spoke no English or German and we spoke little Turkish, the conversation proceeding in fits and starts by pantomime. We escaped after sitting staring at each other for half an hour, Mary speculating that grandma likely had tuberculosis but happy we'd contributed a bit of chocolate to their lives.

A bolt pulled out of the bumper on a rough road, costing $2 in garage repairs; completely stocking up on groceries cost 2.2 million lira ($18). Because Turkey boasted more antiquities than Greece we saw dozens of spectacular sites on the Turkish south coast to the border with Syria.

Turkish hospitality was on constant offer everywhere. Rain threatened at the Xanthos site so the curator offered half price tickets for 65 cents: Byzantine ruins jammed with carved-rock tombs shaped like miniature houses on high pedestals below ruins of an Akropolis high above, overlooking a rotund theater, obelisks written in Lycian script and the Tomb of the Harpies on 50 foot pedestal. St. Nicholas was born in Kalkan where we unforgettably saw twin tornadoes descend from voluminous coal-black clouds onto the bay, becoming twisting waterspouts.

We invited Germans, their overheated RV at the side of the road, for tea when two camels inside a house poked their heads out the windows. I missed this great shot because I'd already taken the day's single allotted photo, one of twin waterspouts, back in the olden days of film. The Germans had wintered in Turkey for five years and were a able to point out favorite places we happily marked on our map. At Rumluca we attended a camel auction held before the annual camel joust, huge shaggy beasts saddled with ornate wooden contraptions, bridles and tassels we'd not previously seen the likes of. The auction was packed with cops, locals and brightly decorated trucks hauling camels, which the Germans told us were used only for fighting.

Mary became depressed in the rainy weather, pining to go *home* to Phoenix, not amused when I pointed out we had no home. But the next day the sun came out and Mary was happy until the next rain. Meanwhile we finally located Yanartos where flames sprouted off a steep rocky hillside in a dozen places, fed by natural gas, the basis for the myth of Pegasus who slew a fire-eating monster and strewed the remains over this hillside.

At the German resort town of Kemer we slowed down to receive mail, finding isolated beach parking near Bildibi with a perfect view of Antalya below snow-capped mountains, a city of over a million people 20 miles north. Mornings were in the 40s when a brilliant red sun would rise predictably out of the ocean. Back in town a rug salesman, while wailing that the Turkish Lira had depreciated 3% in one week, said he saw perhaps four Americans a year. A Shell station insisted on washing the RV gratis, competing against a British BP next door plus a Mobil and Italian Petrol Ofisi across the street.

Four days at the Kemer campground waiting for mail cost $42 including metered electric to fire the refrigerator and space heater and free propane stoves and ovens for cooking; ours was the only RV among pine trees smack on the beach. We withdrew 20 million lira at an ATM, feeling extremely flush for $170, buying doses of Cipro for 50 cents each to treat Mary's perpetually upset stomach caused either by flu or sensitivity to local water, no prescription required.

The luxury of a bought haircut in Antalya included an eyebrow and nostril trim, topped off by a Q-tip dipped in alcohol and lit to singe unsightly ear hair, $5 including tip. Ancient Perge was a miniature Jerash, pocked with standing Roman columns and 20 busloads of Germans. When parking at the archeological site of Side we noticed Norm's RV and began sidling through ruins to town along the waterfront while looking every which direction to avoid detection. Distracted while escaping a rug merchant we were collared by Norm and Paulie who insisted we drive east with them. We hemmed and hawed a bit, casting about for inspiration, finally announcing a long-planned trip to Selge, north into the mountains. Whew: saved again.

A few mornings after the Selge detour two Turkish soldiers knocked on the door and asked if we're heard shooting; when we said no they jogged away with their automatic rifles. The next day two sets of soldiers knocked on the door, including ones from the previous day, all friendly. In addition to copious soldiers Turkey seemed under construction everywhere, particularly new townhouses and apartments near the water.

At Silifke we began a 225 kilometer loop recommended by the German RVers, passing two-story rock tombs with carved columns sprinkled at random in fields. By lunchtime we hit the snow line and had parked at a wide place in the road with no traffic when two guys on a tractor went by, backed up and handed over nine apples, refusing payment. We paused on the River Goksii at the spot where Barbarossa drowned on July 10, 1190, putting a damper on the 3rd Crusade. Silifke was dominated by a massive Crusader castle and picturesque bridge. The nearby Caves of Heaven and Hell cost the usual 65 cents: Hell was a pit 100 feet wide and 300 feet deep with no way in; Heaven could be entered by a steep trail and 452 steps into a long slanting cave with an old Armenian Church at the entrance, the reputed underground river audible but inaccessible.

In the hills above Kizkalesi Crusader castle that sat on an island 200 meters offshore we prepared for overnight parking with unimpeded views of new apartments on the ocean. It seemed like a good idea at the time but at 11 p.m. four police showed up and ordered the RV moved because of dangerous *terrorists* in the area, who we assumed were Kurdish rebels. I asked where to go and they had no answer, finally gesturing to stay put. Kurds are only a dangerous to Turks, not tourists. But at 1 a.m. some guy knocked on the door with a large flashlight yelling something we couldn't understand. With Mary shaken we drove down to the beach we'd thought too busy in the daytime and a nice chap at the hotel said we could park overnight. The disco finally quit at 2 a.m., rendering the balance of the night restful; Mary slept in but I simply had to get up to listen to the *Red Dwarf* science fiction spoof on the BBC at 6:30 a.m., quite hilarious. It only took two days for Mary to calm down after our rousting. A little old lady at the fruit and vegetable market in Mersin thought I should carry all the bags, taking them from Mary and thrusting them at me, helping improve Mary's spirits.

After a cloudburst outside Ceyhan we stopped at a huge O/Pet gas station and asked whether we could park overnight. The typically friendly Turkish attendant said *no problem*, whereupon overnight parking at sprawling Turkish service stations became a habit. In thanks we partied down with the Turks in the restaurant, attached to most Turkish gas stations, paying eight cents a glass for tea. Next morning with 48 degrees inside and a cold north wind we fired up the propane heater for the first time in a year.

We braved raucous winds to see the sprawling Yakacik/Papas ruins, huge bubble-topped Arab baths around a castle and mosque with a 1000-year-old olive tree in the courtyard.

Akmet, a guard at a resort deserted for the winter, invited the RV to park overnight, well sheltered from the wind in a courtyard surrounded by new townhouses 100 meters from the ocean. We weighed having mandatory tea, finally parking and meeting the family, making difficult small talk with no common language, declining dinner after half an hour reviewing 8-year old Damla's homework. Next morning Akmet handed over two fresh loaves of bread; we gave him 100,000 lira, then down to 80cents, and a Phoenix postcard for his green-eyed wife.

Little was left at Antakya, ancient Antioch, except fragments of a castle on a high hill; however we immediately met Yilmaz, the director of the excellent museum, who spoke fluent English. He issued the usual invitation for tea after we browsed extensive 2nd and 3rd Century mosaics, Roman and Hittite relics, statues and sculpture. After tea Yilmaz suggested lunch the next day and a personal tour of old Antioch, which we said we'd like. Parking on the beach at Samandagi, 25 kilometers south and practically on the Syrian border, we'd reached the end of the line in Turkey. We were reluctant to head north in the increasingly cold weather, snowing the day before in Istanbul and across most of Turkey, sparing only the south coast.

Next morning the icy wind was steady at 35-40 knots, gusting to 50 knots, on occasion lifting a wheel of the RV off the road. Four cops came by at 11 p.m. asking to see our passports, a discouraging trend. But we had a nice breakfast at a restaurant where the owner's son spoke English and explained Antakya was the capital of a country called Hatay until 1939 when Turkey and Syria almost went to war over who got it; Hatay opted for Turkey.

Lunch with Yilmaz was skipped, blamed on the wind and reluctance to wait around until noon. At Iskenderun we chatted with a Turk we'd met a week before who said 25 convicts had escaped five days ago. Ah, now we knew why there'd been so many police roadblocks where we'd see drivers hastily fasten their seat belts to avoid a big fine, and why we'd suffered nocturnal visits by soldiers and the police.

CHAPTER SEVEN
End Game in Spring Time

At Ceyhan a Turk pulled in next to the RV, saying he ran a caravan factory and was curious to see *Grendel II* inside, which we happily showed him. We enjoyed a long chat, forgetting to inquire about RV parts we needed. At Tarsus we turned north toward the mountains for Cappadocia, a primary highlight of Turkey we'd always wanted to see. By Pozanti we had snow flurries, the first in years; Mary reminded me that Phoenix had been 94 degrees the day before. We stopped at a big O/Pet gas station, debating what to do besides freeze to death, still hoping to see Cappadocia. The weather was so dismal we turned around and drove 50 miles south to the coast, finding a rest area behind Tarsus, completely deserted and quiet.

The Attempt on Cappadocia

The next morning's brilliant sun with no wind encouraged a long day's run into the mountains to see two crater lakes next to a campground. If the weather held we'd drive on to Cappadocia. Before leaving we stocked up in Mersin and totally out of character, lunched at McDonald's. At the next table sat a blonde guy with a crew cut, a two-year old blonde girl and red-headed blue-eyed mom: Captain Paul was stationed with wife Betsy at the U.S. Air Force Base in Adana, loving Turkey as much as we, fulminating an hour's chat. They were headed to Konya, the whirling dervish capital, she was 6-weeks pregnant and they'd stay in Turkey as long as allowed by the U.S. Air Force.

We had brief snow flurries through the mountains and then a major storm, finding the crater lakes uninteresting. The RV was stopped by cops who accused it of crossing a solid white line when passing a truck, the same as a dozen Turks before. They wrote the fine as 7 million lira, $60. I counter bid, suggesting a kitty of only 250,000 lira, $2, turning pockets inside out, pleading I'd have to find an ATM for money. They finally waved the feckless RV off in disgust; in 15 years driving around the world I've paid two traffic fines, actually bribes to escape police traps: $10 in Java and $10 in Panama. The mood in the RV greatly improved as we drove off laughing, stopping within sight of the police to fill with diesel for 2.2 million lira. North over two 5000 foot passes we found snow everywhere, stopping to see a city and old monastery carved into solid rock from the 9th Century at Eski Gumus near Nigde, according to the guidebook covered with colorful frescoes, but it was closed on Mondays.

The biggest concern was whether there might be a campground open in Cappadocia because light snow covered the landscape near the end of March, 1997. However, the snow rendered Cappadocia a wonderland of fairy chimneys and carved rock cities, magical and exhilarating. We found an open campground near Goreme, covered in snow without a single other camper; having no choice we signed on to pay $9.50 for absolutely essential electricity, to keep the RV's pipes and systems from freezing. The young caretakers cleared snow from the bathrooms and a trail to the RV but the campground pipes were frozen, nixing hot water showers and rendering the toilets unflushable. This should have alerted us to something, but no, not us.

I was frantic about having sufficient antifreeze in the radiator, walking to a close-by Shell station in the burgeoning blizzard. The Shell had no antifriz, but I'd learned a new Turkish word. The helpful Shell manager found a Turk Petrol station with antifriz, called a taxi and we forged through a full grown blizzard over roads frozen with glare ice, three liters of antifriz for $6, a deal. I siphoned water from the radiator, added the antifreeze and ominously the snow stopped, the skies cleared and the temperature plummeted below zero.

The space heater ran full blast all night, gradually losing ground as the temperature dropped to 51 degrees inside and below zero outside; we were in trouble. The fresh water pump was frozen, the kitchen and bathroom drains wouldn't drain and the RV was covered with icicles. The propane was almost solid, inadequate for lighting the stove or water heater, which was beside the point with no water pump. But I'd done something right in buying antifriz. Still, the engine wouldn't start. We ran an extension cord to the space heater and placed it on the engine. By 10 a.m., after an hour, it'd thawed to the point where it'd turn over slowly, sounding like an anemic single cylinder engine.

The caretaker had called the owner, who'd come by the night before promising hot water, now refusing to take money and begging that we stay for free as long as we wanted. We explained the pipes had frozen and we had to leave but he refused money. After two miles the RV overheated and the radiator blew up, creating the opportunity to take the only photo of a tiny portion of the snow-covered fairy chimneys and rock carved

city. Either the radiator was frozen or the engine block was cracked, sayonara trip. The engine cooled rapidly and we added water with the last of the antifriz, the engine starting right up. With eyes glued to the heat gauge we shoved off through Nevsehir, narrowly avoiding two accidents. Nevsehir roundabouts are apparently the only ones on earth where those inside the roundabout DON'T have the right-away.

We headed south as fast as we could pedal, which was slowly, the engine unable to attain substantial RPMs. Near Nigde we couldn't resist turning off for the monastery at Eski Gumus where the ticket seller, seeing us rolling through town, came running up to accept 65 cents each and mutely lead us through bright frescoes, bones in open crypts and a monastic city carved from whole rock, miniaturely similar to Ethiopia's Lalibella.

At 4 p.m. we reached a deserted rest stop near the coast, unvisited because the freeway ended in a muddy track a mile south. We tried to unstop the sink, after two hours finding the water pump seemingly kaput, deciding we'd have to visit the friendly caravan man for repairs in Adana. I was exhausted and Mary was saying *I want to go home.* Though I figured she'd be bored in a week I carefully avoided saying we had no home. Next morning the water pump worked perfectly so I backed the RV over a curb under the curious stare of the rest stop's caretaker, crawled underneath and disconnected the gray water pipe. Slushy ice easily drained with the encouragement of an ice pick, unplugging the drains. The caretaker and I were equally impressed.

Springtime in Turkey

In Mersin, a large city with over a million people, we found the automotive industrial area and a paint shop that could fiberglass and paint the rear corner of the RV scraped by the lady in Brussels. The insurance had paid $550 and the two hour repair cost $24, a good job though the touch-up paint was slightly crooked. We also bought a replacement side mirror, drinking mandatory tea at both repair shops. However, we couldn't find the right size windshield to replace our cracked one.

Over-nighting next to the castle at Luman Kilesi we saw the Hale-Bopp comet in brilliance. The next afternoon we drove past Norm and Paulie buying bananas at the side of the road, hoping they hadn't seen us. Parking on the beach at Anamur West we walked around the sprawling ruins at Anemourion that we'd missed the previous week; the gatekeeper awarded Mary a bouquet of flowers.

While Mary was cleaning the RV she closed the inside windows, apparently taken as a snub by four Turkish girls who tossed a couple of pebbles toward the RV. I told them to go away. Fifteen minutes later they reappeared with four boys and began throwing rocks. I chased them behind a building where their parents were having lunch, told the parents they'd thrown rocks and the boys' parents slapped their faces as I left.

Intermittent rain cells created hazardous driving along the Turkish coast through Antalya's usual terrible traffic, the Turks habitually turning onto the wet slippery streets without looking either direction. To pass a two-bus and van accident we drove off the road into a ditch and back, past windshields blown out, vehicles crumpled and a broken leg someone was trying to set before the arrival of an ambulance or the police. We parked in a Pamukkale campground at one of the ancient world's seven wonders, my third visit and Mary's second. Disappointingly, most of the famous travertines were dry. We passed on the $6 admission to the hot pools with Greek ruins on the bottom where we'd had snorkeled with friends after a 1985 sailing trip.

Aphrodisias rated a short backtrack and we arrived mid-afternoon, a great site I'd explored in 1972, a year after it was discovered and written up in National Geographic Magazine. Benjamin from the jandarma granted permission for overnight parking next to the museum. We watched out the picture window for two hours while five separate German tour buses disgorged hundreds to resolutely walk the site in driving rain. We crossed our fingers that morning would bring sunshine. The clouds cleared at sunset for vivid views of Hale-Bopp and news of 39 suicides in San Diego. Morning was dazzling sun. Before the arrival of tour buses we were able to walk the Brobdingnagian oblong stadium and through perfectly preserved marble tombs surrounded by snow-drenched peaks.

At a rustic campground without electric on the Guzelcamli peninsula we immediately had a flat tire, difficult to change on muddy ground when distracted by a sunset over the Greek Island of Samos ten miles across the Aegean. After a hard day's sightseeing the closest gas station confirmed the tire was ruined; we passed on a used replacement, having learned something in Morocco. Adding to the gloom was a week of weather so rainy and windy we hadn't been running. Lunch on the large lake at Camici Golu recalled my older daughters had loved wading there 25 years ago on my first trip to Turkey.

New Pirelli tires in Bodrum cost $78 each, a deal, mounted in forty minutes by an eight-year-old jack-wielding kid who spun off lug nuts like ringing a bell; the child labor was excellent though we were afraid the RV would fall when he ran underneath to set a second jack. I clipped a Turkish Times story about the University of Arizona winning the NCAA basketball tournament and mailed it to a friend in Tucson who later expressed amazement at worldwide coverage. We also sent a postcard of Bodrum, site of one of the ancient seven wonders' mausoleum to a friend in Newport Beach who'd captained a second boat on the 1985 Greek sailing trip and had really enjoyed Bodrum.

Having seen Ephesus on two previous trips we skipped it for the extensive ruins at St. John's Basilica and tomb in Selchuk, below a large fortress on the hill. We found a pleasant grassy area on the ocean near Doganbey for lunch and relaxed the whole day and overnight, disgusted with the weather, which when bad destroys the fun of traveling. Mary additionally had concluded the Turks were too friendly for privacy. Because of the continuing bad weather we finally ruled out a retry for Cappadocia, extremely disappointed, finally returning in 2006 for a great month including a drive east as far as Mt. Ararat near the Iranian and Armenian borders.

The west coast of Turkey was a mud hole. In Izmir we easily found a new Fiat windshield for $130, installed in half an hour by working clowns who demanded we undergo the usual tea ritual, adding an oil change and new air filter for $47; we continued to love Turkish prices if not Turkish winter weather.

Pergamum's marvelous ruins on a mountaintop two miles above Bergama were charming in the snow, particularly impressive for Mary on a first visit. We spent an hour wandering the acropolis, the Temple of Trojan and the steepest theater on earth where lots of Japanese, British and German tourists stood on the top row to see the stage between their feet. The next morning at Ayvalik was 38 degrees, the coldest we'd had inside the RV, fogging the air with our breath and demanding the clicking on of the trusty heater an hour before rolling out of bed, boosting the temperature over 60 degrees by breakfast.

The RV turned west at Edremit following the olive Riviera, stopping for a scenic lunch at Assos and driving up to Behramkal with its 400 B.C.E. temple where Aristotle studied four years, across the Aegean from Lesbos.

This was pastoral Turkey, rolling countryside dotted with olive trees, sheep munching grass, locals in baggy pants with crotches at their ankles, smiling and waving, tractors pulling wagons loaded with families, nightly fires sponsored by pyromaniacs, revered archeological sites and fancy gas stations for peaceful overnighting.

Near Gulpinar we found a sunny spot overlooking Dalyan and the Aegean close to the Alexandrio Troas archeological site but two dogs barked half the night. With 45 degrees in the morning we declared a heat wave. We skipped paying admission to Troy, having visited on previous occasions, but used the daily photo on the great fake Trojan horse. The ferry left Canakkale Bogazi at noon, costing $9.60 and 25 minutes to transit back to Europe from Asia Minor. We lunched overlooking Gallipoli, which the Turks call Gelibolu, along the bay of Saros Korfezi, a 35 knot wind practically pushing a loaded bicycle backwards as the rider desperately fought up the road.

Greece: Home Sweet Home

Back in Greece the wind amazingly stayed at 35 knots. When meeting a truck the wind would disappear for a tenth of a second, then we'd veer all over the road. Still Mary was happy to be back in her grandmother country. However, at 7 p.m. it began raining for 24 hours making the next day exceptionally miserable; we'd been psychologically expecting unending sunshine in Greece. The wet weather induced a driving compulsion of 291 kilometers (175 miles), among the most during 2 ½ years. In Kavala a car rear-ended the RV at a stoplight. There was no real damage but the poor guy kept saying in English, *It's all my fault,* and I kept saying, *I know, I know.* We drove onward and wetward. The cutesy villages with picturesque harbors became nothing in the rain.

At Stavros we headed south for the Halkidiki peninsula, parking on the beach in pouring rain, Mary pleading to go home. I said we'd be in the UK in three weeks to sell the RV and we couldn't drive there any faster, Mary swearing she couldn't last that long. Fortunately the next morning was sunny though cold with the snow line 100 meters above the beach. We climbed to a 500 meter plateau for excellent views. The scenery was brilliant in the snow and sun, at Poligyros providing a wide view of the three 30-mile long peninsulas of the Halkidiki spread below: Athos, Sithonia and Kassandra.

We began the Sithonia finger on an east coast loop, signs everywhere saying *No free camping*, probably because there were so many campgrounds though all were closed. We found an overnight view of the Athos peninsula, bays with sandy bottoms making a pale turquoise sea. What a difference the reappearing sun made, Mary suggesting she could live overlooking Athos for perhaps a whole month. At Nea Pltidea a canal severed Kassandra from the mainland and offered great views of Mt. Olympus, its snow-capped peaks seeming to float on ether. We diddled three hours walking through Kastoria's 36 Byzantine and 40 post-Byzantine churches on the narrow causeway between the island and mainland. Though the churches were unremarkable the scenic location was striking, furs for sale everywhere, stretched and drying. An elderly Greek man beckoned, we rolled down the RV window and he said he'd worked at Ford Motors in Dearborn for 30 years, living in Detroit where Mary was born to a Greek family, old home week with the man saying *God bless USA* at least ten times.

At Thessaloniki we found the blessed U.S. dollar had dropped 5% since we'd left Greece in November, a few short months, a fact we got used to in most countries during the bulk of the next ten years. We overnighted in a picnic area below a large fortress castle at Platamonas below the brilliant peak of Kato Olympus covered in snow, whizzing to the Kalambaka campground where we'd ordered mail. It was our nicest campground anywhere in Europe: marble bathrooms, actual toilet paper and lots of hot water at the base of the spectacular Meteora mesas precariously topped with monasteries. The mail arrived before lunch and we spent the afternoon climbing up a butte and down to Kalambaka town, the verticality rather upsetting Mary.

Mary had stayed with her father's family at the neighboring Amelia Hotel during the summer of 1994, looking up relatives from this small part of Greece. We drove to the villages of Mary's grandparents a dozen miles southwest on a glorious sunny day, finding her grandmother's village at the end of a snaky five mile road spiraling upward to Pefkofite. No one spoke English and it was chilly. Mary found her cousin, a priest, but without a common language he couldn't understand who she was and we left after ten minutes, enjoying great views down the mountain. The rest of the day we relaxed, watching little girls traipse about with Easter baskets covered in flowers.

Meteora's monasteries were shadowed by a heavy cloud cover the next day but we drove the 11 mile route, sad to miss sunny photos of the precarious Greek Orthodox architecture perched high on skinny rocks. The road was crowded with tour buses full of Germans and Japanese, like being behind the front lines in WWII; the Japanese snapped photos in perfect unison. When we checked out of the campground the lady presented us with an icon, a postcard of the campground and a book of scenic Greek photos.

The skies cleared for a gorgeous sunny day at the top of 1705 meter (5500 foot) Kitares Pass, high snow-capped peaks all around on the 225 kilometers (140 miles) of twisty road toward Igoumenitsa for the ferry to Venice. We lunched at the Ioanina viewpoint over the lake where we'd overnighted the previous September by Perama cave. It took an hour to negotiate the twisty up and down road to Igoumenitsa where we found ferries for Venice left on Saturdays and Wednesdays; since this was Sunday we had 2 ½ days to wait. Competing travel agents cornered the RV; I went with one and Mary the other, playing them against each other for a final price of $270 that we'd thought would cost $360. We spent two days poking around the peninsula south at Swota, Marirtos and Arilla, all with lovely deserted beaches, aquamarine coves, no traffic and easy overnight parking.

The Ferry to Venice

After picking up boarding passes in Igoumenitsa we found an overnight spot on a grassy sand spit two miles north of town, went to bed at 9 p.m. and were up by 4 a.m. for loading the 5 a.m. ferry and a grand surprise. The ferry had reserved a spacious lower deck with cathedral ceilings for easy RV clearance. The deck would hold 50 RVs and only ten had boarded. We plugged into electric next to two large open windows with a western view, waking from a two hour nap to a rolling ferry, happy for electricity and a space heater. The other RVs were seven Germans, a Dutch and a New Zealander. We chatted for hours with Kiwis Heather and Patrick, retired dairy farmers. They were on their way back to the UK to sell their 6 ½ meter (22 foot) 1989 RV after two years RVing Europe; Patrick had Parkinson's disease that required medication every four hours, hoping to travel until he packed it in. They were off to Italy, Austria, Switzerland and Germany before the UK, then to Australia and the U.S., if Pat were able. They loaned us the MMM English camping magazine so we could copy the list of dealers advertising used RVs, in case we needed help selling *Grendel II* in London.

The next morning we watched Venice glide by at 6:30 a.m., passing a few meters off St. Marks in the barely rising sun. We promptly got lost in Mestre, unable to find a good breakfast place until 8:30 a.m. It became a difficult day for good parking, whether for breakfast, lunch or overnight, finally pulling into a quiet cemetery well off the road near Molinetto. The RV was becoming difficult to shift; because I've always been unmechanical I wasn't sure whether it was the clutch or something serious. The Italian lake district was so commercialized it was onerous to find the waterfront. We finally gave up and headed for the tunnel under Mt. Blanc to France.

Good overnight parking was available after Ivrea on the raging Dora Baltea River beneath a castle near a long waterfall. It rained all night starting at 9 p.m., clearing the next morning to reveal the tops of the Alps. At Donnes the highway was blocked for a bike race. The police directed traffic into the narrowest lane on earth, an inch clearance on each side of the RV for over a mile, and top clearance problems, a nerve-wracking drive that Mary had to direct from the outside. The townspeople couldn't believe we were actually driving through town, standing mouths agape, but neither could we, blaming the cops. The drive after Donnes was dramatic with castles, chateaus and villas surrounded by high Alps along sheer green hillsides dotted with perfect Swiss chaleted towns next to the raging river, driving within 18 miles of the Matterhorn. We skipped the steep windy road to the mountain because the Alps had become shrouded in cloud.

The Mt. Blanc tunnel cost $33.50 for 12 kilometers (7 miles) and presto we were in France, where it was raining above Chamonix. We took a crazy scenic route to avoid Geneva and Switzerland's $30 road sticker, heading south at Sallanches through deep gorges past chalets beneath snowy peaks through the Gorges D'Arly. It had rained every time we crossed France, five times in 2 ½ years. This time we made it across in three days, 175 miles or 275 kilometers a day, a big deal for normally slow-moving us. We stopped at a Fiat dealer to diagnose the difficulty of shifting gears and he said it was a bad clutch plate. He had none in stock so we decided to wait for easier communication in England. France was cloudy through Bourg, by Nantua and the lake through the Gorges l'Ain, the high point the old walled city of Beaune with quaint streets, old churches, arches, gates and citadel.

We passed the source of the Seine, following the River most of the day to Troyes and through Chalous sur Marne and Rheims, suffering continuous problems with the clutch. We parked near Abbe de Vauclair where we'd overnighted 1 ½ years before in a quiet forest near a musty lake and old Abbey, later stopping at our favorite walled town of Laon, at the Continent Supermarket to stock up on groceries. When we turned onto the canal at Marquion for lunch we realized we'd overnighted there several years previous, a great spot for watching barges and topping up water. Calais was a traffic jam of Brits over for the weekend, stocking up on cases of wine, beer and booze.

The European End Game

The Chunnel offered a lower fare of $115 after 10 p.m. We tried to drive on and were tartly informed the train was full. Finally aboard at 11:30 p.m. we found the Chunnel shuttle the exact width of the vehicles with a tiny walkway added on either side. The train was split into separate cars with six vehicles each, drive on and drive off the entire length of the train upon arrival in the UK, taking 45 minutes with extra precautions because of the disastrous fire the year before. The UK appeared after midnite, the day of Tony Blair's election as Prime Minister on May 1, 1997. The Crystal Palace campground was located in London on the northwest corner of the site hosting the Great Exhibition of 1851, immaculate landscaping and the most expensive we'd stayed at for $24 a night, surely doubled by the early 21st Century.

Nearby shopping offered 33 ethnic restaurants, a huge Safeway's and an ancient public library with index cards and manual typewriters. We phoned many of the Brits we'd met over the years and said hi. England had no RV-trader magazine but locals suggested we consult close-by Turner's, an RV dealer that bought used RVs. At Turner's a salesman took a look and said the value would normally be 11,000-12,000 £s, then $18,400-20,000, but the high mileage would knock it down to 10,000 £s; we'd originally paid the equivalent of 12,000£s. In addition the *Q* license plate would drastically drop the value to 8,000 £s, which meant well-meaning Mr. Turner couldn't pay more than 5,000-6,000 £s, $8400-10,000, bottom line. But call him back if we couldn't find a better deal.

We called ten dealers from the listings copied off of Patrick and Heather's RV directory on the Venice ferry, and they stuck to the same story about the *Q* plate and high mileage. We couldn't put an ad in the largest newspaper dedicated to selling miscellany in London, *The Loot*, because we had no call-back phone number and the campground wouldn't let us use theirs. A cell phone would have remedied this dilemma, making it easy to sell an RV anywhere on earth, but there weren't any in 1997. One dealer said he wasn't interested in a *Q* plate at all. We hadn't a clue the detriment of the *Q* plate two years before, thinking we were smart and lucky. But that dealer said call Steve at Painham Motorcaravans, who we'd already talked to on the far eastside of London.

Steve spent a lot of time discussing a potential purchase, finally saying he'd pay 5500-6000 £s, *depending* on how it drove, concluding the *Q* plate and left-hand drive cut the value in half. We were shell-shocked because we'd hoped to get between 8000 and 10,000 £s. We told Steve the RV needed a new clutch plate, despondently driving across London to the campground in heavy traffic. The apparent solution was the purchase of a magic marker and fluorescent cardboard for a window sign: *For Sale; 9999 £s OBO.* We'd take the RV to the big *Aussie* used camper market near King's Cross station, barely north of downtown, meanwhile inviting Kerry and Adrian, who we'd rescued in Spain several years previous, to dinner and cards. Adrian had begun driving moving vans to Germany and Kerry was a traffic warden.

We were totally stumped on how to sell the RV but next morning drove across Westminster Bridge by Big Ben and the Houses of Parliament past thousands of tourists in occasional sprinkles, around Trafalgar square and 10 Downing Street, finally finding the *Aussie* market. It consisted of a dozen VW vans and small campers parked on both sides of the street, prices from 2000 to 4000£s, mostly sellers and few buyers. *Grendel II* was way above this market. After five hours reading the Sunday Times and chatting with other sellers we decided to stay the night and try the next day. The *No overnite parking* signs were ignored by the half dozen vans also staying overnight. After another fruitless day we drove to Steve's motor-caravan office for the night. Calling around the next day we found a new clutch plate would cost $400. At Painham Motorcaravans we negotiated with Steve for two hours, including a test drive, arriving at a final deal of 5750£s ($9600) for *Grendel II*.

Mary canvassed shipping companies to dispatch the detritus of this expedition back to the U.S., finding they were all located at Heathrow Airport. We drove over, 61 miles, dumping loads in the trash while Mary schmoozed with Wilson Shipping, associated with Nippon. We were required to pack everything in boxes, driving to the closest large Tesco supermarket a mile away and packing 22 banana boxes in 41 hours while befriending a security guard who let us stay overnight, twice. After two days and 13 hours of packing we were exhausted. Meanwhile I called bucket shops and travel agents to find the best airfare to Phoenix. Every newspaper ad was deceiving, listing student fares. The best price was 622£s for two, $1066 on Sabena from London to Brussels to Atlanta to Phoenix, taking 18 hours; leaving at 7 a.m. London time and arriving 5 p.m. Phoenix time.

The bikes were rusty and difficult to fold, resulting in a keystone cop routine. We donated remaining food to the Tesco security guard, including half a case of beer. Shipping 22 boxes cost $645 including two bikes, totaling 510 lbs. We drove to Heathrow for the plane tickets, finding the cheapest hotel room was $125 at the five-star Radisson, normally $192 a night way back in 1997, probably double that in 2009. Driving halfway around London took over an hour. We left *Grendel II* with Steve for 5757£s in 20£ notes and a fiver, a big bundle Mary hid in a daypack, clutching it to her chest for two days. An employee of Painham Motorcaravans took us to the tube station at Upminster, the last stop in furthest northeast for travel to furthest southwest London, taking over an hour to Heathrow and the shuttle to the ritzy hotel. After blowing the balance of miscellaneous British money at McDonald's next door we spent the evening at the hotel's fancy health spa and collapsed in the room, hoping the plane tickets would be at the counter at 6 a.m. for the 7 a.m. flight; oh, the olden days.

The next day took a horrific 20 hours. We hadn't seen a movie for 2 ½ years and both flights showed *Jerry McGuire.* It was a balmy 98 degrees in Phoenix where prices seemed ultra-cheap. However, the best exchange rate for British pounds was $1.59, netting $9,198 for the RV upon exchange.

Years in Europe: The Bottom Line

During almost three years in Europe we'd averaged $20 a day for depreciation and fuel, driving an average of fifty miles a day and getting twenty miles per gallon, concluding that diesel was the only way to go. Overall, considering the difference between the purchase and sale price of *Grendel II*, plus food, oil changes, excessive tires and fuel costs, campgrounds, mail forwarding, admissions and sheer fun, we blew $50 a day, including the cost of side excursions to Russia and Egypt. This grand total of $1500 a month should perhaps be conservatively doubled in 2009, especially for those who prefer staying in campgrounds, which in Europe may be closed half the year. We would have netted much more on the resale of *Grendel II* in the era of cell phones with a phone number for internet or newspaper ads easily available, far different from as recently as 1997.

Now we'd sell the RV online or through a classified ad in a newspaper or RV trader, instead of to a dealer, making more money, which is exactly what we did when reselling RVs in Australia and New Zealand. But we wouldn't change a single destination. We saw it all in forty countries in Europe and environs, from stem to stern, warts and all, and that's what we set out to do. However, we've become increasingly more careful of RV security, always parking safely in cities, in for-pay parking lots, which we'd failed to do in Florence.

In South America we learned to never park on the street, but always in an estacionamiento (covered and secured pay parking, available in every South American town and city), but only after thieves had entered the campervan in Ica, Peru, stealing a backpack and daypack with lots of vitamins and gear for two years driving around the continent. With a single exception detailed later we've never suffered a personal threat during years of continuous world travel.

A few days after landing in Phoenix, while staying temporarily with Mary's sister, she solicitously inquired: *When are you leaving?* Within a week we'd bought a 1984 Lazy Daze for $11,000, cherry condition, naturally christening it *Grendel III*. We were off to South America, we thought.

CHAPTER EIGHT
Rving After Europe

Rolling Stones: Off Again

Grendel III was prepped with two years of spare parts when we headed *toward* South America, planning to bridge the Darien Gap by shipping from Panama to Cartagena in Columbia. Having no schedule we spent the first year in Mexico, reveling in grandiose Copper Canyon, the old colonial cities and silver boomtowns wealthy before Jamestown was thought of, and particularly the underground colonial city of Guanajuato where we spent a month in Spanish school. Better equipped in Spanish we headed for ancient Pazcuaro and the district of old volcanoes, the dozens of spectacular Mayan ruins on the Yucatan Peninsula and all of Chiapas from Palenque to San Cristobal de las Casas. After Belize and Tikal in Guatemala at the end of October, 1998, we hit a brick wall called Hurricane Mitch. Mitch wiped out the roads and bridges in Honduras, Nicaragua and Guatemala, making further travel south, impossible.

- ## Changing Plans

Grendel III executed a U-turn toward Alaska via Western Canada, where we photographed bears, glaciers and rugged Rockies, following the mighty Yukon River through Whitehorse to Dawson and into Chicken, Alaska. We drove every paved road in Alaska, truly no big deal, and took the Aleutian Islands ferry as far as it goes, from Homer to Dutch Harbor, sleeping on deck (inside), and meeting marvelous characters before driving to Denali and north of Fairbanks to the Arctic Circle, which was eclipsed by Arctic Norway. Taking the car ferry from Haines to Juneau, Sitka and Ketchikan, we disembarked in Prince Rupert to drive the legendary Canadian Rockies through Jasper to Banff, then on through Calgary to Waterton Lakes National Park in Canada and Glacier National Park across the border into the United States. We retraced much of this route in 2009, pulling a 26' trailer with a diesel 4x4 truck.

Years in Australia and New Zealand

What next? Truly simple places to travel were getting scarce but the two easiest were still ahead from October 1999- April 2001: Australia for thirteen months and six months in New Zealand. In Brisbane we bought a twenty-foot camper bus, driving it for great adventures completely around Australia and down the middle, a country the size of the United States without Alaska. We encountered crocodiles up close in the Northern territory, mind-boggling national parks, the two best being Karijini and Purnululu—also known as The Bungles in Western Australia—and Tasmania. The Great Barrier Reef required four dives and snorkeling visits. For old times' sake we chartered a yacht in the Whitsunday Islands, quite incredible scenery and snorkeling. After driving down the center to Alice Springs, and Ayer's Rock, also known as Uluru, we sold the camper bus back in Brisbane, flew to Auckland and bought a six-berth RV.

New Zealand was mind-bobbling scenery, to which we returned for five months in 2009-2010: on North Island the Tongariro Crossing, Waitomo Caves, White Island's active volcano and charming Wellington before heading to the real highlights. South Island bewitched us from the Banks peninsula south of Christchurch, to Dunedin, Stewart Island and the phenomenal hiking every which direction from Queenstown. We cramponed the glaciers on the back side of Mount Cook and hiked seven three-day backpacking trips to a few of the 900 huts available in New Zealand's wondrous system of national parks. When we're too old to continue gallivanting the world we may live six months in New Zealand and six months in Australia.

- **Intermittent RV-less Years**

On September 10, 2001 we flew to Hong Kong and spent the next eight months backpacking through China, Laos, Cambodia, Thailand, Vietnam, Malaysia and more, for the first time mostly without personal transportation because of driving restrictions in China and Myanmar. It would have been a much better experience if we could have driven our own RV but try telling that to the repressive governments of China and Myanmar.

We'd intended to backpack through Mongolia, Nepal and India before going to South America but Nepal erupted in a Maoist revolution while Pakistan and India seemed inclined to nuke each other over a variety of non-reasons at the turn of the century, religion aka Kashmir. We hiked all over Nepal, India and Pakistan in 2004, after returning from two years driving around South America.

The highlights in Nepal were the Annapurna Circuit and trek to Everest Base Camp. Annapurna was three weeks of easy hiking, excluding the strenuous day up, over and steeply down 17,769 foot high Thorung La Pass. The Circuit is perfect for those who love stunning scenery, Nepal's Himalayas, around some of the world's highest mountains. This is perhaps the world's most popular long trek and also one of the easiest because it's a series of day hikes between zero-star guesthouses. Swing over suspension bridges above glacier-melt rivers and through quaint villages beside brilliant green rice paddies to pig-out on international cuisine because with daily hiking no one gains an ounce. After three weeks of amazing scenery we left for the hike to Everest Base Camp.

Tackling Base Camp begins with a flight from Katmandu to Lukla for a trek of twelve days, round-trip. I took part in a high altitude acclimatization study and made the trek, as could anyone of average fitness, by hiring a Sherpa porter for the duration: total cost $100. On night three I stayed in Jimmy Carter's suite at a Namche Bazar hotel. The next morning dawned with Everest on the horizon fifteen miles away. These fifteen miles took four days and three blizzards, sprinkled among some of the most extravagant scenery on earth. I finally made it to base camp, immersing myself in the politics of the fifteen expeditions seeking the summit in 2004.

The highlight of Northern India was Kashmir, unfairly tarred as a war zone by the media reports of a strife-torn and splintered province, the focal point of the eternal fracas between India and Pakistan. In reality Srinigar, Kashmir is idyllic and one of the world's most romantic destination for honeymooners from lowland India.

In 1867, a Kashmiri Brit built the first fabulously carved Moorish Palace to float as a houseboat on perfectly reflecting Dal Lake in Srinigar. On the Everest Base Camp hike I'd met a grand dame who told marvelous stories of the perfect months she'd whiled away in an opulent house boat on Dal Lake, thirty years previous. I simply had to go after meeting a Srinigar native in Nepal, who invited me to visit. I found Kashmir home to some of the world's most beautiful scenery in nearby Pahalgam and Gulmarg, surrounded by glaciated peaks above mountain meadows cut by crystalline rivers and reputedly, the world's highest golf course.

I made a special effort to visit northeast Pakistan's Karakoram Mountains, which boast six of the world's highest fourteen peaks within a small radius and one of the most scenic hiking areas on the planet. This area of Pakistan is well away from the iffy-part, which borders Afghanistan near Khyber Pass, and well north of the 2005 earthquake. After months among these gorgeous peaks in Pakistan we crossed into China, amazed by the changes, elevated wealth and sophistication of the Chinese people, compared to three years earlier. After relaxing in Bangkok we flew to South Africa for several months' exploration of Africa. We were truly amazed by the ease of getting around and the excellent roads in East Africa

- ## The South American Connection

During 2002-2003 we drove around South America. We'd planned to ship a Dodge Ram diesel four-wheel drive with pop-up camper to Guayaquil, Ecuador in a standard container. Instead we found a nicely tricked out Dodge camper van in Quito, Ecuador, with Canadian plates, the plates being a large part of the deal. An RV, for example bought in Argentina where they're readily available, can't be taken across many South American borders. A camper plated anywhere outside of South America can easily cross any border south of Central America, and Central American borders too.

Two Germans from Stuttgart, Barbara and Andreas, had refurbished the van and offered it for sale in Quito, advertising its availability at http://www.saexplorers.org. We were impressed by their email of a dozen pictures showing the inside and outside of the van, striking a tentative deal, subject to in-person inspection. We flew to Quito, took a look at the van and found it as advertised, buying it on the spot for $5500. This saved the $6000 it would have cost to ship an RV to South America and back in a standard container, and all the problems inherently involved with international shipping, about which more later.

Beginning Africa

The next year we Land Rovered up the East Coast of Africa from eclectic South Africa through freaky but safe Zimbabwe, Idyllic Zambia, along the incredible rift lake dividing Malawi and fell in love with Tanzania, from the exotic island of Zanzibar to the incredible natural zoo in Ngorongoro Crater, adjacent to the equally astounding Serengeti, meanwhile climbing three fabulous mountains culminating in Kilimanjaro, the world's largest birthday present from Queen Victoria to her cousin the German Kaiser. Then there was Ethiopia, a don't-miss country among the world's top dozen.

From 2006 to May 2007 we trucked through the northern half of East and West Africa, untouristed parts of Egypt, the length of Sudan and back to the magnet of Ethiopia; from the oceanfront paradises of Cameroon through fascinating and indelibly fragmented Nigeria, the voodoo strongholds of Togo and Benin, the peace of Oceanside Senegal, checking out music festivals and sacred catfish in Burkina Faso, ending in my African favorite, Mali, home of the world's oldest market and largest mud mosque at D'Jenne, up the Niger to Timbuktu and a trek through mystical Dogon country. The truck trek wrapped up through Mauritania, the Western Sahara and the feeling of a *hometown* return to Morocco, having wintered there in 1995-6.

A Few Highlights

Though we aren't done yet some of the best overnight sights and experiences during years of continuous international travel were obviously available only by RV, some previously described, over-nighting within or next to:

- The Heights of the Horns of Hittite where the Crusaders met their final demise above Lake Kinneret, aka The Sea of Galilee, Israel, visited by helicopters,

- Mt. Cook out the 270 degree back windows on South Island, New Zealand,
- Surrounded by kangaroos on a remote beach in New South Wales, Australia,
- Overlooking the phenomenal ruins of Ancient Petra, and definitely by ourselves in remote Wadi Rum where Larry of Arabia hung out, both in Jordan,
- Watching a full eclipse of the moon atop an RV in Alice Springs, Northern Territory, Australia,
- Many overnights in the wind-hewn canyons of the Negev Desert, Israel,
- Over-nighting next to a French Canal, or an ancient French Monastery in a primeval forest,
- On Hobart Bay, and beneath Cradle Mountain in Tasmania, Australia,
- In the orange and black striped mountains of the Bungle Bungles, Purnululu National Park, and at the confluence of sandstone slot canyons in Karajini National Park, both in Western Australia,
- On the waterfront in Ushuaia, Argentina, southernmost city in the world, watching ships leave for Antarctica, and in Tierra Del Fuego National Park, outside Ushuaia, at the foot of the last of the Andes, on the Beagle Channel,
- Near the top of Vesuvius overlooking the Bay and lights of Naples, relieved it wasn't erupting,
- Milford Sound, all to ourselves after the tour buses had gone home for the night, South Island, New Zealand,
- On the canals of Brugge in Belgium, and Venice in Italy, but unfortunately not by RV for the canals of Suzhou, China,
- Surrounded by reindeer on lakes in Finland,
- On the waterfront in Stockholm, Sweden,
- On Lake Titicaca in Copacabana, Bolivia, and next to hot springs at Mt. Sajama (6542 meters or 21,000 feet), Bolivia at about 15,000 feet, and a few kilometers away on the border with Chile where a perfectly reflecting lake doubled twin Fujiesque cones.

And a hundred other scenic spots on the planet, available overnight only by tent or RV.

What about the States? Shouldn't everyone first see the U.S.A. in their Chevrolet? We're saving the States until foreign RVing becomes too much trouble and our walkers won't fit through turnstiles. But the States won't be new travel because we've already scoured forty-nine of the fifty, all but West Virginia.

We've been on the road sixteen years, living in a hundred forty seven countries with *only* forty-four left to go, based on U.N. membership, which we figure will take another ten years, or so. Someday we may run out of countries to live in but places like Vesuvius exist on the moon, don't they?

APPENDIX:

Europe's thousands of campgrounds are listed in detail in easily available European campground guides. See www.camping.info listing twenty-some thousand European campgrounds and http://www.europe-camping-guide.com. But campgrounds are seldom necessary, often a waste of money, usually boring and often crowded with noisy people. We prefer wilderness, rivers, mountains, canals and the like for quiet and inexpensive overnights. With the single exception of a Buenos Aires city park we've never been menaced in 15 years. To find an RV in Europe Google *Buy Used Campingcar Europe*, which is what RVs are called over there. Also search online in the classified ads in English-language newspapers in Europe, under *Campingcar or caravan for sale*, the terms often used interchangeably. Buy the most detailed road atlases available, a boon for free camping, showing every little alley, road, ruin, lake and campground, many free, quiet and remote. For example, several towns in northern Italy provide free municipal parking for RVs, hook-ups included. French rest stops are RV friendly with overnight parking allowed, the same as we think we found in Denmark and Sweden. European countries with difficult free camping include the UK, though roadside lay-bys work tolerably well, UK parking lots height restricted and Poland with farms fenced up to the roads, and probably Switzerland, though we've only traveled there by train and plane, avoiding what was a $30 road tax, perhaps doubled by now.

CHAPTER NINE
How About RVing the World?

Life is a book; those who never travel outside their country of birth read a single page.
David Rich (Dissimilar to St. Augustine, except in their youths)

Curious souls who'd like to see the world's most fabulous sights before they die may be disheartened by extremely limited travel options, often grossly unappetizing though popular. These range from the boring and hectic rat race of **tours** and the outrageously expensive cattle-call of **cruises** to the often filthy, difficult and unsafe travel conditions associated with achy breaky backs propping up luggage, aka **back-packing**.

Instead of risking a scurrilous range of hotel beds we prefer to sleep in our own bed every night, avoiding suspect restaurants by fixing our own excellent meals, occasionally hazarding the risk of eating out. We prefer to avoid choosing among scabrous hotels or paying hundreds of dollars for a bed and interminably schlepping our own luggage.

Anyone can easily find excellent English-speaking doctors and medical facilities in every country, even Myanmar, the majority with at least one hospital better than the average in the States, at a tiny fraction of the cost. Health insurance is unnecessary for anyone who can afford to travel because excellent foreign healthcare costs far less than American medical insurance, unless entirely paid for by an employer.

Veterans of foreign travel find post 9/11 fears of terrorism are merely fear itself, indistinguishable from balderdash. The USA is Al-Qaeda's prime target, not Timbuktu, or the Karakorams of Pakistan, or fascinating South Korea or outback Australia. Non-travelers are shocked to learn that 99% of the world, with a minimum of precaution, is safer than portions of any large U.S. city, including the city where they live. A country such as Yemen, away from the border area with Saudi Arabia, is overall safer than parts of any big city in the USA.

It's easy to keep in touch with family and friends anywhere in the world, except Myanmar, to instantly reach out and rub anyone raw with travel photos and fabrications. The internet and Skype are available in every little town most places, even Timbuktu as I can testify: flat screens with broadband in the electronics lab at Timbuktu High School.

Those who've taken over-hyped tours, poorly conceived package deals, hectic week-end getaways, luxury cruises spent mostly at sea, eating horribly fattening foods, and shuttling ship to shore or have tried back-breaking backpacking, may have unconsciously, at least, found these modes of travel seriously wanting.

Who wouldn't prefer intimate comfort, ease of travel, sleeping in their own bed every night, stopping where and when they wish next to babbling brooks, gorgeous lakes and scenic canals, atop hopefully extinct volcanoes, beneath snow-clad peaks or next to ancient antiquities?

Travelers often feel disconnected from the sights they've come to see and from local people because they're a) herded around like cattle, b) packaged in claustrophobia, c) spend most of the time getting there and back home again, c) see little except the ship's buffet and pesky little tenders motoring to sterile tours on shore or d) return with a nearly broken back, perhaps crippled for life. We prefer seeing the world's most incredible sights up close, safely and intimately without the crush of other tourists, finding little known gems and meeting interesting locals, avoiding know-nothing tour guides and forcible routing through sleazy tourist traps.

What would-be travelers haven't unconsciously feared terrorist attacks, worried about foreign medical emergencies and avoided travel to stay in close touch with family and friends? It's simple to jettison frenetic see-nothing know-nothing travel and connect with the land, the real land and real people, and see the world the way it's meant to be seen: one on one without hotels, restaurants, fattening buffets, tourist traps and hideous personalities attracted to the travel industry to serve no one but themselves, and to do it safely without losing touch with family and friends or risking cataclysmic medical perplexities.

Of course there's a catch. RVing requires a skill, a single skill. One must be able to drive a motor vehicle, about all there is to driving an RV. Then anyone can see the world's incredible sights without the crush of other tourists, being herded around like brainless birds or subject to the lectures of boring tour guides, safely, with excellent medical care readily available while keeping in close contact with family and friends.

Traveling outside the country of birth, as a practical matter, involves one of four choices. The first easy option is a tour or cruise, often populated by dependent persons with little inkling where to go, or why, except they might have heard of Egypt.

Tours and Cruises

The alternative to buying or renting personal transportation is public transportation and hotels, or tours and cruise ships. The latter dynamic duo feature the mindless toting of those having little or no say in where to go, what to see or how long to see it, waiting, forever waiting for the slowest in the group, suffering interminable lectures and bounteous buffets, forced to visit sleazy merchants selling chintzy wares at outrageous prices.

Tours and cruises are anathema because we find them shockingly expensive for the value, deadly boring and so restrictive of independent movement that to us they feel like solitary confinement, making us cringe. We've never found a tour guide more knowledgeable or quieter than a guide book. The only extended tour we've taken, eight long days in Cairo and up the Nile from Aswan, featured a colossal know-it-all bore and stuffed shirt mixed with antiseptic hotels floating the Nile, boring affairs filled with often boring people on a fortnight's vacation.

The fun part of travel is being able to wander when and where the impulse carries, at our own pace, which varies substantially from that of the typical tour. The best way to travel doesn't require exorbitant payments for a stifling experience. In sixteen years of continuous international travel we've stooped to tour a few times out of sheer necessity. For example, the only way Americans can legally enter North Korea, which we did in 2005, is by an unstructured group tour from South Korea.

No-brainer tours and cruises appeal to those who can't, don't or won't read a guide book, do simple basic research or Google. They pay big money to take big chances that the particular tour or cruise will be interesting, joining a herd driven thither and yon with no latitude for the individuality of moo cows. And oh, the prices: we could buy a condo in North Dakota for the cost of an around-the-world cruise. My elderly cousins love cruise ships because they have physical difficulty getting around, missing many shore excursions and spending enough in five years to buy the Queen Mary. But they have no other choice to see the world, which is consequently restricted to tiny portions viewable from a cruise ship. For those physically able there's a far less expensive and more satisfying way to see the world, their own way in their own sweet time.

Package Deals or Independent Travel

A second popular travel choice is by package deal, usually limited to a single city or location, but including hotels, meals and perchance a rental car. Package deals often offer short term bargains for those with limited interests, a yen for the latitude of a single degree on the compass and little or no free time, providing excellent means to break up the monotony of the work year. Naturally it's more interesting to travel fulltime, recognizing that even a lifetime is insufficient to see the world in depth.

The third and fourth choices are independent travel or joining the Navy. For those who'd rather avoid the Navy or are too mature the only palatable alternative is independent travel. Of course there are two ways to travel independently. Traveling the world like a backpacker, by bus, train, hotel and restaurant, is primarily for the financially challenged who don't mind grungy inns, unsanitary eateries, decrepit trains and maniacal bus drivers, and are very very young.

Unfortunately there are countries prohibiting foreigners from driving motor vehicles, relegating tourists to buses, trains and bicycles. These include China, Myanmar and Bhutan. Also entire continents, most of Asia and Africa, offer few or no RVs or campervans for sale, requiring intercontinental shipping or driving an RV or campervan to the continent of choice; or the local rental or purchase of a car, necessarily coordinated with the inimitable experience of hit or miss hotels and restaurants. These options are later dealt with in detail.

Forgoing personal transportation means putting up with rickety buses that may break down or fall off mountains or trains crowded with rowdies and no flexibility. Meanwhile travelers may suffer lots of dirt and association with those of questionable character and bathing habits. RVing and public transportation cost about the same. Tours are far more expensive, geared to those with little time or who are too inexperienced, timid or infirm to plan personalized travel, and who don't mind or have no alternative to being herded around like expensive sheep.

The Independent Travel of Public Transportation

Preferring to travel the way the locals get about—by bus train and ox cart, is an urban myth. Surely that's the way to meet the locals, experience a colorful culture and understand local lives. The theory is marvelous in the abstract. However, in many developing countries decent public transportation is mostly or only for tourists, there are language barriers to becoming more than superficially acquainted with locals and local buses cram passengers elbow to chin, choking passengers on chicken feathers or taking days to get anywhere.

A tourist bus may take eighteen hours during which the occupants see little or nothing along the way, with no means to take the picture of a lifetime or visit the bathroom. Many foreign buses, though advertising on-board toilets, actually have none. Many with an on-board bathroom padlock it shut or offer the equivalent of a gas chamber. Public buses are often a terribly uncomfortable means of transport but are necessary in some countries including China, where buses are excellent and first class trains a palatable alternative.

We've never been timid to drive in a foreign country. However, driving a humongous RV on narrow roads with funny traffic rules across cities no one could navigate unless born there might contribute to temporary timidity. Before exploring alternatives it's edifying to look closely at one country where no foreigner will drive an RV, considering the pros and cons of personal transportation, if it were allowed.

About the worst traffic we've experienced was in the world's third largest country, China. Cairo, Vietnam and Java were perhaps tied with China for ugly frightful traffic but China stood out. The traffic in China's many large cities was horrific, partly because of non-existent and ambiguous traffic rules. Crossing the street would challenge a world-class computer gamer.

The terrible Chinese traffic was tempered by the fact a non-citizen can neither drive nor rent a vehicle. Only citizens of China are allowed to drive motor vehicles, except motorcycles, relieving most tourists from personally coping with nigh impossible traffic. Tourists who fail to hire a Chinese driver must rely on public transportation.

Chinese buses come in all classes and conditions from fourth class and decrepit to luxury liners with stewardesses, waterless bathrooms and pirated videos. Passengers may watch the latest pirated Hollywood epic or a melodramatic soap opera, clearly understood though in Mandarin or Cantonese.

The ever-present, beckoning and ubiquitous minibuses of China become more jam-packed at every stop. By the time unfortunate commuters reach the closest city, legs tucked under chins would be better off asleep. Instead lower extremities will feel like they've been stung by venomous spiders, promoting staggering and literally falling down the aisle on exiting. A bonus will be the small urchin who's never seen a foreigner, who spends twenty minutes running grimy fingers over the arms of adjacent Westerners. The Chinese are either hairless or their hair is practically invisible, making foreigners a kid-magnet, the highlight of an urchin's week and rural lifetime. He'll tell the story to his yet-to-be-thought-of grandchildren. *Ah, yes, sons of my son, it was in the fall of the year of the rooster, back in 'ought-one, when I had a gringo under these very fingertips, and hairy beasts they are.*

Chinese trains offer four classes of accommodation, from hard and soft seats to hard and soft sleepers. The maximum time for comfortable travel on a hard seat is thirteen seconds, assuming it's possible to dislodge the occupant who has SRO tickets, a fifth class unavailable to foreigners. Naturally the occupant will pretend to speak no English whatsoever.

Hard sleepers offer six beds in open compartments where everyone smokes like a factory. The sole palatable berths are the bottoms, incidentally the only places to sit by invitation of the owner. The lucky owner becomes instant friends with the occupants of the car's forty middle and top berths: *Oh, hi, new best friend, and yes, I am thanking you in advance for sitting on your bed.* Often the *thank you* is difficult to translate from languages spoken by the Korean, Chinese, Pakistani and other friends attracted on any trip in China. New friends will use the bed as an ashtray and adjacent lungs as a receptacle for exhaust gases from cigarettes and beer. The dear, though temporary friends met in this fashion will persuade the average tourist to rely exclusively on soft sleepers.

Soft sleepers are four berth rooms with fancy embroidered lace curtains, inexhaustible thermoses of scalding water for tea and instant noodles and attentive attendants at only half the price of a plane ticket. But soft sleepers are equipped with doors and often unshared, no smoking allowed.

Travel Really Independently, by RV

Independent souls seeking relief from the vast sea of public transportation incompetence can easily explore our vast blue orb when, where, how and with whom they please. Instead of being crammed into public transportation as a co-captive with the unwashed it's more felicitous to see it with under one's own direction, by RV if possible. This is precisely how we've probed all of Australia, New Zealand, North, Central and South America, and Europe, plus much of Asia and parts of Africa, for most of the last sixteen years.

Those preferring independence to lumpy beds, ptomaine palaces, fat and alcohol-cramming cruises, boring captive tours, the Navy and public transport fit for those of little sensitivity, can easily RV the world. It's a piece of cake, the only means to truly experience any country up close and intimate. This mode of travel is quite unlike that utilized by those who fly from airport to airport in a race to rack up a hundred countries they've not even had a whiff of. Rudyard Kipling got it more nearly right when he said, *The first condition of understanding a foreign country is to smell it,* better outside the confines of Chinese hard sleepers.

What to do Thursday Next?

I shall be telling this with a sigh somewhere ages and ages hence: Two roads diverged in a wood, and I - I took the one less traveled by, and that has made all the difference.
Robert Frost

A depressingly small percentage take or make the opportunity to savor in-depth and long-term world travel. Whether wannabe travelers or travel dabblers we work until we keel over. This makes sense for those who enjoy working. We should all do what we love. I personally prefer a permanent vacation.

On a ski trip to Colorado we met a pharmacist who said he wasn't interested in travel because he liked his job so much. We'd always heard drugs could be fun but forever pushing pills, for me, would take the sixties to extremes. Similarly, most lawyers never retire, they just lose their appeal. As a recovering lawyer I appreciate lawyer jokes and trust many pharmacists also harbor a sense of humor. For those in a less-than-fun occupation having to drag themselves out of bed every morning, perhaps to perform the same nasty job each and every tedious week, month and year—something as traumatic as going to court to joust with unsavory attorneys in front of hardhearted judges—RVing the world can be the gateway to a real life and tons of fun.

Perhaps few are cut out to travel the world. Many are too timid to venture beyond their turf of birth. We suspect other countries are more dangerous or less safe, afraid we can't drink the water or that other people's primary preoccupation may be spotting the odd American to assassinate—silly us, except for the water. But beware that continuous foreign RVing could make render one, as the irate Norwegian told me I'd become, a foreign-born idiot.

The same as those unable to understand a passion for travel I've never understood people uninterested in world travel or travel of any description, except to visit Mom and Dad in Cleveland every tedious Christmas, preferring to drive the same streets all the days of their lives because they're familiar and therefore considered relatively safe. The familiar may be safer but is also more boring. We have the choice of embracing a constantly changing tableau or a tiresome existence of quiet desperation.

Americans inherently believe we live in the safest country on earth notwithstanding the fact that, except for countries actively engaged in war such as Iraq and Afghanistan, the United States boasts the highest per capita incidence of violent death on the planet. Simply put, it's safer almost anywhere outside the United States.

The few Americans traveling the world and the average American know little or nothing about the almost two hundred countries outside our borders, basically oblivious. *Canada*, they ask. *Where's that?* Most world travelers come from outside the United States, illustrating our essential insularity, timidity or lack of interest. Perhaps those travel voyeurs uninterested in personally visiting other countries may enjoy finding out how easy and safe it really is. And who knows? Indulging in armchair travel might motivate some to try the real thing, minus hotels, restaurants, buses and trains. I'd probably never have plunged into unending world-RVing had it not been for a ninetieth percentile curiosity and a family that loved and encouraged truly independent travel.

It's easy to rationalize working forever, remaining an armchair travel voyeur and never traveling the world. Those living in developed countries such as the States, Europe, Australia, New Zealand, Korea and Japan, and enjoy a half-way decent income can easily travel the world. The choice is a life of working until we drop, RVing a single country like most U.S. retirees or wide-ranging world travel. Not that working hard forever or biodegrading in a single country out of the over 200 in the world is inherently bad; just *boring*. The preference for unending hard work, driving up and down U.S. freeways forever or seeing all there is to see may depend on personality, or impairment thereof.

Hesitate Not; Just Do It

Twenty years from now you will be more disappointed by the things you didn't do than by the ones you did do. So throw off the bowlines, sail away from the safe harbor. Catch the trade winds in your sails. Explore. Dream. Discover. Mark Twain

The biggest hurdle to RVing the world is giving up the security blanket of a staid mundane existence, the compulsion to see the same fast food restaurants and shopping malls every day of our lives, the ability to perpetually shop until we droop. Why do people enjoy this lifestyle; it couldn't simply be a lack of *cajones* to leave it?

Many women have asked Mary how we can possibly RV the world. They suggest they *need a home*, a place of refuge, lest the security blanket frazzle. Susan Chitty and Thomas Hinde expressed it well in *Making Each Day Extraordinary; How to Multiply Your Memories,* in a 1977 issue of *Quest* magazine:

> *Days at home pass pleasantly enough, but one is very like another, and they leave little mark behind. By traveling, you make each day extraordinary and cheat time into giving you more than your share of memories.*

Or more succinctly by Caskie Stinnett: *I travel a lot; I hate having my life disrupted by routine.*

Another excuse for staying home is *my friends and family are there*. They'll still be there, stuck at home, no matter where we go. We can stop by and see hidebound friends and family every few years, or even yearly when absence makes both our hearts pound like a migraine. We should avoid being tied down by obstacles, imagined or real, in the sheep's clothing of friends or family. There are tons more interesting friends on offer in the big wide world than we'll stumble across in the fast-food neighborhoods of home. Plus the characters we meet on the road are 99th percentile more interesting than those languishing at home. Those who stay firmly at home are worse than in a rut; they're in a gorge, a drudge—not an entirely bad thing, as comfortable as a yawn. Why prefer the familiar instead of seeking out the interesting? Do we always suspect the interesting is more dangerous, in line with the ancient Chinese curse: *May you live in interesting times*?

After almost three years RVing around Europe, North Africa and the Middle East, Mary had become increasingly homesick for family and friends, severely tried by the unending rain and bad weather. She was ecstatic when her mother and a sister met us at the Phoenix airport after years away from *home*. Happy homecoming, chitchat about the weather, not a single question about the trip. It took her sister, where we were staying, less than an hour to ask when we'd be back on the road again, *please*. After the few days we spent looking for a suitable RV to romp through Central and South America her sister pointedly asked when we might become the dearly departed. Five days had been four days too many for the close-up pleasure of our company.

During the first week back Mary had difficulty making appointments to see her family. They were busy with school, work, soccer practice, affairs, relationships and the everyday debris of living. We should never stay home thinking family or friends will pine away while we're off traipsing abroad. They won't. No matter ineffectual protestations everyone is mostly concerned with themselves. The other guy, no matter how closely related or how tight the friendship, is and always will be the other guy who's unlikely to miss us more than fleetingly, if at all. For persuasive authority we couldn't do better than *The Death of Ivan Ilyitch*, by Leo Tolstoy.

Those with a family more copasetic, closer and caring can buy a bigger RV and take them along. As Dave Barry said:

> *That's the wonderful thing about family travel: it provides you with experiences that will remain locked forever in the scar tissue of your mind.*

Anyone can stay in close touch with family and friends almost anywhere on earth. The Internet guarantees daily contact with anyone who'll put up with it. We're closer to children and relatives than when living in the United States, working the rat race to make a living. Now family and friends, willingly or not, are the recipients of multiple color photos weekly, and two or three stories a month, illustrating precisely where and how we've been making mischief. *Every* country in the world, with the minor exception of Myanmar (formerly Burma), has readily available Internet. The Internet is not only worldwide, as in worldwide net, it's in every hole in the wall restaurant and library in most towns and bitsy bergs. In the next decade even Myanmar, finally the entire world, may have Internet for checking on NBA scores and the latest Hollywood gossip.

Outside developed countries Internet access is dirt cheap. Internet in China, for example, averaged thirty-seven cents an hour, waiting patiently in every little canton and dozens of grungy gaming parlors in most cities. Sometimes the machines were borderline archaic and the modems a tad slow, exacerbated by 900,000 Chinese government spies slowing it to a stroll, but the price was right.

In developed countries the Internet is free at most libraries, few levying even a nominal charge. At first-world Internet cafés I hide my wallet, extracting only what I can afford to lose, which may buy a few moments of checking e-mail. But now Wi-Fi is sweeping the planet, available free or nearly free at coffee shops, tourist offices, hostels, hotels and campgrounds worldwide.

Keeping in touch abroad is inexpensive because international phone rates have plummeted. Phone calls to the United States from most countries cost nineteen cents a minute, or less; Skype costs far less, about 2 cents a minute. Only a few countries, those without telecommunications competition, remain in the dollar-a-minute range. In those countries Internet offers free or inexpensive phone service via Skype. Or five hundred dollars will buy an unlocked Blackberry, Treo or Iphone allowing email in most countries, except Myanmar.

The old folks at home are the most common excuse for not traveling. Anyone can fly anywhere in the world on a day's notice, often for about the same as it'd cost to fly across the United States without a seven-day advance purchase, especially for those facile on the Internet. See http://airbrokers.com, http://airtreks.com, http://www.travelzoo.com, http://www.lastminuteairfares.com and http://smartertravel.com, among many possibilities. Internet fares are among the cheapest in the world. Some of the world's largest and most expensive airlines, such as Lufthansa, offer last minute bargain fares. Thus the excuse of elderly parents simply doesn't wash. If they're able to travel they can go along. It'd probably do the old folks good to get out of the house, assuming everyone enjoys each other's company and someone can locate a big affordable RV in an exotic locale upon which everyone can agree. Guaranteed family intimacy; ho, ho, ho. Mark Twain said: *I have found out that there ain't no surer way to find out whether you like people or hate them than to travel with them.*

Funny as it may seem the only real difficulty with RVing the world is what to do with old photo albums, those left behind by 21st Century technology. Photo albums are the only things that can't be sold. What to do with them? Leave them with family or friends, or scan them. I scanned ours and put them on a CD but because the average life of a CD is only five years I finally backed them up onto an auxiliary hard drive. Then it makes no difference what happens to photo albums, which regardless of what anyone thinks are a treasure only to the photographer and *perhaps* immediate family. When was the last time *anyone* begged to see a photo album?

A lovely couple off the east coast of Australia on Magnetic Island asked us what they could do with precious antiques, their only barrier to RVing the world. We gave them the same advice my father-in-law gave me, unsolicited, about an old Volkswagen camper van: sell the van, buy a dog, and shoot the dog. Sell the antiques and boost the travel kitty. Unless the antiques are valuable no one likely gives a hoot except immediately lurking family. Real Louis XIV antiques will bankroll travel for a very long time. Don't let mere sentiment stand in the way of lifetime adventure—RVing the world.

Particular travel interests depend on individually warped perspectives. We like mountains and antiquities, geographic magnificence and hiking. With few exceptions we have little interest in beaches or cities. Everyone has their own irrational travel biases. One thing most share, however—we'd rather play than work. RVing the world is the independent answer. Those giving it a try may possibly, no matter how remote, love it like we do.

The greatest collateral benefit of incessant travel is around-the-clock education. We figure each year of international travel is the equivalent of at least a year of college, which makes us professional students. We're learning how the whole world ticks, not just the tiny patch of real estate we were born on, where most will exclusively live and die. Mark Twain said:

> *Travel is fatal to prejudice, bigotry, and narrow-mindedness, and many of our people need it sorely on these accounts. Broad, wholesome, charitable views of men and things cannot be acquired by vegetating in one little corner of the earth all one's lifetime.*

Other systems of religion and government may lead to interesting comparisons and conclusions, perhaps suggesting many are half-baked or corrupt, including those back home. The world offers every shape, size, style and shade of people. But I've found we're more alike than different no matter where we live or how much money we make.

The few crooks we've run across were common thieves, police or politicians. The vast majority in all countries are just folks, overwhelmed trying to get by, day-to-day, to make ends meet, to eat. We found the overwhelming majority of people friendly, honest and anxious to go out of their way for a stranger, no matter their country of residence.

Everyone outside developed countries has more time for the foreigner and people in general, finding money far less important than we do because they often have little. It makes no difference whether they're Chinese, Afghans, Aussies, Brits, Serbs, Argentineans, Indians or whatever else—which leaves another 184 national labels to experience—only religions, governments and government policies differ. As Aldous Huxley said, *To travel is to discover that everyone is wrong about other countries.* People are generally the same everywhere; governments differ only according to their degree of corruption and ineptitude.

When we travel we soak up information related to our interests; everyone does the same. Those who love beaches become experts. Those into politics will find enough to go around. For collectors of figurines the world is a bonanza, and for everything else too.

A whole world beckons, waiting for us to live, experience and RV. Why spend a lifetime in a single country, reading a single page of life's book when there are hundreds of pages to read for those who have the gumption, interest and know-how to do it? The next chapter tells how. Gumption is a matter of self-acquisition. There are 200 countries to explore, to relish and understand. Really live—RV the world.

> *Clay lies still, but blood's a rover;*
> *Breath's aware that will not keep.*
> *Up, lad: when the journey's over*
> *then there'll be time enough to sleep.*
> A.E. Housman 1859-1936: *A Shropshire Lad*

Or more succinctly by Hans Christian Andersen: *Enjoy life, there's plenty of time to be dead.*

CHAPTER TEN
How to RV Wherever

Things to Write Down:
You can't fly away until the airplane arrives. Author
Luckily Anonymous

Over-generalizing, the three bare-bones choices for RVing the world are:

- Shipping an RV to the continent of choice
- Buying and selling an RV on almost every continent before moving to the next continent, or
- Shelling out bundles of money to rent an RV.

Which choice fits best must be determined by individual budget, personal preference and risk tolerance.

There's a world of decision-making imbedded in the simplicity of where to buy an RV or RVs to drive all over the world, and how to get you and an RV there at a reasonable cost. This is the kind of simplistic-sounding statement Mary always responds to by saying, *Gee, I'd better write that down.*

To Ship or not to Ship

We've met several people who have shipped a single RV to serial destinations. A British couple we met in New Zealand had shipped an RV to North America and then to Asia, and finally to New Zealand where we met them. They'd spent years driving around North America and Asia between shipments. They'd had to master a delicate science to determine the best shipping gateways and destinations on the six drivable continents. RVing Antarctica can be ignored except by those seeking an entry in the Guinness Book of World Records and perfecting freeze-proof RV plumbing, though we did see a small private sailboat amongst Antarctic icebergs.

• How to Ship

Shipping information is easily available on the Internet. Google *shipping companies [continents of embarkation and destination]* to corner shipping possibilities in .1 seconds. For example, to ship an RV from North America to Europe enter *shipping companies North-America Europe.* URLs and shipping prices will appear instantly. Shipping between far-apart continents requires a standard container. In 2004 its rental and transportation cost about $3000 between continents separated by a major ocean. It's inexpensive to ship on a local ferry between Europe and Asia, and free to drive the bridge across the Bosporus from Istanbul to Kadiköy, and equally simple to ship from Spain to Morocco. The expensive shipping is across the Atlantic, Pacific or Indian Oceans, or from North to South America. Beware, however, of at least two pitfalls when shipping over long distances.

• Shipping Pitfalls

The first problem is having everything stolen off of and from inside a vehicle, even when *safely* locked inside a container. The usual advice is to personally drive the RV into the container and lock it yourself; then stand and wait up to 48 hours or much longer, watching the container until it's loaded onto the ship. However, based on stories we've heard this may accomplish nothing, the vehicle will likely still arrive completely stripped. Dock workers and merchant-marine mariners are among the most accomplished thieves in the world.

The cost of shipping will include insurance, but good luck on collecting from the shipping company or the insurance company without days and weeks of extended bureaucracy, red tape and constant headache. *Once the RV arrives* it may take a week or more to refurbish stolen items, such as side-view mirrors, and replace anything inadvertently left inside. This means don't ship dishes, utensils, pots, pans or anything else inside the RV, though the average person might consider them untempting to thieves. Buy these things upon arrival. They're easily available anywhere in the world. RVers we've known have flown to the RV's destination point and experienced the extreme frustration of shipping problem number two, just when they would have rather been RVing a new and exotic continent.

- ## Shipping Delays and Worse

Shipping problem number two is waiting for the RV to arrive, which means shipping delays. Seemingly all ships are delayed, often by weeks and sometimes months. We met a couple from Canada on a cruise up the Amazon and they told a sad tale: They'd gone to South America with an RV tour and caravanning group out of McAllen, Texas. The groups' RVs were shipped from Texas to Iquenque, a duty free port on Chile's northern coast. But the ship didn't arrive and didn't arrive for a full month, by which time everyone was *so* bored sitting in Iquenque. Having visited Iquenque on three separate occasions I know a day and a half in Iquenque is the outer limit, after which anyone would be bored stupid. When the ship finally arrived in Iquenque one couple was so frazzled by the waiting that they jumped in the RV and left on their own, forfeiting hefty tour payments, last seen heading south down Chile's 2500 mile-long coastline. The McAllen, Texas RV-master had explained that the company was not responsible for shipping delays; no money would be refunded, though the tour would lose an entire month's itinerary and tough toenails.

An unanticipated delay-related problem happened to our German friends, Andreas and Barbara, who loaded a Dodge campervan into a container in Panama and confidently flew to Caracas with certain knowledge: their container ship was leaving Panama the next day and would arrive in Venezuela a few days later. They were perfectly correct. The ship did leave Panama the next day and, wonder of wonders, arrived in Caracas exactly on schedule. However, the shipping company had left their container, with the Dodge camper inside, sitting on the dock in Colon, Panama. Oops. When the ship arrived in Caracas without the container Andreas and Barbara came within an inch of giving up on international RVing. After flying back to Panama and driving the campervan from Panama to Seattle, friends convinced them to try shipping the campervan to South America, again. They finally did so successfully, from Miami to Buenos Aires. Otherwise they wouldn't have had a Dodge campervan to sell to us in South America. Thanks for hanging in there, Barb and Andreas.

Buying and Selling RVs Abroad

On the other hand we've always flown to a chosen continent, bought an RV there and driven as far as we could go in every direction. Then we sold it and moved onto the next continent. Naturally, there are pros and cons to either approach. Those actually RVing the entire world may have to juggle a combination of strategies.

For two reasons we've always bought an RV in the area of the world we wanted to see: 1) this avoids shipping nightmares and 2) replacement parts are easily available in the RVs geographical region of birth. Someone shipping an RV made in the USA, for example, to Australia, will have an enormous problem obtaining parts and repairs. American RV brands are basically unheard of in Australia and Australian customs duties on imported parts, as in most countries, are outrageous.

• Shipping Replacement Parts through Customs

Shipping parts into Australia, or anywhere in the world, except duty free ports such as Singapore, Iqueque and Dubai, will embroil the shipper in a customs' nightmare with which no one wants to become familiar. When we were in Australia in 2000 we found onerous across-the-board duties on most things foreign. Governments seem to specialize in protecting local industry, even when they don't have the particular industry they're protecting. For this reason motor vehicles and many other items are horrendously expensive in Australia, which has customs duties up to 100%. Imagine shipping an RV part that costs $500, paying hundreds of dollars for express shipping and then paying $500 to Australian, or whatever customs, while waiting a month for the part to be shipped, work its way through customs and finally be installed, all while you sit in some place like Iqueque. As a Japanese friend of mine would say, *Yuck*.

On the other hand, the extended chassis Dodge campervan we bought from Barb and Andreas, driving around South America for two years, was fairly easy to find parts for and repair. When looking for a camper in South America we had two main concerns. We first thought we needed a four-wheel-drive to negotiate South American roads but were quickly disabused of that notion by Internet research and Andreas. The second concern was finding a reliable camper with out-of-South-America license plates, precisely what Andreas offered.

Fortunately we seldom had to search for Dodge parts or fix the van in South America. We rapidly learned to remedy two reoccurring problems, the alternator and front end, or find someone to fix them. I practically became a journeyman mechanic in South America, for example learning to adjust the carburetor for major altitude changes. Only a diesel engine will purr from sea level to 15,000 feet in a few hours, such as from Arica, Chile, into Bolivia. The Dodge camper's carburetor required constant adjustment according to altitude, a real accomplishment for a mechanical klutz extraordinaire such as me. The parallel problem of acclimatizing one's body to a 15,000 foot altitude change, in a few hours, is completely impossible.

We considered shipping the camping bus we'd bought in Australia to New Zealand but found the red tape would have been formidable. However, by the time we'd driven all over Australia and Tasmania for thirteen months we were tired of our pre-used Toyota Coaster, though it'd been slickly converted to a camper. Thus we never had to worry about the intricacies of New Zealand customs or Australian shipping. However, if we'd headed a few miles north of Australia, to Indonesia or Malaysia, we would have had to ship an RV or camper because there are few available in most of Asia.

Only the Japanese are familiar with RVs or campers, tooling around in the cutest, narrowest little RVs we've seen, specially made narrow by U.S. manufacturers. However, used vehicles are almost unavailable in Japan. The Japanese buy vehicles new and keep them almost forever, decimating the potential domestic market for used vehicles. Most used Japanese vehicles are shipped to countries where people will actually buy products touched by other people's grimy hands. My Japanese friend would describe pre-owned vehicles as, *Yuck*.

• Better RVs are Diesel

The average gasoline-guzzling American RV is better left in North America because foreign-made RVs, easily purchased abroad, are primarily diesel. Diesel engines last far longer and use much less fuel than the gasoline engines found in most large American RVs, which may burn a gallon every five miles. European and other foreign-made RVs extract two or three times the mileage, or kilometrage. Plus huge American RVs would easily fit on few European, Asian, South American or African roads.

The best RV we've owned was a Class C Ford diesel, 25 feet (almost 8 meters), made in New Zealand. It slept six, making it extremely comfortable and spacious for two. It sparkled with 270 degree windows around the rear where we slept in a king sized pedestal bed, the better to see Mt. Cook and Milford Sound through the wrap-around picture window. If the steering wheel had been on the other side we would've shipped it back to the States and all over the world.

The New Zealand RV was a success story from start to finish. Before arriving in New Zealand from Australia we'd searched RV-rental companies and used-RV dealers on the Internet, to no avail. However, these searches told us where to start looking when we landed in Auckland. Within an hour of sallying forth we found a large used-RV dealer in a north Auckland suburb. Mary instantly spotted the final choice, falling in love with it on the spot. Who doesn't like big picture windows?

While test driving the New Zealand RV we met a local named Jim. He wanted to trade in his RV and buy Mary's favorite. We beat him to the punch, but only barely because Jim hadn't yet sold his old RV. When we'd finished seeing almost every square meter of New Zealand we advertised the RV for sale in the New Zealand Camping-Car Club's Newsletter. On the day after the ad appeared we received a frantic phone call from Jim: *Don't sell that RV to anyone else. I'll buy it as soon as you get back to Auckland*. And he did. The difference between the purchase and sales price was less than $1000, excluding fuel, very inexpensive insurance and one small repair, to RV all of New Zealand for six months.

• Renting RVs Internationally

Those with beaucoup bucks can rent an RV in dozens of countries. However, right out the chute RV rentals may cost $200 a day and up. Then add the cost of fuel and campgrounds, which may mean costs will reach $300 a day. Of course, there'll be no maintenance or repair expenses, which is the big risk avoided by renting. Plus rentals provide a wide choice of luxury amenities, from satellite TV and GPS navigation, to microwaves and generators for a soothing background to snooze by. Of course these can easily be installed on an owned RV anywhere in the world.

Checking out foreign RV rentals on the Internet requires familiarity with the various names by which they're known outside the US: motor home, campervan, motor caravan, camper, camping car in most of Europe, Wohnmobile in Germany, autokaravanu, auto sleeper, campingvogn and more. Keep this list handy when firing up a search engine to find an RV rental in the countries of choice. At least one Internet site lists 30 countries alphabetically, continents and parts of countries, where RVs can easily be rented, for a price: Alaska, Andorra, Argentina, Australia, Canada, Chile, Corsica, Cuba (we saw none there), England, Estonia, Finland, France, Germany, Great Britain,

Hawaii, Holland, Ireland, Italy, Namibia, New Zealand, Portugal, Russia, Scotland, Spain, Sweden, South America, South Africa, Thailand, UK and the USA.

Thus the choices are simple: buy, ship or rent. I can hear Mary saying, *Gee, maybe I should write that down.*

CHAPTER ELEVEN
What It Costs to Travel Forever

*I'd like to live like a poor man--only
with lots of money. - Pablo Picasso*

It's crucially important to understand that fulltime world travel can be mind-bogglingly inexpensive, cheap even. We're frequently asked, *how cheap?* At dinner with friends we suspect of less than sincerely soliciting an opinion, he asked, *Dave, do you think we'll be able to go wherever we want on what we have available?* My eyes popped because he must have been having me on. His wife had just retired with a pension of $10,000 a month and $500,000 in back-up savings. He'd sold a business it took thirty years to establish, likely for a cool million dollars. We really think they'll be able to scrape by. And though it might be nice to have that kind of cushion anyone can enjoy RVing the world forever, on much less, in fact practically for peanuts.

What You Need to RV the World Forever

The minimum *monthly* costs needed for full-time travel are simply derived. The only equipment, gear and possessions needed, besides a passport, are a slew of guidebooks and maps, food, shelter, transportation and minimal clothes: donate dress clothes to charity and sell the jewelry. Add these few items up to see how incredibly cheap it *can be* for two people to RV the world, month by month.

- **Passport**   **$2**
- **Food and Treats**   **$400**

- **Eating out**   **$100**
- **Health care**   **$120**
- **Accommodation: RV Expenses & Amortization**   **$400**
- **International Airfare**   **$200**
- **Clothing**   **$50**
- **Guidebooks and Maps**   **$20**

                                                $1292

A passport costs a hundred dollars every ten years, rounded up to a dollar a month per person because a new passport is needed every nine years: entry to all countries requires a passport valid at least six months.

Food, for those fixing nutritious feasts instead of eating in restaurants, will average $300 a month for two people. Add another $100 for treats, including alcoholic beverages, totaling $400 a month. Throw in another hundred dollars for eating out, sampling the local cuisine, an amount that should be matched dollar for dollar by contributions to a health-care kitty.

Health care for the healthy, including dental costs, will average ten dollars a month for those seldom eating out and exercising at least an hour a day. These are bare minimums: health care will cost more for many. However, we spent far less for dental and medical care during the last decade and a half, averaging $200 a year per person, $35 a month for two. Walking around gawking will satisfy the exercise category, year in and year out.

Accommodation costs are the amortization of the RV's purchase or shipping costs. Those relegated to hotels and local transportation may experience a less enjoyable and relaxing experience but can *get by* spending the same minimal amount. Amortizing the RV will cost about $400 a month including fuel, maintenance and depreciation; hotels and local transportation outside developed countries can cost about the same for two people. This excludes airfares to exotic destinations, which will add another hundred dollars a month per person, for those who avoid flitting too rapidly from continent to continent.

The total to this point is $1292 a month, which means foreign travel can be dirt cheap. Those preferring campgrounds to *free camping*, or who prefer fancier hotels, must add another $300 to $600 a month, still keeping the budget below $2000 a month.

Unfortunately these calculations ignore taxes back home, which for many people will eat up at least $200 a month, boosting a minimal budget to $2000 a month. Thus most can get by on $24,000 a year, $2000 a month, for two people. We've lived on far less in developed countries, but there's always the inflation calculation.

Prices in Europe, when we revisited in 2006, had spiraled out of control, partially because the dollar had lost a third of its value in ten years; Scandinavia and Japan have always been pricier. What it costs to RV the world depends on where you go and what you want to do when you get there, detailed in the next few chapters.

Property Back *Home*

Fancy cars and sprawling haciendas are unnecessary for those RVing the world. Houses and cars are exactly what fulltime world travelers don't need, unless someone has a security fetish or wishes to travel less than fulltime, perhaps six months a year like several couples we know.

- ## The Downside of Property at *Home*

Property requiring maintenance and up-keep at *home*, or tenants and renters necessitating supervision and coddling, are potential headaches. How would any traveler abroad react upon hearing the pipes had burst and flooded the house back home? Management companies can handle renting a house and keep up maintenance but that's often a losing and continually worrisome proposition. Trusted *compadres* or relatives back home may not mind taking care of property, renters, maintenance and taxes, allowing some fulltime travelers to avoid ending up homeless like us. But the easiest way to travel fulltime, enjoying a minimalist existence, is to opt for *homelessness*.

- ## A Minimalist Existence can be Fun

A minimalist existence is no burden for those who've retired early to travel; that's how they got there, being frugal and saving every penny. We're so used to pinching pennies it's difficult to stop. Based on years of *mentalis frugalis* we're unable to spend an extra ten dollars for a shirt because that'd double the price. Whoa, twenty dollars for a shirt. But those who've planned properly will be able to spend much more without the slightest threat to the budget because they'll have a ton of money saved. Those who can't handle a minimalist existence should either make sure of a nearly unlimited budget or stop reading now. Otherwise they could become hooked on RVing full-time, internationally, for very little money.

Cost Depends on Destination

How much money is needed to travel indefinitely depends primarily on destinations. The healthy low-maintenance homo sapien couple can easily get by on a clear $2000 a month almost anywhere, excluding urban Japan, northern Europe and the big cities of first-world countries, details in Chapter Twelve. There they'll have to scrimp on $2000, while $3000 a month is a no-brainer. Prices in Europe, after introduction of the euro, have drastically increased, especially against a sagging U.S. dollar. The higher prices in northern Europe have been bolstered by inflation, while those in the south have increased because the single currency allowed Europe-wide price comparisons and pressured prices into parity. Europe as a whole has ended up with relatively uniform prices, way higher.

Excluding Japan and an ever more expensive Europe leaves most of the world where living like a king or queen is easy on $2000 a month, an amount sufficient to avoid major sacrifice. Traveling the ninety percent of the world outside really expensive places lets anyone live well on a relative pittance, compared to what it'd cost to live back home.

As Time Goes By: Plan to Spend More

We've recently upped our monthly budget to $3000, but usually spend $2000 a month or less because we've most recently been traveling in developing countries. These countries are inexpensive for almost everything from restaurants and food to transportation and hotels.

In a few years our budget will increase to $4000 a month, then to $5000. The method in the madness is simple. We felt it better to spend less money when we were younger, when it was easier to *rough it*, or at least less traumatic, when we didn't care as much about pure unadulterated comfort. This is slowly changing, which means we're regrettably maturing. When we hang up our spurs in ten years or so we'll have budgeted $5000 a month.

• Needs versus Wants

No one *needs* $5000 a month to travel less expensive destinations, which include vast swathes of exotic Asia, Africa and the Americas. An occasional hiking companion in the Himalayas got by on ten dollars a day, or $300 a month. It drove us crazy traveling with him because scrimping that much on zero-star inns and negative-star hotels, trying to spend five dollars a day or less on accommodation, wasn't fun. He spent most nights in backpacking dorms while we opted for private rooms with attached bath. But he was living proof that anyone can get by, traveling internationally, for very little moola indeed.

CHAPTER TWELVE
Great International Travel, With or Without an RV

I haven't been everywhere, but it's on my list. Susan Sontag

After accumulating a bucket of cash, perhaps selling the family homestead from underneath the kids and giving the boss the old heave ho, the world becomes an oyster, but which part? There are places to go first, such as where the folks came from, no matter how many generations back, Europe, Africa or Asia. As Isaiah Berlin said:

Only barbarians are not curious about where they come from, how they came to be where they are, where they appear to be going, whether they wish to go there, and if so, why, and if not, why not.

But for those who've already been there and done that, or aren't interested in genealogy and antecedents, then what?

A Place to Go…First

Peculiar travel suggestions are dancing lessons from God.
Kurt Vonnegut, *Cat's Cradle*

Why go to all the effort of scrimping, saving, amassing and banking a bag of dough in order to get out of town, without knowing where to go? For those who have no big-time druthers we've found interesting devices for making where-to-go decisions.

- **Cat in a Hat**

A happily married couple wrote every place they'd especially like to go on slips of paper, threw them in a hat, stirred them about and pulled out two, selecting a first combination trip. The two places were on opposite sides of the globe. However, recent shopping around located around-the-world fares allowing a year to complete a trip with four or fewer stops, slightly over $1500 a person. Enter *around-the-world airline tickets* on any search engine, and dream.

- **Spin the Globe**

We've played *spin the globe*, poking a finger arbitrarily to pick a general area to jaunt. This often points near the equator, which isn't a particularly appealing part of the world. One equatorial exception is Ecuador. The capital, Quito, sits at 8000 feet, practically on the equator. The mountainous center of Ecuador preens in year-round spring, a conic string of perfect volcanoes covered with eternal snow. Skip the rainy season from November to March and spend little time in Quito because most of elsewhere in Ecuador is less crowded and more interesting.

Anywhere near the equator is best spent at altitude where the weather is palatable and the humidity wanes to a comfortable level. Fortunately, the Ecuadorian string of volcanoes and mountains stretches from Mexico south to Chile and the tip of South America, forming the magnificent Andes, a fabulous mountain playground.

How about the Caribbean?

If you come to a fork in the road, take it. Yogi Berra

OK, it's difficult to RV the Caribbean but there are many little bitty places immune to RVs, mostly islands in the Caribbean and South Pacific, plus big ole China and small Bhutan and Myanmar. But to see it all the Caribbean is one place to go, which Mary is busy writing down. My adventures in the Caribbean chanced upon another way of deciding where to go next.

Sailing the Caribbean decades ago I jumped ship with friends, escaping a cranky captain who compensated for an inability to sail with the manners of a Captain Bligh. Our small sailboat had been hit by a killer storm in the Bermuda triangle, the mainsail had shredded and four of us were hopelessly lost somewhere off the coast of Florida. No one knew, with the roiling cloud cover, the way to the Bahamas. Any island in a storm, years before GPS.

• Avoid the Bermuda Triangle

Everyone on board was sicker than a hospital, lolling around with a chartreuse sheen, up-chucked out, bruised from being thrown against bulkheads, tired of sailing and tired of life, with one exception—me. I never get seasick, no matter the weather, with the single aberration of once when hung over, which I fortunately wasn't that day. As the only one not seasick I took the wheel, hanging on for dear life, thrown to and fro for eons, ravenous from lack of food and beat from no sleep, unsure of a future. After hours at the wheel I finally yelled for the dear captain to take the wheel so I could stagger below and grab a handful of anything edible.

The captain's grass-colored face bobbed up from the cockpit where he'd collapsed in a heap. He vaguely nodded his head, weakly taking the wheel with shaky hand. I swung down the steps into the galley, tore off a hunk of the bread swinging wildly in the hammock below and galloped back to retake the wheel. The captain turned a bleary, accusatory eye, and said, *You don't tear the bread. You cut the bread.*

• Going Stand-by

Cutting the captain's throat was not an option, but cutting bread instead of tearing it was the last straw in a long series of ruptured camels. Upon the serendipity of finally stumbling onto Bimini we jumped ship and left the captain with a tattered mainsail and good riddance. The three mutineers took a puddle-jumper to Miami and went standby on the next four flights out, having agreed to go wherever all three could get seats first: Cancun, Jamaica, St. Croix or St. Maarten. An hour later we were in St. Croix for an idyllic week of recuperation from the mad captain of the Bermuda triangle. We popped over to St. Maarten for a few days and a glorious time was had by all.

Surprise Thyself

I am going away with him to an unknown country where I shall have no past and no name, and where I shall be born again with a new face and an untried heart. Colette

Going last minute, by the seat of the pants, when all destinations require the same wardrobe, can be fun, especially when off for a few weeks instead of months or years. Of course this can't be done RVing the world, which takes advance planning. However, with the incredible last-minute fares available on the Internet, occasionally playing the surprise game is a feasible alternative to over-planned travel and a nice vacation from fulltime RVing.

Those who'd rather avoid suspense and surprises can sign up for last minute specials from designated cities, or to preferred destinations, worldwide. See for example, http://www.smartertravel.com and http://www.airfarewatchdog.com. The *Smartertravel* newsletter lists weekly airline specials for whatever departure or destination cities you select, the same as the airfarewatchdog website. For the URLs of the incredibly inexpensive cut-rate airlines springing up all over the world, see www.thebigproject.co.uk/budget and http://www.whichbudget.com, the latter listing cut rate airlines from and to every country on the planet. When in Asia check out http://www.airasia.com, headquartered in Kuala Lumpur, featuring some of the lowest fares on the planet, including to London and Australia.

Many last-minute fares are a fraction of advance purchase fares, often in double or low triple digits.

- ## Experimental Travel

A vivid series of forty blueprints for strange, weird and by-the-seat-of-your-pants travel was contained in **The Lonely Planet Guide to EXPERIMENTAL TRAVEL** (2005). See www.lonelyplanet.com/experimentaltravel. Suggestions ranged from: Chance Travel, finding or inserting the name of your hometown alphabetically in an atlas, throwing the dice and moving that number of cities above or below, identifying the next destination; to Confluence Seeking, which requires visiting the intersection of a whole number of degrees of latitude, such as 32 degrees North, with a whole number of degrees longitude, such as 120 degrees West, which is approximately San Diego. Document and photograph the confluence point and submit the results to www.confluence.org. The record for the most confluence points visited in 2005 was held by Captain Peter, a sailor from Sicily. Things discovered by these off-the-wall approaches to travel may be serendipitous, which Julius H. Comroe defined in 1911 as *looking for a needle in a haystack and finding the farmer's daughter*.

What Plans?

Never hesitate to change plans mid-stream, whenever necessary or when an alternative seems more interesting, such as jumping off a sailboat onto worldwide land yachts, or vice versa. We've never had a master plan, except an extremely simplistic scheme to see it all. We know no one can see it all but that doesn't stop us from incessantly puttering about. Unfortunately, there will always be countries barring foreigners and iffy countries suffering intermittent artillery fire.

No One Wants to Go THERE!

When we started fulltime travel we had no interest in Southeast Asia, except to someday see Angkor Wat. Because Southeast Asia is next door to China, where we were going anyway, we finally went. The experience was an eye-opener with Thailand's fabulous temples and friendly people, and so much more in neighboring countries, though we'd never been big fans of dripping hot places averaging one hundred percent humidity, such as Florida and India. Maybe we'll try Florida sometime. We've learned: there are no uninteresting countries, with the possible exception of horrible Haiti.

Our Favorites? Everywhere!

A year to go around the world! A whole twelve months of scenes and curious happenings in far-off foreign lands! You have thought of doing this, almost promised yourself that when you got old enough, and rich enough, and could "spare the time," you too would go around the world. Most of us get old enough; some of us get rich enough; but the time! the time! - to spare the time, to cut loose from goods and lands, from stocks and dreary desks, quit clients, patients, readers, home and friends - ay, and our enemies whom we so dearly love! Full many a promise must be broken and few the voyagers round the world. D.N. Richardson, *A Girdle Round the Earth,* 1888 ***Money***

The answer to *where to go* is *everywhere*. As Simon Raven said, . . .*life is short and the world is wide*. For ultra-friendly people go see Turkey and Ireland, Thailand and Burma, Australia and New Zealand, Ethiopia and most anywhere outside the first world.

Friendly Turkey Visited and Revisited

On an expedition to Istanbul after sailing the Greek Islands in 1984 we accompanied a fellow captain into the basement of the Hilton where he'd intended to gamble. He was barred because he'd forgotten a dinner jacket. The ballroom next door was jammed with a raucous party. We peeked inside and the occupants of the closest table cordially invited us to enter, bodyguards for the mayor of Istanbul; his bodyguards insisted on free drinks for all. The mayor's son was celebrating his circumcision, something I'd have never thought of celebrating. What a party, though with copious free drinks the details remain fuzzy.

- ## Amazing Cappadocia, Finally

Cappadocia waited patiently in central Turkey until we could return to actually explore sans blizzard in 2006, underground churches with colorful ancient murals, cave houses carved into ten-story high cliffs and curious volcanic tufa sculpted by rain and wind into chaotic shapes, mostly tall, round and pointy. The epitome of the visualization was realized in the Love Valley, a photo worth a thousand uncensored words.

The Goreme Open Air Museum was one of the world's great bargains for $6, buying hours of ducking into ten churches carved from solid rock around the time of the crusades, 800 years ago. The churches and a multi-story nun's convent were covered with murals from pale to vivid blue and burnt sienna, others starkly white and red, plus fancy columns, arches and embellishments, and apostles and saints with big golden haloes looking like Green Bay cheese-heads. Goreme was the heart of Cappadocia, hosting daily morning flights of a dozen hot air balloons in a rainbow of colors that fired bursts of gas and roared like Puff the Magic Dragon.

The balloons hovered above what looked like a field of giant Ku Klux Klanners potholed by 3D caves guarded by classical Romanesque columns. Touts offered camel rides on beasts that smelled like Puff the unwashed dragon. We skipped the perpetually sour-breathed brutes, permanently unflossed and grubby.

The valleys of Zelve and Pasabag provided striking hiking, the latter hosting the world's sexiest police station inside a macho pointy hill. The valleys surrounding Goreme were packed with shapes seldom found in geologic nature strewn along eight valleys tinted rose, red, marshmallow pink, honey and yellow, culminating in the Love Valley, packed with giant sex symbols outstanding in their field. I heard one lady exclaim, *They look just like little huts on stilts*. Not exactly.

Aimless wanderers couldn't get lost. Notorious landmarks were always visible to port and starboard, from Uchisar's soaring cave cliffs to the pink wadis of the Rose Valley. At sunset all protuberances glowed golden, making stunning photos, particularly in the valley of the fairy chimneys where pointy hills were topped with saucy black hats like French raconteurs amongst hundred foot stones gracefully swirled with dairy queen heads.

In towns surrounding Goreme, from Uchisar to Cavusin, Urgup and Ortahisar, cave cities were built into hills like Swiss cheese stacked hundreds of feet high, forerunners of the big city condo, bargain leases available. The original intent was defensive, for protection against ruffians on major trade routes. The locals built a hundred underground cities with copious space for ancient living requirements from household horses, cooks and the dead to granaries and pit toilets, buying safety from siege for three thousand years.

Aboveground was jammed with excellent restaurants featuring soft local wines that tasted like a grape juice soufflé. At nearby Avanos whirling dervishes with white beards and tall black hats twirled every night in skirts to cow a fifties teeny bopper, jitter-bugging in a single direction for hours, like a kid's game of *twirl until your get dizzy and fall down*. But these guys amazingly didn't.

- ## The Crazy King of Mt. Nemrut

From Cappadocia we reconnoitered mystical Mt. Nemrut (2150 meters or 7000 feet high), littered on top with six-foot tall stone heads, the scene adorning the cover of Lonely Planet's recent Turkey guidebook. The heads on the east side of the mountain were arranged in front of the towering statues from which they had been lopped by earthquakes and the sands of time; those on the west sat forlornly alone. These monoliths were built by the grand-daddy of all delusions of grandeur, Antiochus I Ephinanes (64-38 B.C.E.), who saw himself as a god-king like Apollo (Persian Mithra or Greek Hermes), Zeus and Heracles. The statues were carved flanking his godly façade, commemorating a kingdom that lasted 26 years. The setting is spectacular, the trail up passing columns topped with an eagle and lion, an old Roman bridge, jagged castle ruins and a perfect stone relief showing Antiochus' daddy shaking hands with Heracles.

- ## The Digs of Abraham

Ten miles from the Syrian border sat one of the world's oldest continuously inhabited sites, at Harran. See Genesis 11:31-32, where it's spelled Haran, the home of Abraham some years back. *Modern* Harran was cheek by jowl with mud beehive houses, cool in the sweltering summers and warm in cold winters, sumptuous inside with lavish Turkish carpets, throw pillows and water pipes among a forest of colorful tassels where it was always teatime. Tiny school kids were dressed like movable rainbows, lending a hand to keep pairs of bathing tots shouting and squirming in red tubs, soapy heads incongruous amid building stones strewn about for 5000 years among the ruins of Turkey's oldest mosque and ancient arch. The Citadel was the grandest ruin, dating from the worship of Sin, god of the moon.

• To Mt. Ararat

On the way to humongous Lake Van, a fourth larger than Rhode Island, we found Kurds on both sides of the Iraqi border pleased with the new American regime. Lake Van's waters were seemingly painted in shades from gorgeous blue to aquamarine, though almost as dead as road kill. The water was bitter alkaline, washing clothes clean without soap; only carp could survive. Still, the setting was stunning, the lake surrounded by snow streaked mountains of reddish, green and purple ores, revealed in an ancient volcanic eruption that covered a former exit river with hundreds of feet of lava. Two miles off the south shore sat an island with an old Armenian Monastery. Akdamar Kilisesi had been built in 921 C.E., plastered with colorful frescoes of Old Testament fables. Castles from ancient dynasties pocked the countryside, including a sprawling complex above Van, a city of half a million nufus (Turkish for people). Van was occupied from the 13th to 7th centuries B.C.E. by the biblical kingdom of Ararat, aka Urartian.

Mt. Ararat dominated the skyline of Dogubayazit, 23 miles from the main crossing into Iran, a dramatic backdrop for the quite incredible Ishak Pasa Palace sitting high on a hill like Alhambra east. The Palace had been newly restored on an elevated plateau four miles southeast of town. Lonely Planet called it *the epitome of the 'Thousand and One Nights' castle.* The setting was backed by rippling cliffs in sienna and purple, fronted by 5137 meter (almost 17,000 feet) Mt. Ararat. For exotic history covering the eastern half of a country twice the size of California try an eastern Turkish delight in a sampler putting Whitman's to shame.

Thai School for Bossing Around Elephants

The Thais and Burmese are among the loveliest people around, most unfailingly polite and charming, bowing and smiling incorrigibly. Too bad the Myanmar government is a callous dictatorship and the Thai government rotten to the core; the people deserve better. The Thais, at least, have an idol they consider worthy, their King, worshipped by every Thai. Think Yul Brynner. For those with three extra days in Thailand and an interest in elephants, consider a course to become an elephant trainer like me.

Kids hungering to join the circus lurk inside random adults. Personally, I've always wanted to boss around elephants. When I stumbled onto the website for a mahout school an hour south of Chiang Mai, Thailand, I knew I'd found my ideal back-up profession: elephant trainer supreme.

• Thai Elephants Only Speak Thai

The Elephant Conservation Center's three-day course had enrolled half a dozen excited students: a young German couple, Dutch sisters, a miniature Japanese girl and me. Supat, the course manager and now a long-time friend on Facebook, escorted the students to home-stay quarters and handed out schedules listing 14 basic elephant commands, all unpronounceable. First scholastic hurdle: Thai elephants only speak Thai.

Donning baggy pants and spiffy shirts in bright blue denim we became instant mahouts-in-training, introduced to *our* individual elephants. I solemnly shook Piajaub's trunk and she shook me down for bananas. Piajaub was a good-natured patriarch 72-years feisty, a 5-ton behemoth of a blimp with a nose for trouble. Her occasional sudden gallops and frisking of fellow elephants were attributed to out-of-kilter hormones.

• We All Lived on Gray Submarines

Uta, a German woman, and one of the nearly identical Dutch sisters, drew elephants that relegated them to gray submarines. Elephants love bathing and these two additionally loved sinking, leaving the ladies soaked to the tops of their frazzled blonde heads. Still, Uta loved every minute, wearing the world's widest grin for three straight days. The Japanese girl was assigned a near-baby elephant that made them an exquisitely matched set. And we were off to the races.

The first assignment was to command *song soong* and climb up the big-gray skyscraper from the side, onto the horny hairy head. When *song soong* was pronounced correctly Piajaub would lift a huge front leg as a step stool. I'd leap and she'd lift, half tossing me onto her back. The execution of *song soong* presumed the immaculate coordination I'd never had, affording bountiful opportunity for repetition. We practiced and repeated 14 commands, sometimes to effect.

On the first trek into the jungle we quickly learned the most used command is *bai*, which means *GO*. The jungle to an elephant is like a chocolate factory to Willie Wonka; every jungle bit is luscious, edible and available. An elephant the size of Piajaub devoured 200 kilos (440 lbs.) of fodder a day, an enormity of leaves, bananas and sugar cane. The result from the Conservation Center's fifty-elephants were reams of elephant dung paper.

• Making Paper

The students were assigned the joy of making paper. Fortunately, the near-National Basketball Association-sized dung had been pre-bleached and washed. Up to our elbows we re-molded it into 400 gram (one pound) balls, remixing the pure fiber with water and jell, swishing it onto screens for drying into elegant papers tie-dyed into in a millennium of pastel hues.

The only downer was visiting the elephant hospital. About half the bulky gray patients had stepped on land mines littering the Thai/Myanmar border. Land mine wounds eventually healed but a bowel-constricted elephant was often on the short list for the big tusk depository in the sky.

Elephants played so well together and with mahouts-in-training that they became big gray dust-bunnies. The last duty at night, after trekking into the jungle, and first in the morning when retrieving our charges, was to bathe the elephants. For the elephants bathing was playtime. For mahouts-in-training it was dodging exuberant trunk showers and playing submarine, while attempting to avoid bobbing paper-wannabees.

The evening jungle trek ended with chaining the elephant to a tree surrounded by an evening's bliss of munchables and dirt for rolling in. On the trek in we'd bob high through verdant green snarls of jungle, chains rattling as the elephants galumphed majestically through the foliage. Sitting on chain loops branded student's butts like Cheerios across a bowl of milk.

• The Morning Fetch for Showtime

In the mornings we'd tote 10-foot long joints of sugarcane into the jungle to begin the jolly giants' day in a good mood. First, we'd unhook the chain and bark, *Non long*. When the elephants played dead, sugarcane clamped in their jaws, we'd whomp them with bundles of branches to dust off the night's accumulation of dirt. Then we'd mount up and galumph off for the splish-splash of their happy morning bath.

Every day was show time for tourists flocking to the Elephant Conservation Center. I sat with Supat as he busily clicked a digital camera at what must have been the thousandth time he'd watched the show. Utterly curious I asked why he was still so enamored of elephants. He lowered the camera a split second and said, *Because they're so dang smart.*

Supat was right on, illustrated twice daily at show time. Four elephants had formed their own jazz band, working on improvisations with marimba, gong, drums, cymbals and percussion, tutored two week a year by a jazz aficionado from New York City. Budding Picassos penned bouquets of daffodils and abstracts paintings. One precocious big-gray chap produced a meticulous self portrait, mahout perched on top. The elephants were unaided in their art; the mahout's only role was to dab paint on the brush.

The daily shows began with a baby elephant raising the blue elephant flag. The elephants gently placed a hat on the mahout's head, kicked around logs, balanced atop logs and stacked logs, played a jazz concert, painted and generally cavorted like kids in a chocolate factory. The mahouts-in-training put the elephants through routines: grab a floppy ear and jump up the side, sliding off trunks, backing up elephants and dropping spikes for retrieval. On the third day those who didn't flub received diplomas, graduating to full-fledged mahouts.

Several nameless mahouts-in-training never properly learned the impossible-to-pronounce Thai commands. Though Supat patiently took us through the unfamiliar words, after days of frustrating drill the students turned inventive. We memorized the show-time routine that was always followed faithfully and perfectly by the elephants, a mental crib-sheet for graduation. As we stood in the spotlight before the cheering crowd and accepted diplomas we realized that we, along with Uta, had been smiling for three straight days. Far more than qualifying in a back-up profession we'd become the world's newest and happiest mahouts.

A World of Friendly People

Other friendly people include the Aussies and the Kiwis, whose language we almost speak. But don't be deceived by a short list of friendly people. The vast majority of people in all countries are friendly or, at least, non-threatening.

As Charles Darwin said:

> *[The traveler] may feel assured, he will meet with no difficulties or dangers, excepting in rare cases, nearly so bad as he beforehand anticipates. In a moral point of view, the effect ought to be, to teach him good-humored patience, freedom from selfishness, the habit of acting for himself, and of making the best of every occurrence. . . Traveling ought also to teach him a distrust; but at the same time he will discover, how many truly kind-hearted people there are, with whom he never before had, or ever again will have any further communication, who yet are ready to offer him the most disinterested assistance.*

The majority of strangers are able to distinguish between the individual traveler and the policies of his or her homeland government; hopefully we can all reciprocate.

First-worlders are often too busy to exercise friendliness, appearing more frigid, though they usually aren't. Broadly over-generalizing forty percent of people, no matter the country, are friendly; thirty percent are neutral, often too busy to put in the effort to be friendly; twenty percent may be unpleasant and in too much of a hurry; nine percent are potential crooks and one percent can be larcenous, thieves or worse, often including the military, customs and other petty bureaucrats on the take. We can safely go most anywhere the fancy strikes as long as the country isn't actively at war or threatened by revolution. Only ten to fifteen countries fall within these outlaw categories at any one time, leaving at least 175 countries for RVing forever.

Several countries are difficult to visit, such as Saudi Arabia, North Korea and Bhutan, though they allow tours, keeping pesky tourists on a leash. Bhutan makes a mint, charging $200 each day of a visit, all inclusive from room and board to excursions. The only way to enter Bhutan for free is to sign up to teach English, which a family we met in Vietnam had done for six months

We couldn't enter Syria or Lebanon in 1997. We can now and plan to visit both soon. Small portions of Iraq and Afghanistan are currently unsafe. Though the governments of many Middle East countries may be an aggregate of halfwit religious yokels, often paralleling fundamentalist cousins in the West, the residents of Iran are super friendly. However, we occasionally misrepresent our homeland as Canada.

Sudan is perpetually at war between its Muslim north and Christian/animist south, though a *final* peace deal was reached in 2005; we spent a month there at the end of 2006. Sudan takes months to issue a visa to Americans, perpetually retaliating for President Clinton's strike on a Khartoum munitions or pharmaceutical company, opinions varying on which it was, when attempting to take out Osama in 1999. The Sudanese government can't be trusted for any purpose whatsoever but a visa can easily be arranged through a Khartoum travel agency, usually via email. Algeria and Somalia continue iffy because of ongoing fundamentalist Muslim revolutions yet we've met people who visit Somalia on a regular basis, but they know the country, having worked there as engineers.

For those who don't mind tours Libya is easily traversable. Some governments can be put in the column of *unfriendly*, such as North Korea, though we visited on an unstructured tour, with 600 other people for three days in 2005, mostly South Koreans.

Local friendliness may not be a priority. Too much friendliness can be an invasion of privacy no matter how sincerely intended. In many countries, such as the tourist areas of China, Vietnam, Cuba and Mexico, friendliness is often a preamble to a sales pitch. Beware of sudden best friends materializing from vacant space.

Ruins and a City or Two

Instead of friendliness we're drawn by antiquities. In person and up close antiquities are our personal cups of java, probably because they're uniformly photogenic. Check out Angkor Wat, which is only one of 275 temples and temple complexes in the north of Cambodia. Or Machu Picchu before it's destroyed by an earthquake. We spent four days hiking to Machu Picchu in 2003, during the first year in South America, re-hiking the Inca Trail in 2008. Bagan in Myanmar/Burma sits on the mighty Irrawaddy River, hundreds of temples ranging from small, perfectly sculpted sandstone monuments to sprawling 200-foot-high temples gilded with gold.

We don't normally like cities but our favorites put Prague, with its World Heritage center, at the top of the list. We also like rococo Vienna, exotic Istanbul, Stockholm's islands, Lijiang and Dali in Western China; Bruges and Ghent, Belgium, Amsterdam, Cape Town in South Africa, Wellington and Dunedin, New Zealand. Everyone will find cities they like even better because they've discovered them on their own. There's no accounting for tastes in cities, beer or much of anything else.

CHAPTER ENDNOTE:

Cappadocia: Turkish Airlines offers reasonable flights from most anywhere in Europe for about $300 to Kayseri, a few miles from Cappadocia. Car rentals in 2006 cost $35 a day if you shopped around, but fuel ranged from $7 a gallon (about $2 a liter) and up. We stayed at the *Local Cavehouse Hotel* in Goreme, double ensuite rooms with a view and swimming pool for $42 a night, hotels available in all price ranges up to $90. The Bakay Hotel in Sanliurfa cost the same and included wifi in the lobby. The Golden Hills Hotel in Dogubayazit rated four stars for $48 a night with great views of Mt. Ararat and the Ishak Pasa Palace. All Turkish hotels included breakfasts of cheese, olives, cucumber, tomatoes, jam, honey, butter, bread and tea. Cappadocia balloon trips with champagne landings cost between $140 and $200 depending on duration. E-Mail dir@balooningdir.com or check out www.balooningdir.com. Also see Goreme Balloons, Phone 90 384 341 5662, email info@goremeballoons.com, or log onto www.goremeballoons.com

The School for Mahouts: See www.changthai.com for course-days, often a month's wait. Supat has posted great photos and detailed descriptions of the various programs offered at the Elephant Conservation Center. The three day course, including excellent Thai home-cooking, was $100, all inclusive, up to $300 by 2009 with the strengthening Baht and sinking dollar. Supat, photography-nut extraordinaire, provides each graduate mahout with a DVD of 1200 photos. These candid shots immortalize their happy little group for a reasonable $25 in 2008. Sign up for a three day smile.

CHAPTER THIRTEEN
The Details of Costs

We know that money isn't everything, but we suspect...deep down...that it is ninety things out of a hundred, that it will buy nine of the remaining ten, and make even the absence of the remaining one tolerably comfortable. - Madson Perie

How much on average it costs to RV internationally depends on many factors but three things stand out: destinations, comfort requirements and preferred activities. Psychologically there are people who can travel only Hilton to Hilton via spa resorts, limousines and first class air. We've known some of these people, briefly.

Years ago when the dollar was weak against European currencies we were able to travel Europe with a budget of less than $1200 a month, far less than $2,000 a month. Naturally we didn't stay in fancy hotels or any hotels at all. But we didn't rough it. We enjoyed gourmet meals, hot water showers and everything needed for comfort. However, with creeping inflation these numbers must be continually revised up, and up and up.

Cosmopolitan Europe and Japan

Travel in developed countries, especially Japan and Northern Europe, requires a wad of cash. In 1996 diesel was $7 a gallon in Norway. By 2006 regular unleaded gasoline in Europe averaged eight dollars a gallon and was rising. For those RVing with other than a gas-guzzling American RV an average of fifty miles a day like us, fuel costs remain doable over the long haul.

The costs of European accommodation and restaurants have doubled in ten years. However, continuing competition among large European supermarket chains, such as Carrefour and Tesco, have kept grocery prices and most common household commodities at almost reasonable levels in Europe, a boon for RVers.

Exotic Asia

Countries outside Europe and Japan are relatively reasonable, formerly downright cheap but with the shrinking dollar, pricier. All of Asia, except Hong Kong, Shanghai, Beijing, Japan and Singapore, is relatively inexpensive except Korea, which is reasonable. Many tourists demonstrate how well you can live in Southeast Asia for $500 a month, and less. Palatable hotels cost between twenty and thirty dollars a night. We're not talking backpacker's hostels, but actual hotels with spacious private rooms, nice bathrooms with all the amenities, cable TV and a refrigerator, though even Asian prices are spiraling against the puny dollar. We stayed at a four-star hotel on the resort island of Penang, Malaysia for twenty-seven dollars in 2002, a special promotional rate often available at many three and four star hotels, especially via the Internet.

It's difficult to spend more than five dollars when eating out in Southeast Asia. Food is uniformly delicious in Thailand, passable everywhere else, though somewhat over-oiled in much of China. Seafood lovers will find favorites both sublime and inexpensive. Avocado dishes are superb in Myanmar and coffee is top notch in Vietnam. Southeast Asian countries colonized by the French came away with a modicum of culinary arts: Vietnam, Cambodia and Laos. Chinese hot pot in Szechwan Province and

Borneo is fabulous and inexpensive. You could cruise practically forever in Southeast Asia and China for very little money outside of Hong Kong, Shanghai, Beijing and Singapore, where prices are similar to the average large American city. With the run up to the 2008 Olympics Beijing and Shanghai became increasingly more expensive.

The Colossus of Africa

Africa is inexpensive except for Southern Africa and the former French colonies of West Africa. For some strange reason, South Africa, which has little to offer outside of Cape Town and a few over-priced game parks, is as expensive as parts of Europe. The popular tourist trek up the East African coast through Zimbabwe, Zambia, Malawi, Tanzania and Kenya is inexpensive, once out of South Africa. Plus the East African infrastructure is far better than anyone would dream. The main roads are excellent and decent hotels are reasonably priced. However, it's shocking to see every other storefront hawking coffins, the primary growth industry in AIDS-stricken Africa.

Morocco, Egypt and most of North Africa are economical for both accommodation and food. Africa, outside of Johannesburg and Nairobi, is not nearly as dangerous as parts of South America, particularly the ever-present danger of kidnapping and robbery in Rio and San Paulo, Brazil and the constant danger of theft in Peru and Bolivia.

Mexico, Canada, Australia and New Zealand

Mexico is inexpensive outside Mexico City and Cancun. There's more to see in Mexico than most gringos can possibly imagine, with ninety percent of Mexico relatively inexpensive and safe for those not competing with local drug cartels. All of Central America, excluding Belize, Panama and Costa Rica, are cheaper than Mexico. Belize, Panama and Costa Rica are in the upper ranges of inexpensive.

Canada has become more expensive everywhere, costing more to traverse than the U.S., and, as anyone knows who's been there, is exactly like not leaving the continental U.S., except for Quebec. The Canadian dollar gained parity with the U.S. dollar in 2007, and surpassed it in value, raising prices for Americans in Canada, at least temporarily.

Australia was reasonably priced and New Zealand slightly less expensive. This judgment in relativity depends on the parity of the U.S. dollar with the local currency, which varies in rough proportion to the ups and downs of U.S. interest rates, government debt and the stock market. It makes small difference that most world markets partially mirror each other, falling or rising similarly because of the interconnectedness of world economies. The continuing imbalance of payments is pushing U.S. creditors, such as China, to consider a massive switch into Euros, perhaps foreshadowing a further tumble for the dollar.

Super South America

Most of South America that isn't cheap, is reasonably priced. As usual, large cities are substantially more expensive for accommodation than rural areas. Argentina used to be the most expensive country in South America but since the crash of the Argentinean Peso in 2002 Argentina has become quite reasonable, though more dangerous with large numbers unemployed and thus at loose ends. Now the most expensive country in South America is French Guyana, but then, hardly anyone goes there because it's difficult to access, along with its neighbors, Surinam and Guyana.

Chile and Ecuador, after the latter adopted the dollar for its currency, are on the high end of reasonable. Ecuador is a must see for the Galapagos Islands, a week's tour of which on any of it's eighty-some live-aboard boats ranged in 2003 from \$330 to over \$2000, by 2009 likely doubled.

Chile is easy to travel with lots to see in the volcano/lake district south of Santiago, the incredible desert in the north and the fjords south of Puerto Montt, the last most easily accessible by ferry to Puerto Natales. The ferry terminus is adjacent to two of the world's most incredible national parks, Torres Del Paine in Chile and Perito Moreno Glaciares, which includes Mt. Fitzroy and Lago Argentino in Argentina, both inexpensive and unforgettable. When in Argentina visit the world's largest and most impressive waterfall, Iguaçu, on the border with Brazil near Paraguay. Once anyone sees Iguaçu the world's other waterfalls become instantly mundane, including Niagara in North America, a third the size of Iguaçu, and the relative dinker of Victoria on the border between Zimbabwe and Zambia in Africa, half the size of Iguaçu.

Though the dollar has plummeted since we spent months in Chile, a 2/3 liter of Heineken is probably still less than \$1 and the wines are not only superb but exceedingly bargain-basement. Viva, Chile, South America's only first world country after Argentina's economic slippage. Still, don't miss Venezuela, one of our favorite countries with its strange tepuis in the southeast, including the tepui from which cascades the world's highest waterfall, Angel and my favorite hike on the planet, onto Roroima tepui.

Big Cities

Only in the big cities of developed countries must the traveler scrimp and mince about, seeking bargains for a couple to survive on \$2000 a month. Forget about Japan, Norway, Iceland, the UK and Switzerland; though the number of expensive countries continue to rise these are only five countries out of 191.

On \$3000 a month a couple can scrape by Rving in Japan and the world's big cities, even New York City, Paris and perhaps London. The further north or the larger the city the dearer the real estate and thus campgrounds and restaurants are more expensive. Conversely, the farther south, except the big cities in South America, and the smaller the population, the less expensive, except for supermarkets and fuel.

How Much Comfort Does One Need?

The amount of comfort required may depend on whether the person is male or female. Females occasionally require more pampering. We have several female acquaintances who couldn't possibly stay in anything less than a four star hotel, which they'd consider roughing it. They'd prefer five stars, thank you very much. We refer princesses to *Lady Windermere's Fan, 1892, Act III: In the world there are only two tragedies. One is not getting what one wants, and the other is getting it.* Bless Oscar Wilde.

How much comfort does one really need? We need very little. Cleanliness beats the heck out of godliness. As long as the joint is clean almost any hotel will do if it has a firm bed, decent bathroom facilities, cable TV and a refrigerator. A refrigerator is necessary to keep the beer cold. However, I can skip cable TV when the NBA finals aren't on, which is almost always in most countries.

We prefer never to stay in hotels or eat in restaurants so this kind of discussion is relatively remote. For others the comfort question will determine how much it would cost to RV the world. The difference between wants and actual needs can be confusing to many residents of developed countries. This book is not for princesses. We recommend the old Polish Proverb: *He is rich enough who wants nothing.*

Before non-princesses read further heed this caveat and beware: Travel is addicting. Those beginning to RV internationally may never, like us, be able to stop. A monkey clambers onto the back, creating the archetypal rolling stone, gathering no moss or attachment to the ubiquitous shopping malls and fast food joints some call home. Variety becomes the spice of life, spawning the realization that there are too many places packed into this world to fully explore though traveling from infancy to age one hundred, much less the few dozen healthy years most have left upon retirement, early or not. Then there's the other question— the activities of choice when going to wherever one wishes to go?

Antiquities

Those interested in antiquities are familiar with our favorites from Petra, Angkor Wat and Machu Picchu to Bagan, most of Turkey, Greece, Egypt and southern Italy. Except for those in the EU, which means Greece and Italy, and perhaps someday Turkey, the others are located in relatively inexpensive countries.

Cambodia, for gawking at Angkor Wat, mostly uses U.S. dollars. Any country using U.S. dollars hikes costs, but the other two countries, Jordan and Peru, are inexpensive to drive around and soak up atmosphere. This assumes luggage and peripherals aren't stolen in Peru.

The Turks are among the friendliest people anywhere. Browsers can't look at merchandise in a Turkish shop without being invited to sit down and drink chai (tea). Then there's Israel, a moderately priced country with intermittent unrest and antiquities up the wazoo; unlimited access to all of Israel's antiquities and nature reserves in 1997 was available on annual passes costing less than $75. Egypt, though known for occasionally massacring tourists—twice in 1997 when we visited—offers what many consider the best array of antiquities in the world, pyramids and such. For antiquity buffs, the world is a cheap enchilada, including such as India and China.

Hiking

The best hiking is also in relatively inexpensive countries. These include friendly and easy to get around New Zealand, which offered 900 hiking huts with most amenities for five dollars a night (by 2009 up to $22-33 with inflation and the up-valued Kiwi dollar), which we revisited for 5 months in 2009-2010; fabled Nepal, which from 2002 to 2006 had a small revolution going on, mostly out of prime trekking areas; the American West and Alaska; British Columbia, the Yukon and Alberta in Canada. Under no circumstances miss the fabulous Karakoram Mountains of northeast Pakistan where six of the world's fourteen highest mountains are crammed into an area of astounding beauty, not only completely safe but north of Pakistan's killer earthquake zone.

Premier hiking destinations include the 5500 mile (8900 Kilometer) length of the Andes Mountains in South America, western China in Yunnan and Sichuan Provinces, and Tibet, and northern India around Manali and Leh, aka *Little Tibet*. Leh is accessible a few months of the year by the world's highest motorable passes over 16,000 feet, almost 5000 meters.

There are many more non-iffy places for scenic hiking, a list of which would stretch longer than a book. We swoon because hiking national parks are us. Those who like adventure sports such as bungee jumping, paragliding, jet skiing, glacier hiking and such, can do it all in New Zealand, fairly inexpensively even now; head for Queenstown, the adventure capital of the world on South Island. South Africa has recently challenged for the world-adventure capital but prices relegate it a runner-up to New Zealand.

Shopping

The good news for those who like to shop is they can do that practically anywhere. All of Asia is exotic, safe and inexpensive, though Indonesia has a reputation problem, which we've habitually ignored, and the southern Philippines isn't exactly a gated community. Our motto jibes with the ancient Chinese proverb: *Don't listen to what they say. Go see.* Media accounts and embassy warnings of violence, outside of active war zones, seem to be uniformly and grossly exaggerated.

China hosts superb shopping, though offering more fake than genuine designer goods. European shopping is overpriced and Japan is astronomical. There's one money-saving grace for those traveling full time—they can't buy souvenirs or fancy stuff to take home because they'll have no place to put it, no home whatsoever. Being homeless means we can't buy a Greek statue to stick up on the hearth, or a Papuan carving for the mantel or a cobra in a bottle of Vietnamese wine, unless we drank it on the spot. But what would we do with a leftover cobra?

The inability of the homeless to buy knickknacks saves a mint of money, adding many years to a budget for RVing the world. Photos and t-shirts are my substitute for buying souvenirs. Photos take far less space on a hard drive while my souvenirs consist of an extensive assortment of T-shirts with pictures of interesting places on the front. RV internationally for a pittance without sacrificing comfort or frivolity.

CHAPTER FOURTEEN
The Ins and Outs of International RVing

Thanks to the Interstate Highway System, it is now possible to travel across the country from coast to coast without seeing anything. Charles Kuralt, *On the Road With Charles Kuralt*

There are RVs and there are RVs, which Mary is busy writing down. The humongous RVs cruising American freeways would easily fit on the majority of highways in few other countries, except perhaps Canada and Australia. On the other hand, wherever there's a road a reasonably-sized RV will squeeze onto it as well as an 18-wheeler, garbage truck or city bus. But many roads in most countries are too narrow and convoluted to comfortably accommodate large American RVs. Besides, with foreign fuel prices (we think US gas and diesel prices are high?) only Warren Buffett or Bill Gates could afford to drive a huge American RV outside the U.S. But American-style RVing, mostly driving Greyhound-type buses up and down interstates, has no particular connection with seeing the world by RV.

Go Anywhere in Four-Wheel Drive

All-wheel drive, aka four-wheel drive, is excellent for the intrepid explorer. We found RVs with four-wheel drive in Europe, manufactured in Finland, and the Hymer RVs manufactured in Germany. A hundred grand and up will buy a diesel 4x4 RV in the States, somewhat less used.

Four-wheel drive is especially handy in Australia where the north floods during the rainy season and most vehicles are equipped with—few believe this but it's true—a periscope. A periscope is necessary on Aussie vehicles so the engine can breathe under water in the world's most arid country. Eat your heart out, Saudi Arabia.

For an interlude during over a year cavorting around Australia we rented a four-wheel drive to explore the Gibb River Road and environs in the remote north of Western Australia, aka WA. Much of WA is accessible only by four-wheel drive, which we've found is about as much fun available with clothes on. Four-wheel drive is necessary to visit Australia's most scenic national park, which is not Ayer's Rock, but the Bungle Bungles. The Bungles, or Purnululu National Park, are a photogenic series of beehive mountains striped in horizontal bands of orange and black, like Halloween without waiting for October. These black-striped pumpkin bon-bons offer mystical hikes into cathedrals of rock, narrow fissures leading to horizons of grandeur and miles of stream beds replete with long-tailed dragon lizards. We forded fifty-three river crossings on the fifty miles of dirt road into Purnululu, obviously requiring four-wheel drive.

We recently bought a 4x4 diesel truck to pull a trailer and re-explored much of the Western U.S., Canada and Alaska. This leaves tons more places we couldn't check out for want of four-wheel-drive, requiring a return to chunks of Spain, Australia, New Zealand, Norway and a hundred other places.

The Proper RV

The best way to comfortably see the whole entire world requires an RV that's stand-alone and completely self-sufficient. This is easily accomplished.

• Potable Water

The biggest limitation, except for those who usually stay in campgrounds, is water. How long civilization can be avoided depends on daily water usage and RV tank capacity. RVs we've owned have held a maximum of fifty gallons, sufficient for four days. Fifty gallons allows four parsimonious showers, one every other day, with enough water left for washing dishes and drinking. This can be stretched to five days, skipping showers in an emergency, allowing an entire week without refilling water. Normally we carry at least one five-gallon jug of extra water, and depending on the circumstances, may carry more. Otherwise, we're dependent on finding water twice a week, most conveniently and usually from gas stations.

The kicker is the water must be potable. This is easily achieved anywhere in the world with a proper filtration system. We've RVed malaria-ridden Mexico without care or complication, relying on a filtration system taking everything out of the water except the H2O. These systems can be found with increasing ease, almost anywhere. Pathogens are executed by adding chlorine or iodine. A good filtration system preserves taste buds by taking out every trace of these potent disinfectants.

• Twelve Volt Power

The second most important requirement is electricity. The appliances in our stateside RV, except the microwave and air conditioner, whirled away on 12 volt. We had no need for a noisy generator, instead doing nicely with 200 watts of solar panels, continuously topping off the batteries while the sun was shining. We couldn't use the microwave unless plugged into 110 or 220 volts. Instead of air conditioning we used evaporative cooling, easily powered by 12 volt. Evaporative cooling fans a pool of water, evaporating the water to cool the RV interior when the outside air is saturated with less than fifty percent humidity. A single efficient and extremely quiet 100 watt solar panel is enough to run evaporative cooling, a laptop computer several hours a day and a VCR/TV for a couple of hours, leaving plenty to power fluorescent lights for hours. Except for those who must use an air conditioner or microwave a noisy generator is unnecessary. Sans generator the quiet of constant solar charging is instantly appreciated. We haven't missed air conditioning or a microwave in most of our RVs, but we've avoided Florida.

A minimum of three batteries are necessary to properly run a 12-volt electrical system, the best batteries available. Buy dual 6 volt marine deep cycle, if possible, because they're heartier. The batteries should be isolated, with two batteries separately dedicated to house functions: lights, laptop, TV and small appliances, while the third battery (12 volt) is used solely for starting the engine (and a fourth for diesel engines), undepleted overnight by household usage. All RVs and camper vans should be and usually are set up in this fashion. Then there is no worry about evening energy use and the vehicle will start first time, every time, each and every morning, unless something untoward happens, such as fuel injectors going kaput in Serbia.

The refrigerator pulls a ton of electrical current rendering a 12-volt system inadequate. But most RV refrigerators run efficiently on propane, which is needed in any event for the typical RV stove and oven. Thus a good-sized propane bottle solves the balance of energy needs.

All RV energy needs are provided easily by one or more solar panels and refillable propane bottles, with one caveat. Most continents, except North America, are a pain for propane bottle refills. European, African, Asian and South American countries employ different thread sizes, refill requirements and hard-to-find places for refilling bottles. The easiest solution across Europe is Camping Gaz containers, the bigger the better. These can be easily exchanged for full ones for a price in most European countries. There's no similar solution available on other continents. However, we've found that propane can be poured by hose between bottles, taking up to an hour and requiring creative hose fittings. South America uses only two types of thread sizes and attachments. The standard seems to alternate from country to country with no two contiguous countries having the same policy on refilling or exchanging bottles, or the type of attachments necessary for their operation.

- ## Diesel: A No-Brainer

The optimal vehicle fuel is diesel. Diesel engines enjoy better mileage than gasoline engines, last longer, generate more dependable power and return a higher resale value. Diesel ranges from slightly less to much less expensive than gasoline in most countries, except the U.S. where diesel is often more expensive. Fortunately, ninety percent of foreign RVs are diesel. American RV manufacturers are only reluctantly—and as slow as molasses in winter—converting American RVs to diesel and then seemingly only the largest. An RV using gasoline will get, at best, between five and ten miles per gallon, whereas the same diesel rig will get up to twenty miles a gallon, an incredible savings in fuel costs and efficiency. A diesel RV will save a yearly fortune in fuel alone and a diesel engine will usually last between 300,000 and 500,000 miles. A gasoline engine is lucky to rack up 200,000 miles. When choosing between diesel and gasoline engines, it's a no-brainer—diesel *über alles*.

The Nitty Gritty of Driving An RV Abroad

The traffic problems encountered in such as Java, Italy and Cairo demand a consideration of the pros and cons of driving an RV all over the world. The pros vastly outweigh the cons, we believe, which may reflect a lack of common sense and represent a mere matter of taste. I'm partial to Marilyn Monroe's judgment: *Ever notice that 'what the hell' is always the right decision?* Well, except for over-dosing.

- ## Those Nutsy Foreign Drivers

I avoid navigating at night in any vehicle larger than a breadbox, including in the States. Night driving is particularly hazardous in countries where drivers presume to conserve battery power by leaving headlights off, such as Turkey. Romania can be hazardous when gypsy wagons, without lights, trundle main roads in the small hours. Or don't drive at night because sights are exceedingly difficult to see in the dark.

Except for driving on the *wrong* side of the road, driving in New Zealand, Australia and the U.K. is no different than driving in the States, except there's no road rage abroad, yet. Countries where the locals careen down the wrong side of the road are only momentarily unnerving. It doesn't take long to permanently remember that the driver, assuming the steering wheel is on the same side as the other vehicles in the country, always hugs the centerline. Cars hurtling head-on in the same lane tend to imprint memory circuits with indelible ink. A friend driving in Northern Ireland experienced two such near-miss episodes before he never forgot again. Unfortunately, his wife nixed further adventures in countries that drive on the *wrong* side of the road. After a maximum of twenty-four hours of trauma everyone remembers which side to drive on. By day number two the RVer is driving like a native, which is often with abandon, especially in Italy, Egypt and Southeast Asia.

The curious thing about crazy local drivers is they're actually quite good, which they must be to survive. Many developing countries have codified what boils down to no traffic laws, or if there are traffic rules few drivers acknowledge first hand acquaintance. It works out to be easy for those who pay attention. Because first-world countries have traffic laws, laws that are sometimes enforced we assume people will observe the laws, resulting in complacency and inattention.

After a year or two of foreign travel, briefly returning to the States to plan the next trip, we're traumatized by the legion of inattentive drivers and it has gotten far worse with the widespread use of cell phones and texting while driving. These are implicated in ¼ of all injury accidents. Half of drivers aged 18-25 drive while texting; 73% of us have used a cell phone while driving: the equivalent of driving drunk.

The leading cause of inattention-caused car crashes was cell phones and radio/CD distractions, soon overtaken by text-messaging. Other diversions included rowdy children, sloppy eating, ambidextrous reading, acrobatic smoking, unruly animals, electrical equipment such as GPS and primping. An inattentive driver would live maybe ten seconds in a developing country where only the attentive and fittest survive. The chaos of no traffic laws produces motorists who concentrate on their driving and thus live to drive another day. Driving in developing countries requires paying attention, all the time, in every direction, to everyone coming from all places, points and positions. After a few days it becomes completely ho-hum, simple reflex attention.

- **Obtaining Insurance**

The cons of a personal vehicle include the machinations necessary to cadge RV insurance, which can be tricky in countries where the owner has no home address. However, there's always a way to scare up a foreign home address. Addresses can be manufactured. Few insurance companies dispatch detectives to inspect a home address. The police are only interested in a card showing proof of insurance if, heaven forbid, someone has an accident. However, if the insurance company insists on mailing the insurance policy and it's returned for *No such address*, questions could arise.

Move to plan B before the company cancels the insurance, which could involve a friendly local who'll lend a street address. That may require dependency on a new friend to forward mail from the insurance company. The easiest solution to avoid all this rigmarole may reside with the RV dealer or private seller from whom the RV has been purchased. We've always been allowed to use the seller's address for insurance purposes, simply by asking. Be creative. There's always a way to accomplish anything though it may take a syncopated song and dance.

In Europe we used the seller's address for vehicle insurance. The dealer obtained insurance from AIG, until late 2008 the largest insurance agency in the world. Way back in 1994 AIG Europe specialized in American servicemen overseas. In Australia and New Zealand we bought RV insurance through their respective motor-caravanning clubs, using their business addresses for insurance purposes. The Caravan Club of Australia can be found at www.cmca.net.au, the Caravan Club of New Zealand at www.nzcma.org.nz, and for our next continent of RVing, see The Caravan Club of South Africa at www.caravanclubofsa.co.za.

In Africa, Asia and South America few motorists carry auto insurance so we fit in well, driving with no insurance like the locals. When in Santiago, do as the Santiagoans. Many African borders' require on-the-spot purchase of vehicle insurance.

- **Complete Independence**

The advantages of a private vehicle are multitudinous, creating a much higher quality of travel experience. The first advantage is complete independence. Using public transportation puts the traveler at the mercy of inconvenient schedules and often less than punctual trains and chicken buses. Trains may be hours late and agonizingly slow, especially in developing countries. Plus many trains are filthy, noisy and verily uncomfortable, such as most in India and Indonesia. Buses may be more comfy, faster and cleaner, though some are the pits. The comparative quality of buses and trains varies not only between countries but also within sections of a country. Trains are far superior to buses in Eastern China but buses beat the stuffing out of trains in most of Western China, both in cleanliness and speed.

Personal transportation makes for a footloose and fancy-free traveler, able to leave anywhere on a whim, stopping when and where the fancy strikes. Those preferring to sleep in instead of hustling a tuckered tush to the 5 a.m. train, the only one leaving all day for a preferred destination, know that glomming onto a personal vehicle is the only answer. Having an RV or camper van instead of a car will save a bundle on hotels and restaurants. No countries we know of require that RVs stay in campgrounds, or if they do it's seldom to never enforced. This allows anyone to overnight free on public lands adjacent to the most scenic spots on the planet.

Overnighting at a trailhead simplifies the early morning hike, assuming the RV can be properly leveled. Sleeping on your head, canted to one side, is good for neither circulation nor relaxation. Most RVs must be parked level, not only for comfort but to avoid damaging the refrigerator, which usually must be close to level in order to avoid burning out the compressor or separating the gases essential to its operation. We learned early to park flat, with or without the aid of simple bubble levels for front to back and side to side leveling. A chunk of wood, or the odd rock under the appropriate tires, delivers smooth and even perfection.

- **Quality of the Travel Experience**

The ability to park where the fancy strikes adds immeasurably to the excellence of travel. Imagine never having to find a hotel, check out the suitability of a room, find another hotel if the first one is shocking, haggle a price (required in many developing countries), carry leaden bags up flights of stairs because the elevator is temporarily out of order, unpack, find a decent place to eat and then throw oneself dead tired on a saggy, too soft or too hard bed, too beat to enjoy the novelty of a new place. Those utilizing hotels must repack the next morning and begin the process all over again.

Those in RVs or camper vans can park beside a river in the early afternoon without having to find strange beds to sleep in, packing and unpacking bags or breaking their back carrying luggage a single solitary inch. The rest of the day is left free to explore something other than hotel options. This avoids transportation hubs, also known as cities, except occasionally to stock up on supplies. Skipping cities obviates traffic jams, road rage, nasty pollution, higher crime rates and parking problems.

Overnighting on public lands triples the reward: 1) excellent scenery, not an attribute for which campgrounds are often known, 2) it's free and 3) the RVer isn't crammed in with a bunch of other campers who've sired nasty frolicsome children, leading to 4) a quiet, hassle-free stay. Overnighting on public lands in a National Forest or on land owned by the Bureau of Land Management is easy and free in the Western United States. The heavily populated eastern U.S. is far more difficult. We RVed the U.S. using topographical atlases for each state, showing every river, dirt track and out of the way place for quiet over-nighting in every speck of the entire country.

The wide world outside the United States is relatively easy to free camp. Most difficult in Europe are Poland, England, Holland and Switzerland where privately owned land often comes up to the road and many parking lots are height-restricted to low-clearance vehicles. It's equally easy to free camp all over Australia and New Zealand, except in the few big cities where inexpensive campgrounds are a better option. No matter the country free camping in big cities should be avoided because they're home to the world's greatest concentration of its most dangerous animal: the homo sapien.

South America varies radically by country. Argentina, Uruguay and Chile are basically first-world countries. Almost no one cares where an RV parks as long as it isn't on their property. Public lands and most anywhere are safe outside poverty-stricken portions of cities. In poorer countries it's safer to park in the town square under a streetlight or at a gas station. In many poor countries they've never heard of or seen campers or campgrounds. In Brazil and most of Peru only gas stations, secure parking lots or campgrounds should be used for overnighting.

Africa is easy to free camp but avoid big cities even more passionately; especially Johannesburg and Nairobi, and at night like the plague. The rest of the many countries in Africa are relatively safe outside those with intermittently active revolutions such as The Congo, Ivory Coast and Somalia, parts of Chad and Sudan, and Algeria. Asia is the safest continent, bar none. Walking around even a large city after midnight is stressless most anywhere in Asia.

Leisurely Seeing It All and Saving a Mint

Tourists don't know where they've been, travelers don't know where they're going. Paul Theroux

Private transportation means complete freedom to change plans on a dime without forfeiting previously-purchased train or bus tickets. We like this not so much because we can change plans without notice but because we don't need plans to begin with. Our SOP in Australia, for example, was to head for a national park but often we'd find a detour or alternative trail (the Aussies call it a track) taking up the rest of the day, leading to unanticipated adventures. When it makes no difference what day a destination is reached, whether the same day, next day, next week or next month, the potential hassle-quotient abruptly drops to zero.

- ### See It All, In-depth
The occupants of a private vehicle can actually see everything there is to see between two points, stopping for pictures or exploration whenever and wherever, which is impossible with public transportation or a tour, cruise or package deal. Public transport simply doesn't go to ninety percent of potential destinations in any country.

I sense disbelief. Take a road map of anywhere. Buses and trains run only between main towns, making no provision for those who may wish to explore anywhere in between or off the well-beaten track. The bus may let someone off at an unscheduled stop but it often won't pick them up. If the bus can be flagged down it's often a day later at an indeterminate time, the convenience of which may depend on whether it's raining buckets or cataclysmically sweltering. In a country such as Vietnam and a hundred others most places are inaccessible by public transportation, such as much of the Vietnamese highlands where a road ghosting the Vietcong trail was recently built. Without private transportation any place off the heavily beaten tourist track is extremely iffy to access, anywhere.

- ## Who's More Trustworthy

Which is more trustworthy, bus drivers in Peru, China and Italy, or our own driving? Prudent conduct before answering might include consultation with a significant other, whose opinion could slightly differ. But even Mary trusts my driving more than the other fellow's, especially the screwball bus drivers we've observed in numerous countries abroad. On occasion, however, Mary's opinion has faltered.

- ## Saving Health and Bucks

An RV or camper van encourages saving a mint by eating in instead of eating out in restaurants of dubious quality. There's a singularly stellar reason why diners are barred from most restaurant kitchens—to shield the shock of the unsanitary, if not downright disgusting conditions surrounding the preparation of much restaurant *cuisine*. I feel better eating street vendor food sautéed in front of my eyes instead skulked over in a hidden back parlor. More importantly, with a little effort, an RV or camper-van expedites eating precisely what we prefer instead of being limited to restaurant entrées, severely limited, over-salted and often pathetic.

- ## Who Can't Cook?

Anyone who can read can cook if they put in a bit of effort reading a recipe. Concededly, many are too lazy to cook for themselves, especially when there's only one person to cook for. But if health is of any interest or concern, preparing one's own meals is of utmost significance. Over ninety percent of restaurant food is high in fat and salt. Neither fat nor salt is particularly healthy or palatable for a balanced diet. Those harboring little or no concern about a balanced diet can eat in as many restaurants as often as they wish because they're relatively inexpensive outside of Europe, Japan and the U.S. Eating out is occasionally easier and faster, though far more expensive, and in many establishments, borderline dangerous.

- ## Easier to Eat In or Out?

A main advantage of toting a pantry is being able to eat when and where the whim or hunger attacks. There's no waiting or interminable trudging to find a potentially acceptable restaurant. Restaurants don't exist where we prefer to travel, out in the boondocks, at a trailhead, on a hike or climb, away from cities. I'd prefer a stir-fry or tacos at the foot of Mount Cook in New Zealand to Maxim's in Paris. Restaurants pale compared to eating favorite food where and when the heart desires. This convenience avoids having to find a truly palatable restaurant, which is never obvious from appearance.

- ## Picking Poison

No restaurant can be accurately judged by its facade. Only after ordering, interminably waiting and finally tasting can we know whether the food is edible; whether it is or isn't we've acquired an almost iron-clad obligation to pay. Food we've personally picked out and prepared is *a priori* superior, assuming we don't ruin it in the process. We'd rather never venture into civilization to find a restaurant, instead fixing our own food while contemplating a spectacular beach, mountain, lake, ocean or river, views offered by few dining establishments. Our food is never too salty, oily, smelly or unsanitary, a daily risk for those relegated to restaurants. Exceptions include countries such as Thailand and Turkey with outstanding cuisine where we relish eating out; it's affordable and invariably *fabuloso*.

- ## Ancient New Year's Resolutions

Those wishing to keep fit need the convenience of personal transport. Otherwise exercise will often have to take place in hotel rooms or on city streets. Public transportation only connects cities, providing little or no access to trailheads or other interesting exercise options. Many campgrounds are in or near cities, providing similar restrictions in pursuing a regimen of personal fitness. This is one reason we prefer to avoid campgrounds or stay at those outside cities, the more rural the better. We'd rather park where fitness activities are readily available such as trailheads and other isolated areas that are usually abundant in natural beauty with unlimited opportunities for exercise. With an RV anyone can travel most of the world in-depth for a pittance, and keep in shape.

CHAPTER FIFTEEN
The Cost: Buying and Selling RVs Abroad

Reserve a packet of capital for the purchase or an RV, camper van or other vehicle of choice. Upon resale, after a year or more of in-depth continent exploration, most of the principal will boomerang back. We began with an expensive sailboat. All sailing vessels are money pits from the get-go, no matter make, model or motor. After investing a portion of the sale proceeds in a $20,000 German RV we worked that down to less than $5,000, but it took ten years. Over time the investment in transportation will take a gradual toll on the pocketbook. The speed of the downward spiral will depend not only on *luck* but skill in buying, selling and maintaining the vehicle, and unforeseen variables too imprecise to generalize. Buying and selling RVs has cost us an average of $1500 a year, less than five dollars a day, or about the cost of a daily 16 oz Starbucks: eminently reasonable.

• Comparing Public and Private Transport Costs

Not only is private transportation far superior to public conveyance but the initial investment is mostly recoverable and the driver will hopefully be more trustworthy than such as the run-of-the-mill Peruvian bus driver. With the miniscule initial investment required to RV abroad there's little reason to depend on surrogates to negotiate traffic. The cost of buying private transportation over months and years is far less than public transportation in developed countries such as Europe, Japan and North America, and little more than public transportation in developing countries, while facilitating comfort, convenience and a superior traveling experience.

• RV Internationally for $11 a Day

After spending $20,000 on a used-RV in Europe, admittedly over a dozen years ago, we were able to drive almost three years in thirty-four countries and, because we were in a hurry to leave, sell the RV to a dealer for almost $10,000. If we'd been more patient, avoided the British *Q* license plate and cell phones had then been invented we would have netted a few thousand more. Even selling it to a dealer meant we spent $10,000 for 912 days of transportation, sleeping in our own beds every night amongst the wonders of Europe, Asia, Scandinavia, the Middle East and North Africa. We seldom stayed in campgrounds more than once a month and then primarily to receive mail. Thus the total cost worked out to about eleven dollars a day, excluding the obvious expenses of fuel and maintenance, far higher than we spent on other continents. Because we prefer seeing places in depth we normally drive not more than fifty miles (eighty kilometers) a day, which is leisurely. With little daily driving the fuel consumption has been minimal, meaning expenses have never been more than the cost of public transportation and far less than any tour yet invented.

• RVing Australia and New Zealand: $11 and $7 a Day

Buying a camper bus in Australia and driving around the entire country for thirteen months, including Tasmania, also worked out to a daily eleven dollars. We stayed in Australian campgrounds about half the time because they were relatively inexpensive, well appointed and usually rural. Because Australia is almost the size of the US with only 7% of the US population, the whole country is genuinely rural.

We bought and sold a large diesel RV in New Zealand after a six-month expedition. The difference between the purchase and sales price was less than $1000, costing $6.70 a day for 150 days. We often stayed in extremely nice Kiwi campgrounds because they were dirt-cheap and usually in the country, costing between five and ten dollars a day. Unfortunately by 2009 the U.S. dollar had halved in value since our New Zealand sortie in 2000-2001. Thus these prices must be adjusted upward by one hundred percent, which means they'd now be somewhat less than *dirt cheap.* Using public transportation we couldn't have seen a fraction of what we saw in thirty-four European countries, Australia, New Zealand, all the countries in South America and four dozen countries in Africa. We spent far less than a regimented tour or the cost of public transportation and the quality of travel was infinitely superior.

Fuel, Insurance and Repair Expenses

The cost of buying and selling an RV in various parts of the world doesn't include fuel, insurance or repairs. Fuel in Europe during the mid-1990s averaged four dollars a gallon but the cost wasn't prohibitive because we had oodles of time, driving an average of fifty-three miles a day. The European diesel RV got twenty miles (thirty two kilometers) per gallon (3.8 liters) so we used two and two-thirds gallons (ten liters) a day. Thus the normal daily fuel cost worked out to ten dollars; the total for almost three years was $9200. By 2009 European fuel prices had doubled.

Insurance was always reasonably priced, a few hundred dollars a year, whether through AIG in Europe or the motor-caravanning clubs in Australia and New Zealand. We didn't carry insurance in Asia, Africa or South America and neither did the locals. Repairs varied widely depending on our acuity in purchasing the particular RV. But we've never spent more than $1000 a year in repairs, including replacement tires.

- ### Down Under Experiences

Fuel in Australia and New Zealand cost less than two dollars a gallon during 1999 to 2001. We drove about the same daily mileage as we'd driven in Europe but at half the cost, about $2700 for eighteen months in the two countries. Insurance was identical at $300 a year. The New Zealand RV required a clutch sprocket, which cost a hundred dollars. Oil changes averaged ten dollars each in both countries.

- ### The *Blue Beast*

The Australian bus, aptly named the *blue beast,* suffered two major repairs. While in Alice Springs we lost a piston, which is a lot of power to lose in an underpowered four-cylinder engine. The original engine was not easily available but, after putting along at an average of thirty miles an hour for six days, we found a six-cylinder replacement. Two ingenious Townsville mechanics installed a *new* engine for AU $900. This paltry sum included the replacement engine and their labor, which in 2000 translated to $460 US. A month later the drive-shaft hit the pavement at sixty miles per hour, unable to cope with the newly powerful engine. This brought us to an abrupt, scraping halt, marooned for a peaceful week in the way outback of Australia. We repaired to the closest municipal campground and waited less than patiently for a replacement drive-shaft to be manufactured and delivered. The total cost for parts and labor was $300 US, including the towing bill. The downside of that experience was a drive-shaft that wasn't exactly the right length. The racket it made upon resale back in Brisbane ultimately extracted at least $1000 from the sales price of the *Blue Beast.* Still, 13 idyllic months in Australia were abundantly worth it.

In a nutshell, we spent $4160 for fuel, insurance, oil and repairs on the New

Zealand and Australian RVs, ignoring the $1000 in depreciation from an inaccurately manufactured drive-shaft. But we took the additional $1000 expense into account when figuring the eleven dollars a day it cost to drive around Australia for thirteen months.

Buying and Selling RVs around the World

How do you buy an RV in a foreign country? Our four experiences in Europe, Australia, New Zealand and South America were very different. In Africa we accompanied a Land Rover from South Africa to Ethiopia, later a truck from South Africa through Namibia and Botswana to Zimbabwe, and an overland truck for five months through West Africa. For the next African adventure we'll buy an RV in South Africa and drive around the continent as far as we can go, before selling and moving on.

• Buying and Selling RVs in OZ and NZ

Before flying to Australia we'd corresponded by email with a nice couple in Brisbane who'd agreed to sell their RV to us. They suggested we join the Australian camping and caravanning club, the easiest way to obtain RV insurance, so we joined up. However, a week before the flight to Australia the nice couple sold their RV to someone else. We arrived in Brisbane prepared to check-out local RV dealers, classified ads and the caravanning club's list of members with RVs for sale. We called the club's president on arrival and he invited us to attend a member's rally the coming weekend. We showed up, enjoyed the hearty Australian hospitality and the next day bought an *RV* from a rally-attendee. The seller insisted we spend two days in his spacious back yard while he took us through the vehicle's many features and helped us load the things we'd shipped over. In less than a week after arrival in Australia we were the proud owners of a Toyota Coaster, aka the *Blue Beast*. It'd been converted by the owner into a reasonably functioning, twenty-foot-long camper bus, and we were off south towards Sydney. When we returned to Brisbane thirteen months later we checked into an RV park, put an ad in the newspaper and sold the *Blue Beast* in less than a week. Then we flew to New Zealand.

Before the flight to Auckland we'd pin-pointed two RV-rental agencies, which we hoped might have used RVs for sale. Upon arrival we found the rental companies farmed used RVs out to various dealers and one such dealer maintained a lot in North Auckland. We spent an hour on the lot and Mary fell in love with a six-berth Ford diesel. We were off on another adventure less than a week after arriving in New Zealand.

• Snagging an RV in South America

We began by searching the internet for a four-wheel drive, diesel RV in South America. Through an ad in the South American Explorer's Clubs' on-line newsletter we found an extended-chassis, Dodge camper-van for sale by Andreas and Barbara, a couple anxious to get back to Germany for a family emergency. They emailed a dozen pictures of the van, inside and out, three pages of inventory and the van's service history, meticulously German. The asking price was $5500, less than the cost of shipping an RV to South America and back, which would have cost at least $6000 and potentially untold headaches. The van was neither diesel nor four-wheel drive, which Andreas correctly insisted were unnecessary. But the van did have the most essential ingredient for easily crossing South American borders—license plates from outside South America, specifically from Canada.

We put a ten percent down-payment on the van sight unseen, flew to Quito, Ecuador, spent two days going over the vehicle at Andreas' insistence and paid him the balance. He accompanied us on a two-day trip to the Peruvian border, driving out of Ecuador to get the van off his passport. In no man's land I took his place in the driver's seat and we checked into Peru, showing them a perfectly photo-copied title with Mary and David inserted in lieu of Barbara and Andreas. We drove into the depths of South America and Andreas took a bus back to Quito.

- **Cell Phones Enable RVing the World**

When we first sold an RV abroad it was difficult for one reason. Sales ads require a phone number and this was before cell phones. Now a used cell phone with sim card can be bought for less than fifty dollars almost anywhere in the world: instant phone number to put in an *RV-for-sale* ad. Sim cards are less well-known in the States but are used in almost every other country. This prepaid chip for variable chunks of airtime can be renewed over the phone by credit card and incoming cell-phone calls cost nothing, outside the U.S. This avoids having to sign a multi-year contract for cell phone use, the main choice in the States.

When selling an RV abroad don't assume a U.S. cell phone will work. It probably won't unless signed up for international service, assuming the carrier is international and the cell phone multi-band. The world is on four separate cell-phone bands. For a cell phone that works all over the world, buy a quadra-band phone from Motorola, Nokia, Siemens or Erickson, among others. They cost about $400. Iphone, Blackberry, Treo and several other companies offer viable alternatives.

In a nutshell it's easy to buy and sell RVs abroad. Only once has it taken us more than a week to sell an RV or camper-van in any country except the United States. The single exception was South America where we left the fully amortized campervan with friends in Brazil.

CHAPTER SIXTEEN
Details of Fulltime International Travel

Fulltime international travel is easy and enjoyable for those who pay attention to little picky things. The quality of travel is directly proportionate to preparation and attention to detail.

The First Question Is Always Weather

The first question we research before each trip is, *what will the weather be?* This translates to, *approximately where should we be when?* The quality of all travel is wholly dependent on weather. If the weather is good, travel is usually excellent. Bad weather can ruin the whole experience, such as it nearly did for us in 1997, springtime in Turkey. It's difficult to see anything in sheets of rain or a blizzard, and depressing too.

• Fickle Europe

It's a bear to find good weather in mid- to northern Europe outside of July through September. We tried to follow the weather during years in Europe but were unfortunately ahead of it all too often. During three years RVing Europe we drove from Ireland to Jordan and Morocco to Finland, starting north too soon, each and every *summer*. In Denmark during May of 1995 we were forced, for weeks on end, to wear fur-lined parkas.

Spring comes late to Europe though this is gradually changing with global warming. Check out an atlas; all of Europe is north of San Francisco. Even the furthest south of Spain, Italy, Greece and all but a small speck of far southern Turkey in Asia Minor, are north of thirty-eight degrees, the latitude of San Francisco.

Much of northern Europe is the equivalent of northern Alaska, only saved from arctic temperatures by the Gulf Stream. Northern Europe instead enjoys sub-arctic temps. Half of Scandinavia, including some of the best parts of Norway, is north of the Arctic Circle. Compare Alaska, which has no paved roads north of the Arctic Circle, but then Alaska lacks a Gulf Stream. The only palatable months to visit Scandinavia are July, August and a bit of September; these months, or portions thereof when it's not raining, are marvelous. The high season of July through early September is the only time you can hope for decent weather in Europe, except for the southern countries of Portugal, Spain, Italy, Greece and Turkey. Forget the rest of Europe except in the northern summer. We practically froze to death buying an RV in Germany's December.

We spent three European winters in Spain and Portugal; Spain, Morocco and Portugal; and Israel. We'd never have visited Israel were it not for a British Jewish couple we met in Spain, who suggested we winter in the Holy Land. Israel turned out to be a super choice for the winter of 1996–1997. From Israel we were easily able to branch off to Egypt, Jordan, Cyprus, Rhodes and Turkey.

• Down Under--Reversed Weather

Weather isn't a factor for visiting Australia, at least for those who wish to see it all and have at least a year to do so. Australia is vast, the same size as the United States without Alaska. Visit the utter far north in the northern winter, reversed weather in the southern hemisphere, and it's still hellishly hot in Darwin at eight degrees below the equator. Even in the southern winter Darwin is almost ninety degrees with ninety percent humidity. I'd surely hate to be in Darwin during the summer. Visit Melbourne, Tasmania and the southern parts of Australia during the Australian summer from November through March.

New Zealand should also be reserved for the southern summer. Kiwi weather is often better when the rain slows and autumn sets in during March and April. Rain was forecast practically every day we spent on New Zealand's South Island. However, we learned to never believe weather forecasts; out of twenty-one days backpacking we were drenched on a single morning for three hours, leaving twenty and a half days hiking in super weather. We simply forged onward, never worrying about New Zealand's uncannily inaccurate weather forecasts.

• Asia's Wacky Weather

China is the third largest country, after Russia and Canada, which means parts are excellent any time of the year. However, the winters can be chilly and sometimes windy. Because Beijing is so far north, slightly north of San Francisco, go during the northern summer and save Southern China until winter, with one exception, the incredible mountains of southwest China. The Himalayas and their foothills, along with Tibet, are best accessed during the summer because they're at relatively high altitude. Lhasa, the capitol of Tibet, enjoys the country's lowest elevation at 12,000 feet. We apologize to China for calling Tibet a country and promise to never think of Taiwan as one either.

Southeast Asia carries a strange pattern of wet and dry seasons. The farther south during the northern winter, such as through Indonesia and the Philippines, the more it rains in sheets, whereas the northern parts of Thailand and Vietnam are dry, and vice versa. The weather pattern makes it easy to see most of Southeast Asia's many countries in a single year. Because Southeast Asia flirts with the equator (Singapore is at one degree north latitude) travelers may prefer to go during the rainy season, when a brief afternoon shower makes the weather palatable. During the dry season the lowlands of Southeast Asia are uniformly sweltering and it's almost all lowlands.

• Fantastic South America

South America offers so many variations in altitude and latitude that anyone can go any time of the year and drive themselves crazy, as we can personally attest. The higher elevations in the 5500-mile-long Andes are a must see, best during the southern winter because that's the dry season. Although it's colder that's when clouds vacate the spectacular mountain tops. The trekking is superb in the South American winter.

South America offers elevations from 23,000 feet to minus several hundred feet. This entire range is available within a few hundred miles in Argentina, from Aconcagua, the highest mountain in the Americas, to a Death Valley-like depression in southern Patagonia.

• Africa's Easy

Because Africa has few high mountains the weather follows standard assumptions. It's always hot in the middle, on both sides of the equator, but more palatable north of the equator in the northern winter and vice versa. The exception is the areas around Mt. Kilimanjaro in Tanzania and Mt. Kenya, both near the equator and great climbs any time of the year. The temperate parts are the far south, from South Africa through Namibia, Botswana, Zimbabwe and Mozambique; and the far north, from Morocco to Egypt, both ranging from twenty to thirty degrees Centigrade; 70 to 90 degrees Fahrenheit. Climbing Morocco's highest mountain in April conjured a blizzard of awesome proportions; altitude always renders weather exceptional.

We research weather in-depth before any trip; it's absolutely crucial to a savory junket.

Inherent Intrigue

Countries where people drive on the *right* side of the road are slightly more chaotic than tooling around the U.S.A., outside of Los Angeles and New York City. This has never been a problem though we've admittedly had other modest difficulties driving in foreign countries, caused more by my mistakes than the actions of others. We'll never forget the wrong turn in Sicily leading the unsuspecting RV to an arch half its height, or after our escape, the standing ovation in the main square.

The flat tire in the far south of Morocco left us without a spare for a few weeks until back in Spain. We survived. We also survived the *Serbian* adventure. Instead of a traumatic experience the Serbian episode was a heehaw highlight during three years in Europe and it gets funnier every year. None of these incidents, the only ones suffered in the first eight years of international travel, had anything to do with local driving conditions.

The primary headaches we've had navigating foreign countries were mechanical, excepting an unpleasant episode in Buenos Aires, about which later. When we began traveling full time I was an incompetent mechanic. Now I've graduated to pathetic; I usually know what's wrong though I still don't know how to fix it.

Free Camping versus Campgrounds

Maps of 20,000-to-one reveal every detail of the countryside, leading the RVer to river parking, public lands and spiffy over-nighting that's aesthetically pleasing and quiet. We never stay on private property without permission or payment, such as at campgrounds. But it's relatively simple to find wonderful places to park almost anywhere in the world, for free.

• Dangerous Cities versus Safer Countryside

The rule of thumb is to stay in campgrounds in cities, but there's otherwise little need to do so in the rural parts of Europe. This rule applies equally to Serbia, Turkey, Cyprus, Israel, Jordan and the rest of the world.

We were unable to drive in Egypt; the government prohibited foreign-plated diesel vehicles from crossing the Sinai. This prohibition enrolled us in a dreaded tour. We also technically took tours, without a tour guide or regimentation, to visit St. Petersburg, Russia, to Tibet by air from Chengdu, Sichuan, China and four-days to two spectacular national parks in the far north of Sichuan Province, China. We toured the Yellowstones of China only because public transportation would have required more time, money and inconvenience. We were the only non-Chinese on the national parks tour, a hoot from start to finish.

South America is an entirely different ball of wax for free camping. Argentina, Chile and Uruguay are easy but other South American countries range from difficult to dangerous. The police in Ecuador and Peru will move those camping near the road. Neither country is physically dangerous. Still, no one should overnight in or near a big city such as Lima, Guayaquil or Quito, unless parking in a secure estacionamiento or parking lot. Plenty are available. Park under brilliant street lights in smaller towns.

• Exceptionally Dangerous Brazil?

Only free camp in Brazil under bright lights at a gas station; otherwise stay in a secure campground, if one can be found; there are few. The locals regaled us with tales of

Brazil as the most dangerous country on the planet. They were either bragging or hadn't snuck into active war zones. According to their unnerving tales Brazil was worse than Columbia. In Sao Paulo robbers supposedly throw spikes under tires and when the motorist pops out to inspect or fix the flat they'd kill for a single *real*, the Brazilian dollar worth fifty cents. Avoid the largest city in the southern hemisphere. Instead, park in secure campgrounds outside Rio and Sao Paulo, taking public transportation into the city while watching everyone carefully. Or consider skipping Brazil. Although it's the world's fifth largest country there not much to miss except for those into beaches, music, dental floss bikinis, the Amazon River and the most incredible colonial cities on earth.

- **Easy Africa**

Most of the African countryside is easy and safe for overnighting. There are few campgrounds outside of South Africa, Namibia and Morocco. The only dangerous areas, as on most continents, are cities where ruffians and similar miscreants congregate. Still, the only truly dangerous cities in Africa are Nairobi and Johannesburg, mostly at night. Avoid the war zones in Chad, The Congo and Ivory Coast, and the continuing revolutions in Somalia and Algeria. The must see countries are South Africa's south including Cape Town, the unbelievable dunes of Namibia, Botswana's Okavango Delta, all of Tanzania, Mali and Ethiopia, plus Morocco and Egypt.

Avoiding tours and driving an RV not only saves a ton of money but the quality improves from a one to a ten. Personal transportation is an essential key to traveling comfortably forever, seeing everything there is to see, a practical impossibility with tours and expensive hotels.

Guidebooks, Maps and Atlases

The best overall English-language guidebooks are *Lonely Planet* and *Let's Go*, but the quality varies wildly from country to country. Several specialty guidebooks cover parts of the world even better, such as the *South American Handbook,* which beats the daylights out of other guidebooks for South America, or any portion thereof. The Handbook series is usually superior for those with private transportation. Thus RVers should always check to see if a Handbook is available for where they're off to next.

- **Buying Online**

Buying guidebooks is cheaper on the Internet, depending on current shipping policies. Many URLs provide free shipping for orders over $25. Because books bought over the Internet are discounted by at least twenty percent and no sales tax is levied, between a fourth and a third can be saved off local bookstore prices. In addition, Internet booksellers carry a large inventory of used guidebooks available from affiliated private sellers for half the cost, or less, of new volumes.

There are two catches: the first is shipping charges for used books, which often run twice the actual cost of UPS, USPS or FedEx. The second catch is that many used guidebooks are older than current editions. Before buying a used guidebook check which edition is most up to date.

Internet bookstores also carry maps and atlases, unequivocally crucial for those with personal transportation. Detailed atlases with scales of 20,000 to one are available for many countries. These are a necessity for those wishing, as our German friend Andreas describes it, to *camp in nature*. The ability to park for the night in the midst of scenic beauty is what, to us, world travel is all about. Our 20,000 to one French atlas provided 200 incredibly detailed pages with graphic maps, a godsend for parking on picturesque canals, below towering Alps, on deserted beaches and beside ancient monasteries.

Detailed atlases are available for all first-world countries. Our favorites for the United States are the topographical atlases produced for every western state by DeLorme. These incredible atlases display every road down to jeep trails and hiking paths, additionally marked with elevation lines and delineating publicly owned land.

The best maps for Southeast Asia and China are by Nelles, a German outfit, also available on the Internet. If we can't find the proper scale of map or atlas we ask Wide World of Maps out of our home-town Phoenix to find it and they usually can do. Any map or atlas can be found by searching the Internet. Google or die, ending up in the boondocks of the world, utterly lost without a detailed-road atlas.

Inoculations

After researching guidebooks and atlases, which for us are half the fun of travel, we reach the un-fun part, dreaded inoculations. All shots should be recorded in a yellow International Certificates of Vaccination approved by the World Health Organization and issued by the U.S. Department of Health and Human Services. This record is available at any doctor's office that provides traveler's inoculations. Carry it at all times, hidden in a waist wallet with passport, credit cards and plane tickets.

At a minimum keep inoculations for tetanus and typhoid up to date, plus shots for one or more strains of hepatitis. The three-shot regimen for Hepatitis A is given several months apart and costs about $100 in developing countries, depending on the doctors doing the stabbing. Consult a travel doctor, who will instruct which inoculations should be brought up to date and when.

Managing Documents

It's crucially important—a basic requirement, in fact—to keep passport, visas, money and important documents safe from thieves, hidden in a device strapped around the waist, neck or leg, somewhere on the person, safely in a hotel room or hidden in the secret passages of an RV. Most foreign crime is simple theft, usually from vehicles or unattended luggage. Big cities in all countries are exceedingly dangerous in poorer neighborhoods, particularly in Brazil, Kenya, South Africa and Peru.

- ## Passport Security

Those who've lost a passport abroad will never do it again. Start out right by never losing a passport. I've never lost a passport or important document, probably because Mary takes excellent care of document security on the grounds that I'd lose my head if it weren't attached. I'm too busy scoping out photos, stories and new brands of beer to pay sufficient attention to passports and security.

We've met people who've lost a passport. The terrible tales of what they had to go through to get a passport replaced are grizzly. At a minimum, copy important documents, including credit cards. Keep the copies separate from the documents themselves. If any originals must be replaced the game is half won with a passport photocopy to show the embassy and the consul for the country issuing whatever visa must also be replaced, and other bureaucracies, including credit card companies

Passports for all countries must be good for six months from entry. We renew our passports every nine years so we don't cut this universal deadline too close. Plus we always request extra pages for new passports, which are free on application; forty-eight pages instead of twenty-four, a necessity for those traveling full time. Still, our forty-eight pages are filled with visas long before each nine-year renewal. Thus we've had to add passport pages in Riga, Latvia; Brunei; Vientiane, Laos; Bangkok, Mexico City and other capitals; a snap at most any American Embassy. Even when we were working and only traveling abroad a couple times a year our piddly-paged passports were stuffed full, long before ten years.

- ## Visa Protocols

Many African and several Asian countries require one or two passport-sized photos when applying for a visa. It's convenient to carry a dozen or so of these small pictures on every trip, better than scurrying last minute for visa photos. We usually order a dozen passport photos at a whack, outside the United States. Passport photos inside the States cost twelve dollars or more a pair. In Mexico and most third world countries passport photos cost about ten dollars for twenty-five.

Visas are issued to Americans and the citizens of most other developed countries at the border or upon landing at most airports. However, many countries require the issuance of a visa by their embassy in your country of residence. One such weird country is Eritrea, which promptly deported me when I showed up at the Asmara airport without a visa. This means the Internet must be searched for the visa requirements of every country to be visited, long before leaving the homeland. Up-to-date visa information can easily be found by entering *visa* and the name of the country. For Eritrean visa requirements Google *Eritrea visa*.

We flew to Hong Kong to begin our first trip to China because we'd heard three-month visas were available there. We should have applied for a visa through a Hong Kong travel agent, the only offices able or willing to procure three-month visas for China. Instead we dumbly applied at the Chinese government office, which only issues one month visas. We had to renew the one-month visas twice in China, an expensive and time-consuming proposition most everywhere. The single exception was Lijiang, out in the boondocks of Yunnan Province, where a renewal only took five minutes instead of the usual three days.

Advance visas are required for Vietnam, Cambodia and Myanmar, most easily obtained in Bangkok. Countries requiring an advance visa often issue them at its embassy or consulate in the home or neighboring country of departure. Pre-check all visa requirements on the Internet or you could also be deported from Eritrea.

- ## International Drivers' Licenses

Driving in most foreign countries requires an international driver's license available for ten dollars to members at any American Automobile Association office. Triple-A affiliates can be found in all developed countries. However, these licenses are valid for only one year. Those absent longer, like us, can take along an AAA application form and mail it with two passport photos a couple of months before the initial international driver's license expires. The new license's effective date can be designated to segue perfectly with the original license. Alternatively, when next in Bangkok, an international driver's license that looks authentic (I've never had it questioned by foreign cops) can be obtained on Khosan Road for $25, valid for ten years; heck of a deal.

Safety and Criminal Activity

What's the general safety situation abroad? Naturally it varies dramatically from region to region and within countries. As a rule of thumb almost any place in the world not actively engaged in war, or threatening war, is as safe as or safer than portions of most U.S. cities after dark. Contrary to common fears Americans are often safer outside the U.S. As Samuel Johnson said, *The use of traveling is to regulate imagination by reality, and instead of thinking how things may be, to see them as they are.*

Those who simply go are continually amazed at the inaccuracy of media hype about conditions in countries ranging from Israel and Mexico and continents from Africa to Asia.

• Safe in Asia

Almost any large city anywhere in the world is dangerous at night, though our experience would exclude cities in China and Southeast Asia, which seem uniformly safe. After an early morning train arrival we walked across Hanoi at three a.m. with never a qualm for safety, though many people were out and about. We've done similar early morning strolls through Bangkok and other Southeast Asian cities.

Safety conditions can change with the speed of a rocket as they did in September, 2001. This change was far from limited to the United States, generating a gross over-reaction worldwide. The murder of a single American tourist in Mexico screeches Mexican tourism to a halt for years, though a large American city such as New York City hosts a murder every single day.

• Theft versus Personal Threat

Our experience with safety abroad has been positive. Not once in the first ten years were we physically threatened, though there were moments of near doubt with the Serbian auto mechanic. During almost three years in Europe, North Africa and the Middle East, the RV was broken into only in Florence, Italy, a city notorious for thievery. The bikes suffered attempted molestation only in Sweden, twice, though most of the population of Morocco offered to buy them. Nothing was touched in China, where they shoot people who steal anything, or Southeast Asia, though we heard tales of theft in Thailand. Tourists seldom suffer violent crime in China or Southeast Asia.

Notwithstanding apocryphal stories circulated by the NRA Australia's bit of violent crime, when we were there, was committed with screwdrivers and syringes. I recall no violent crimes in New Zealand during six months there though the populace had grown restive when, just before our arrival, someone cut down an important tree in what was formerly *One Tree Park*. Mary says I blanked out the crime in New Zealand, which she says primarily consisted of vandalism and rowdiness associated with Maori alcoholism.

Kids stole two bicycle wheels in Mexico, the only untoward incident in two years of living on the sailboat and in an RV immediately south of the U.S. border. We know it was kids because I chased them away once and went back to sleep. They must have been frustrated at not being able to steal the bicycles too, poor little tykes.

• At Gunpoint in Buenos Aires

Theft abounds in the poorer countries of South America. Brazil is notorious for armed robbery in Sao Paulo and Rio. In our eleventh year of international RVing, while guests at a local city park, we were robbed at gunpoint in Buenos Aires. This was not an RV park because there are none in Buenos Aires or surrounds. Unfortunately the park placed the RV in a dark area instead of under a light, but then we should have known better. The armed robbers we encountered were extremely nervous and I never looked too closely at their guns to see if they were real. They took the only two objects of financial value, a laptop computer and digital camera, which I flew back to the States to replace.

We returned a few weeks later with the latest models. I could have replaced both in Buenos Aires but prefer Windows in English and the latest digital camera. Computers and digital cameras purchased outside the States are outrageously expensive because of high customs duties. Duty free exceptions include Dubai, UAE; Malaysia; Iqueque, Chile; and Singapore.

- ## State Department Hoaxes

The U.S. Department of State provides information on areas of the world it considers dangerous, plus visa, passport, health information and trip planning publications. Warnings do not include Buenos Aires. Call (202) 647-5225 or visit http://travel.state.gov/travel_warnings.html. We've found that almost all safety warnings, whether by government or rumor, are vastly overblown. But be careful in Buenos Aires, Rio, São Paulo and any big city, notwithstanding a lack of warning by anyone.

- ## Travel Hysteria

Travel hysteria was rampant while we traveled parts of Europe (Northern Ireland, Serbia), Asia (Israel, Myanmar and China) and Africa (Egypt, Nairobi and Johannesburg). We postponed a trip to Nepal and India in 2002 because Nepal was undergoing a Maoist revolution, though not particularly close to trekking areas. On a trip in 2003 we found Nepal packed with charming people and great hiking. However the Maoists fire-bombed a bus we had intended to take to the Annapurna trailhead, the day before we were scheduled to go, requiring an extra two days of hiking just to reach the start of the hike. A peace agreement was signed between the rebels and the Nepalese government in 2006.

India and Pakistan were threatening nuclear war in 2002, though denying it daily. Though the media portrayed it as a combat zone we found the Kashmir regions of both countries charming and safe in 2004. We skipped Columbia during two years in South America, except for flying to Cartagena from Caracas for a several gorgeous days in that fabulous colonial city, in 2007 sailing the entire Columbian coast from Venezuela.

Language Challenges

How the heck can anyone get around in a foreign country without knowing the language? The answer is, *relatively easily*. Mary speaks fluent Spanish while I can scrape by. I used to be fluent in German, but no more; however, I can still muddle through.

People in most countries, even China, speak English as a second language. In fact, more people speak English in China than in the United States. It's an excellent practice, however, to impress the locals and grease acceptance by learning ten words, at least, in the language of any country traveled for more than a few days. Speaking with a perfect accent is unimportant; it's only important to attempt the local patois on appropriate occasions, which the locals will greatly appreciate.

- ## Easy Tricks for Getting by in any Language

The few words needed in every language are: *please, thank you, hello, goodbye, good morning, how much, where is (whatever), beer* and *ice.* Someone else's list may vary slightly but learning these few words in the local tongue will win friends, soothe the local beasts, take anyone far and find most anything.

We've all played charades. This ability cultivates a talent for preservation. Or do as we did in Bulgaria when we'd almost run out of sugar and couldn't find it in a local store, taking in a sample and leaving with a bulk purchase.

There's usually someone anxious to practice English. The odds of this have seldom failed us. We've had escorts galore: Chinese finding the correct train and train station, Belgians finding a propane refill, Turks leading the way to a reasonable hotel, Aussies who simply stared and a Norwegian who called me a *foreign-born idiot*.

- ## The Portable International Translator

If these ways of communicating fail try the International Translator. It's easier and more effective to use than a computer translation program. The translator is a colorful hunk of plasticized cardboard with hundreds of pictures on front and back, folded into fourths. It costs less than five dollars from GAIA Communications in Alexandria, VA, (703) 370-5527, or email kwikpoint@his.com .

The card contains pictures of every conceivable object from planes, trains and automobiles to condoms, bathrooms, money exchange, all sized batteries, cosmetics, birth control pills, family relationships, computers, stationery supplies, entertainments, sports, foods, games, wines, eating out and everything anyone could possibly think of, including the part I like best—pictures of dark draft beer, dark bottled beer, light draft beer and light bottled beer. Point to the object of desire and anyone, anywhere in the world, will understand what's being asked for, guaranteed. We carry an International Translator but have only used it in China to order vegetables at restaurants. The card pictures twenty-four varieties of vegetables.

Don't worry about not speaking the local language. Anyone can usually cope with almost any situation.

Mail

How to get mail? Depending on friends or relatives to forward mail is a hassle for them and could lose someone a friend or inheritance. The alternative of a professional mail forwarding service likely exists in every state. When we signed up with our Florida service it was employed primarily by circumnavigating sailors, which we haven't been for eons. But it still takes our money and sends out mail upon request for fourteen dollars a month plus shipping costs. St. Brendan's Isle can be reached at sbi@boatmail.net or (800) 544-2132.

We order mail once a month and it's shipped anywhere in the world by UPS, FedEx, Airborne, DSL or whatever is most efficient and inexpensive to wherever we happen to be. It usually arrives three days after ordered by e-mail or phone. Only Israel and Canada have taken longer; the Christmas holidays anomalously delayed delivery in Israel, taking a week. Canadian customs delayed our mail over a month.

In Europe we'd call the target campground immediately before ordering mail, confirm its address and phone number, order the mail sent and check into the campground three days later. The mail was always waiting or arrived the next morning. The biggest expense was the express shipment of magazines. Because of the weight they cost a fortune to forward. Still, they provided an intimate link with *home*. We've gradually cut down from ten magazines to five. Because of magazines our mail forwarding usually cost between 50 and 90 dollars a month. In the States mail-forwarding is cheap, only a few dollars via USPS regular or Priority Mail.

Reading Material

Mary reads a heck of a lot of books, an average of three hundred a year. The hundred-dollars it cost to ship two huge boxes of books to Australia was well worth it because, similar to England, books were price protected, even used books. This meant they were exorbitantly expensive. We usually pay bargain prices at U.S. library book sales and take a huge batch on each trip.

- ## Used Books

Used books in England and Australia were expensive with two exceptions: thrift stores and Hay-on-Wye in England/Wales, the used book capital of the British Isles. The other most common place to find books was one-to-one exchange at many campgrounds and youth hostels all over the world. Otherwise, in non-English-speaking countries, it's difficult or expensive finding books in English; often, however, stopping by any hostel or guesthouse in many countries will provide lots of book for trade.

- ## English Language Newspapers

English-language newspapers exist everywhere except Central and South America, even in China, though the quality is often dreadful. Real news in China is as rare as transparency in government. The *Hong Kong South China Daily News* is an exception and is excellent, as is the *Singapore Times* and the *Bangkok Post*. Most European countries that aren't English speaking have a decent English-language newspaper available countrywide, including Turkey where we kept up on the NCAA sixty-four through Sweet Sixteen down to the Final Four.

In Commonwealth countries, such as South Africa, Australia and New Zealand, coverage of American sport is nonexistent, except for those who count soccer. But politics and everything else are there for a dollar a day. For news there's always the Internet, anywhere, anytime. Everyone's hometown newspaper is accessible online for an hourly rate of less than the newspaper costs back home.

Getting Plugged In

Being from one of the few 110-volt countries and traveling the world where plugs vary like the wind requires a converter from 220 to 110 volts for appliances such as hair dryers. Most laptop computers handle both currents. Buy a complete set of adapter plugs or a single universal plug for twenty dollars at Wal-Mart, a travel store or online.

Travelers outside the U.S. will learn to convert kilometers to miles, recasting distances into more familiar terms. It's easy to multiply the number of kilometers by .62, perhaps drop the .02, to get miles. Thus ten kilometers is 6.2 miles rounded off to six miles. Liters are 3.8 to the gallon, 454 grams to the pound and 1000 grams for an obvious kilogram. After a few months it'll be second nature, needed in every country outside the United States, which continues to march to its own drummer. The U.S. remains pretty much oblivious to the rest of the world, including the United Kingdom, from which the U.S. adopted miles, feet and pounds, and which changed to metric years ago.

Other Essentials

Other than books for the addicted reader what does anyone need for extended travel abroad? Other than clothes we needed a laptop, medicine, camera equipment, guidebooks, maps and essential documents. Missing favorite foods, the stuff we simply couldn't do without, was an early fear rapidly dispelled. For starters Wal-Mart and Sam's Clubs pepper Mexico, China and elsewhere. The large French and English grocery chains, Carrefour and Tesco, have opened many stores in China and Southeast Asia, and also the U.S. Every country outside the really backward ones, such as Myanmar, sells most anything and more. In Europe we initially missed Bigelow Teas in the little sealed packets but found English teas as good or better, and available most anywhere.

Foreign beers, to my taste buds, are generally better than American beers except U.S. microbrews and such as Anchor Steam and Samuel Adams. American mainstream beer tastes more like *water* after Victoria Bitter, the most popular beer in Australia. Less than two percent of Australians drink Foster's, which is essentially water and similar to American beers. What American beer could rival real Guinness on tap in Ireland?

- ## Delightful Food Abroad

Favorite foods anywhere are a matter of taste. The average traveler won't miss what's unavailable and will instead experience new epicurean delights, such as the most popular dish in Ecuador, cuyo, whole fried guinea pig. The list of great foods unavailable in the U.S. yet available abroad is nigh endless.

The tastiest blue cheese I've found was in the Pico de Europa area of Northwestern Spain. Don't miss Tajin, the famous savory meat pot of chicken or lamb in Morocco; delectable Moroccan spices are piled high in every local Kasbah. Spicy-roasted piri-piri chicken is a star in Portugal. Succulent French bread is available wherever the French colonized. Delectable cheeses exist the breadth of Europe. Chocolate is great in Belgium and Switzerland. Sample single malt scotch in Scotland, though it's less expensive anywhere else in the world. Guinness is great on draft in Ireland, *for your health*, better than Geritol. The rikjtafel is a gourmet feast of up to thirty imaginative samples, the idea imported by the Dutch from Indonesia. Try bratwurst in Germany and Wisconsin. Scandinavian smorgasbord offers more than a glutton could glom. Greece offers dozens of feta cheeses along with gyros. Italy features fabulous gelato, Chianti and fancy coffees. Most food and coffee in Turkey and Thailand are excellent. Don't miss the coffee in Vietnam, Chinese hotpot or Tibetan bobis. We loved Israeli falafels, Jordanian flatbread and seafood in every country with a coastline.

- ## Ubiquitous American Fast Food

The list of incredible food abroad is practically endless. Still, those hankering for McDonald's, Pizza Hut and KFC will find them in every country except parts of Africa and such as Myanmar. A combination KFC and Pizza Hut sits less than a hundred feet from the crumbling nose of the Sphinx in Egypt. McDonald's and other fast food outlets are society hang-outs, where the beautiful go to be seen in such as Turkey and many developing countries, including the Caribbean.

CHAPTER SEVENTEEN
Living on Investments, Taxes & Voting

"I am a great believer in luck, and I find the harder I work the more I have of it."
Stephen Butler Leacock

Segregating Now-Funds from Money Needed Later

Earning a relatively high rate of return from the stock market, real estate or business investing is not luck. Over the long haul the luck needed to make money in the market consists of paying attention and occasional hard work; nothing more or less. This initial hard work requires reading books on stock market and bond investing, readily available in any library.

- ### Taking on the Market

RVing the world practically forever requires a viable investment strategy. Investment return depends on the health of the market, varying enormously from year to year. But on average, over the long haul, diversified market investments have returned between eight and twelve percent a year, often averaging almost one percent a month.

If and when the market racks up returns approaching one percent a month anyone can travel full time indefinitely with a kitty of slightly over $250,000, which should yield about $2,000 a month. And that's without touching principal. This means when RVers hang up their spurs after exploring the world in depth for twenty or thirty years they could still have the entire principal left. Naturally, there are caveats, considerations, pitfalls, inflation and things to watch out for.

- ### The Rate of Return

The first pitfall is the market rate of return. During the 1980s and early 1990s, when we were furiously saving every penny toward early retirement, market returns averaged over twenty percent. Few markets stay this robust for years, much less a decade. The first few years of the new millennium were lousy, reaping negative returns in many sectors, but when averaged with the eighties and nineties the market still returned the historical average of almost one percent a month. Though the market took most of these gains back in 2008-March 2009, it then shot up 50% in the next 6 months. It apparently can't be timed.

However, anyone who pays attention to the market can tell when it's either tanking (so get out) or shooting up (get in). Though no one can precisely time these upheavals, anyone who pays attention can get the jist and take advantage of broad market or particular sector momentum.

- ### Short Term Money

Those RVing the world full time are necessarily retired and no longer working. Short-term capital—that needed for the first five years of travel—should be in investments with fewer vagaries than the stock market.

For safer investments over the short run of five years the market earns less than one percent a month. With conservative investments only stars rack up eight percent a year, 2/3 a percent per month. Over time no one can count on even six percent a year or half a percent a month. Much depends on the phase of the interest-versus-equity return in the market cycle. From 2000 to 2005 short term investments were lucky to get three or four percent a year, unless fully invested in energy, China and Latin America. For safety the overall size of a travel and retirement kitty must be increased because the return will halve for each running five-year period.

Short-term money for five years of travel should be in near-cash equivalents: CDs, treasuries, bonds and money market. Figuring on an annualized six percent, or an even lower return on a five-year running horizon, gives a cushion for those who do something careless or unlucky, or if the market falls behind its historical averages for more than a few years.

Kitty allocation can be calculated by dividing the number of years a nest egg must last into running five-year segments, keeping all but the immediate five years of funds invested in the stock market or other subjectively comfortable investments.

- **$260,000 Could Buy $2000 a Month Forever**

Those retiring at age forty-five need an early-retirement travel fund for twenty years, until a pension or social security kicks in, requiring approximately one third conservatively invested and the other two thirds in the stock market or similar. Sufficient funds should be transferred once or twice a year from the stock market to short-term investments. This will keep the conservative portion of the current five-year kitty intact.

For example, those drawing $2000 a month will need at least a $260,000 fund, setting aside $90,000 before taxes and keeping the $170,000 balance in the market. Of course these figures are rough guesstimates. Everyone must estimate the expected rate of return and assess their ability to handle investment volatility and risk. But be conservative dealing with money that can't easily be minted after retirement. Benjamin Franklin accurately gauged the value of money, including money earned before retirement, when it's not so difficult to replace: *If you would know the value of money, go and try to borrow some.*

Tax Implications

Drawing $2000 a month from tax-sheltered savings will incur federal taxes of about ten percent. On the other hand the amendments to the 2002 tax code required withholding of twenty percent, netting only $1600 month. Monthly budgets will suffer cramps though half the withheld money may eventually be returned. Because the tax code is amended yearly, sometimes radically, its amended impact must be re-researched yearly.

- **Mixing and Matching Tax Sheltered Funds**

Travel kitties can be mixed and matched, taking $700 a month from a tax-deferred plan and the balance from savings on which taxes have already been paid, structuring withdrawals so no federal income taxes are owed. Seven hundred dollars a month was the threshold for individual tax liability from 2002 to about 2008. Those traveling on $2000 a month could withdraw $1300 from funds on which taxes had already been paid, from a money market account, bank accounts, treasuries or certificates of deposit, taking the other $700 from tax-deferred savings. This $700 threshold will change, requiring confirmation of the threshold yearly when shaping plans for the future.

If the threshold continued two individuals filing separately could exempt $1540 a month from tax-deferred funds before they'd be liable for federal income taxes. Getting by on $2000 a month for two would require the withdrawal of an additional $460 a month from unsheltered funds, incurring little federal income tax liability. The details of individual circumstances are endless and should be carefully analyzed on the *life events planner* of TurboTax, or similar software program. And don't forget to calculate state tax liability.

- ## State Tax Liability

Those traveling the world fulltime will likely be subject to few taxes other than state and federal income taxes. But each individual's tax situation takes in-depth planning far beyond the scope of this modest tome.

Sheltered income is taxed in the state where earned though the employee no longer lives there and, in fact, lives nowhere in particular, off RVing the wilds of Borneo for years on end. Before deep-sixing the boss we researched which states were most advantageous for residency, examining those without an income tax. We'd hoped to avoid paying for services we'd never use, or need, while traveling abroad. But there were two insurmountable problems.

We settled on Florida for a mail forwarding address because Florida had no income tax. However, this was irrelevant because a large part of the money we'd saved for travel had been accumulated in a 401(k) plan through the State of Arizona. Neither state nor federal income taxes are levied on 401(k) funds until withdrawn, thus the fund grew tax free during years of savings and employment.

Once we began drawing funds Arizona income tax kicked in though we no longer lived in Arizona. In one way we were lucky. We hadn't realized that Florida, in lieu of an income tax, levied a tax on stocks, mutual funds and similar intangibles. Florida's Department of Revenue sent a notice ordering our payment of intangible taxes in 1994. We laughed out loud because the previous week the Florida Department of Elections had sent a notice stating we were ineligible to vote in Florida because we weren't legal residents. The Elections Department concluded, based on an Attorney General's opinion, that because we had only a mail forwarding address we weren't bona fide residents of Florida. We sent the Florida Department of Revenue a copy of the Florida Attorney General's opinion and have heard from neither since.

Voting?

Being residents of nowhere has prevented voting since early retirement. We've tried to vote by registration through overseas embassies but U.S. Embassies, no matter in which country, only help citizens obtain extra pages for a bulging passport. They otherwise primarily exist to process applications by locals for a U.S. visa. We've personally experienced this ambassadorial attitude in Riga, Latvia; Copenhagen and Sydney, Australia. However the U.S. Embassy in Sana'a, Yemen, was extremely helpful in facilitating an Eritrean Visa from the Consul for Eritrea. But they were too late; I'd already been deported from Eritrea.

A U.S. Embassy can be depended on in no circumstances whatsoever beyond obtaining additional passport pages. We've tried to vote online without luck, perhaps because our permanent stateside address is only for mail forwarding.

CHAPTER EIGHTEEN
Save a Mint on Airfare

If God had really intended men to fly, he'd make it easier to get t[hr]o[ugh] the airport. George Winters [as amended]

Remember Mary writing this down: *you have to get yourself and your RV to the part of the world targeted next*. Save a chunk of change by shopping for airfare on the Internet. The Internet doesn't always come up with the cheapest airline tickets, only usually, and it improves daily.

Internet Deals on Airfare

Several excellent Internet sites e-mail weekly airfare specials, including many airlines. They include last-minute fares that are often in mere double digits. We've found fares from Miami to South America on LanChile for $200 one-way and roundtrip for less than $300.

Many airlines offer last-minute specials on their Web sites, typically published on Tuesdays and Wednesdays. Promotional fares are often posted in the middle of the night; check early in the morning for the best chance of getting cheap seats. Sign up to receive the *special airfare* newsletter emailed weekly by favorite carriers. Weekly specials are often amazingly cheap, featuring dozens of destinations.

Last-minute Internet fares can save hundreds of dollars. Those who can stand waiting until the last minute to know exactly which airline they're flying can search for *last minute travel*, which is often deeply discounted. Staying flexible when leaving and returning will also unearth better fares. For last minute travel see http://smartertravel.com and for last-minute international travel, www.lowestravel.com.

- ### Amortizing Airfare

Traveling continuously saves money by amortizing expensive airfare over a long period of time. Most people wouldn't fly to Australia for a two-week vacation because, unless they could find a last minute deal, it'd cost $1500 for airfare alone. However, specials to down-under can almost halve this cost, such as our 2009-2010 roundtrip tickets to New Zealand for $830.

For those who decide to *do* Australia it'll take a year to see halfway properly. A $1500 airfare amortized over a year works out to less than five dollars a day. The principle downside is that all airline tickets are limited to a year. Those wishing to stay longer will forfeit the return flight.

One-Way Tickets

We buy one-way tickets when we're off for more than a year because no airline ticket is good for longer. Airlines selling one-way flights often charge little less than for a round-trip ticket. Somehow airlines have never gotten a handle on basic economics but this is gradually changing. Concentrated Internet searches will often turn up reasonable one-way airfares but they're still a bear to find.

- ### Ongoing Ticket Requirements

Watch one pitfall when buying a one-way ticket. Most countries purport to require ongoing tickets before they'll issue a visa. Fortunately, the requirement is often observed in the breach, particularly in South America. However, many airlines enforce the requirement because the alternative is a government fine for allowing a passenger to board an international flight without an onward or return ticket. An exception is Yemeni Airlines, which let me travel to Eritrea, where I was deported for arriving without a pre-issued visa; I'd been assured visas were available on arrival. Yemeni Airlines charged over $300 for my one hour deportation/return flight. Those who can avoid it should never fly Yemeni or Aeroflot Airlines.

- ## Evading the Ongoing Ticket Requirement

To make certain we'd be allowed to board a flight to Quito, Ecuador we bought a refundable ticket from Quito to Lima, which we cashed in after Ecuadorian visas were issued. We were required to show ongoing tickets when boarding a flight from Bangkok to Singapore; fortunately, we had tickets for an eventual return to Los Angeles. Otherwise, we couldn't have boarded a one-way flight to Singapore, notwithstanding that anyone can easily buy a one-way bus ticket to Singapore from anywhere in peninsular Malaysia. These countries hate illegal aliens sucking off their welfare systems or competing with locals for jobs, notwithstanding that most countries outside Europe have piddly welfare systems and offer jobs few would want to fill. An open return or fully refundable ticket is more expensive and will require some time, effort and cost to cash in, but it overcomes the ongoing-air-ticket requirement

The no-boarding-without-an-onward-ticket requirement can always be evaded, such as we did flying Buenos Aires—Phoenix—Buenos Aires. When Phoenix wouldn't let us board without an onward ticket from Buenos Aires we bought the cheapest fully refundable ticket on the same airline from Buenos Aires to Montevideo, Uruguay and cashed it in at the airline's desk minutes after landing in Buenos Aires. A return or onward ticket is always needed when traveling to French Polynesia.

Courier Flights

Courier sites provide the cheapest air travel, as little as ten percent of normal fares. However they severely limit the amount of luggage, theoretically allow little layover time and fly only between a few world cities. Couriers companies also exact a yearly membership fee to become eligible for their cheap flights. However, with the low cost of courier flights luggage could be shipped over separately and still save a bundle, forfeiting the return flight to stay as long as desired. But this strategy could cause the courier to dispense with your services.

Around-the-World and Pacific Rim Tickets

Other sources of cheap airfare include around-the-world and Pacific Rim tickets, their prices based on the number of stops, providing an essentially open ticket good for a year. We've used Pacific Rim tickets with excellent results. One such ticket from Los Angeles to Tokyo, Hong Kong, Bangkok, Honolulu and back to Los Angeles, over eight months in 2001, cost $930. Generally for around the world and Pacific Rim airfare see http://airtreks.com, www.aroundtheworldairfare.com, www.around-the-world.com and http://airbrokers.com.

Around-the-world and long-haul roundtrip tickets are cheaper when bought in less expensive countries, such as Australia, New Zealand and Thailand, before the dollar plunged. An acquaintance who travels to Southeast Asia every year purchased a one-way ticket to Bangkok. Upon arrival he bought an open-ended, round-trip ticket to Oregon for half the cost of the same round-trip ticket in the States, returning to Bangkok on the other half the next year, *ad infinitim*. Research the Internet and easily improve on these modest suggestions.

Travel in Low Season

Flying to destinations in their low season saves money though some might suggest that low season means bad weather. But that's not necessarily true. Low season is only bad weather in Europe. Australia and Asia, for example, are so large that toothsome weather can be found any time of the year.

- ## Low Season Examples

Low season is often, though not always, the rainy season in Southeast Asia. We don't hesitate to travel to Southeast Asia in the rainy season when it's cooler and rain is a brief refresher every afternoon for a single hour.

Chartering a sailboat for two weeks in the Caribbean during low season, also called hurricane season, costs the same as one week in high season. We had no hurricanes in the neighborhood during five charters over ten years, always chartering in mid- to late summer, never later than September when hurricanes, back then, began in earnest. With global warming hurricane season can begin in July or before. Ignoring the occasional hurricane, Caribbean weather is the same year round, warm or barely warmer, while the trade winds blow an average of fifteen knots, perfect for sailing and keeping cool. Low season is often a good time to fly, especially for ski bums, to take advantage of bargain basement fares.

Frequent Flyer Miles and Credit Cards

Those flying relatively often should tally frequent flyer miles. We earn a free trip every few years to wherever we're off to next. The fiscally responsible majority, who pay off credit cards in full every month, never incurring exorbitant interest charges, should consider a card that provides free frequent flyer miles, a mile or two for each dollar *charged*. Buy everything with the card, including groceries and gasoline. Just make certain it's paid off in full every month or it'll cost a fortune in interest, which with penalties can run well over three percent a month. Also, shop around for the right card because most earning frequent flyer miles charge yearly fees ranging up to seventy-five dollars. Unless the card is used perpetually while religiously paying it off monthly it may not be worth the yearly charge.

Trip Insurance

I wouldn't buy trip insurance unless I envisioned the possibility of a trip cancellation due to such as weather or health. After 9/11 trip insurance rates rose over ten percent, making it extremely expensive compared to the risk insured, which ranges between five and seven percent of a plane ticket or tour. Those with an elderly parent on the cusp of disaster may foresee the possibility of cancellation based on health. Those insisting on trip insurance should buy from an insurance company instead of a travel agent. A trip insurance policy for six months can cost as little as $75. Check rates and compare policies on the Internet. See sites such as http://travelguard.com, http://alltripinsurance.com and http://www.csatravelprotection.com, The prices are outrageous for the level of risk insured against. Policies and costs can be compared at http://insuremytrip.com and http://tripinsurancestore.com. The cost for the risk covered by trip insurance describes obscenity better than the Supreme Court knowing it when it sees it.

CHAPTER NINETEEN
Outfox Banks and Credit Card Companies

Education is what you get when you read the fine print; experience is what you get when you don't.
Pete Seeger

Banks and Credit Unions

Banks and bank look-alikes can be annoying or exorbitantly expensive for those RVing the world. Credit unions charge less than banks for services and loans of all kinds, often waiving fees for checking accounts. Most banks charge up to a hundred dollars a year for a checking account not maintaining an astronomical balance. Few banks offer checking accounts without a monthly fee and many slap an exorbitant surcharge on customers dropping a dollar below the minimum balance. A credit union may be the best overall bet because, among other things, most charge nothing for ATM withdrawals; banks charge up to $3.50 for each and every one.

Most banks levy an ATM charge when customers withdraw money from their accounts abroad. No one's hometown bank maintains ATMs in other countries except for those with accounts at such as Citibank and HSBC. Banks love to double dip ATM fees, charging at least $1.50 for each transaction while some ATMs tack on another fee approaching $3.50, up to $5 next week.

- ### Using Foreign ATMs

Foreign ATM fees vary, most without fees while others charge up to two dollars; many in the States charge up to three dollars and fifty cents. A credit union's often low daily limit may require four ATM withdrawals costing up to ten dollars in ATM fees. It may be less expensive to maintain a bank account, which often allows up to $500 per withdrawal, saving money overall. The bottom line for using foreign ATMs is to make the fewest monthly withdrawals possible. On the other hand we never liked to tote a lot of cash in countries with high inflation. A vast daypack was required to carry $100 worth of Laotian or Zimbabwean currency.

- ### Direct Deposit: A Necessity

The direct deposit of travel funds from savings, mutual funds or daddy's annuity enables RVing the world. If funds were instead mailed to the recipient abroad, who then mailed them to a financial institution back in the States, the money would become available far too late, especially if carried by camel caravan for 52 days from Timbuktu. A deposit mailed to a bank or credit union would be received long after the depositor had slimmed down considerably. RVing the world requires the direct deposit of all funds.

Bank Interest

The interest paid on savings accounts varies from black to white. Credit unions aren't much better than banks for paying a reasonable interest rate, which can always be improved upon by shopping around. The business pages of many large newspapers list the best rates for savings accounts and certificates of deposit. CDs pay more interest than a regular savings account, but impose a penalty, usually all interest accrued, if funds are withdrawn before term. For a near cash equivalent high-grade corporate bonds held to maturity or U.S. Savings Bonds may be better. We always shop around for the best place to park money.

Two Credit Cards Needed Abroad

Because most credit cards charge an annual fee its better to pare the number down to a maximum of two—one Visa and one MasterCard for convenient ATMing anywhere in the world. *The Millionaire Next Door* reported that millionaires have no more than a single Visa and MasterCard, plus perhaps a Sears' card. We confess to a single Visa credit card and a Visa debit card.

We always look for cards with the lowest annual percentage rate while watching the small print. Many offer an initially low annual percentage rate but double or triple it if a minimum payment is missed, or after a set period of time. Many credit cards entice with a *mere* twelve percent introductory interest rate; if a payment is one day late the rate may jump to twenty percent or more. The post office wouldn't inadvertently deliver a payment a day late; of course not, especially from abroad.

- ## Credit Card Caveats

Using a *credit* card to obtain currency abroad can be expensive. Those who know how much they're going to charge each month and religiously prepay that amount another month in advance may still end up with unanticipated charges for interest and penalties when traveling abroad full time. A modicum of efficiency requires either a long-suffering and highly responsible friend or relative to forward mail, or a mail-forwarding service. In either event the credit card statement will always arrive after its due date. A check mailed the same day a credit card statement is received abroad will fail to reach any U.S. credit card company before interest and penalty charges have ballooned. Many credit card companies discourage pre-payment, automatically remitting credit balances by check and destroying the possibility of advance financial planning. The best solution is to ATM only with a debit card and arrange for credit cards purchases (never obtaining cash advances) to be paid automatically out of checking or savings accounts.

Even these precautions won't solve the problem of using a credit card at a foreign ATM, which constitutes a cash advance. Exorbitant credit-card interest begins accruing the second the card is used, sky-rocketing the cost of obtaining local currency abroad. By the time the due date for the credit card rolls around, even if the payment is automatically made from a checking account, outrageous interest charges will have accrued.

Only those with online credit-card-paying capabilities should even consider obtaining a cash advance. Using an online bill payer within a few hours of making a cash advance charge may avoid the accrual of interest. The efficacy of this possibility should be tested before leaving home. Paying off a credit card online means finding an Internet terminal after obtaining each cash advance, a chore for those who might rather be off sightseeing. The simple and easiest rule is never use a credit card to obtain local currency abroad. Never bring travelers' checks or home currency for the bulk of expenses, except in Venezuela where ATMs dispense money at a very low exchange rate while black market rates for exchanging dollars with most merchants will net three times the official exchange rate. Always and only use a debit card to obtain cash, a hair-pulling experience in Brazil.

Debit Cards and Travelers Checks

The only good card is a debit card, which requires living within the means of a checking account. Debit cards, Visa more widely accepted than MasterCard, are a boon to international travelers because almost all countries offer a multitude of ATMs affiliated with the Cirrus and Plus networks. These allow the downloading of local currency at international exchange rates, transactions processed through large international banks, which exchange foreign currencies at the world's best rates. This is the rate received when withdrawing local cash with a debit card, whether Visa or MasterCard. Unfortunately, Visa and MasterCard have recently tapped into another source of revenue, tacking on a one percent conversion fee for the withdrawal of foreign currency.

- ## ATM Costs versus Traveler's Checks

Never buy travelers' checks or exchange currencies if it can be avoided. Banks and exchange shysters charge a *minimum* of three percent to cash a travelers' check or change dollars, Euros or yen into local currency. Saving between three and six percent of a budget means those living on $2000 a month, or $24,000 a year, will save between $720 and $1440 a year using a debit card to withdraw local currency. Adding together the fees charged by the bank back home and the ATM bank will total between three and five dollars for each transaction. Limiting withdrawals to $500 four times a month will cost between $144 and $240 a year in ATM fees, substantially less than the $720 minimum it'd cost to exchange travelers' checks or currency. The $720 figure is a likely minimum.

Most currency exchanges and travelers' checks cashing facilities claim to charge no commission. Instead they apply a rate that averages five percent and up. Only those who can do the math in their head or carry a calculator will realize how much it costs to exchange currency or cash travelers' checks: uniformly exorbitant.

Never ever carry traveler's checks. These prehistoric dinosaurs will cost a fortune compared to ATM withdrawals. In addition, travelers' checks are horrendously difficult to cash, anywhere, anytime. In most towns only a single bank will convert travelers checks and then only reluctantly after the holder has waited in a very long line. Secondly, banks charge a five percent commission, or more, for the privilege of *never leaving home without travelers checks*. Compare the typical ATM fee, which costs half a percent on transactions of $500 or more, plus one percent gravy for Visa or MasterCard.

Beginning in 2005, banks, debit and credit card companies began charging one percent to obtain local currency from ATMs in Batavia, Bangkok, Buenos Aires and everywhere other than from their own ATMs. Until a hotshot class-action lawyer goes after these vultures this additional fee will permanently burden all travel budgets. Thus the relative value of using plastic has dropped, except for the convenience of not having to carry large wads of currency. Still, the value of international exchange rates, won through the use of foreign ATMs, has only been reduced by one percent; the cost of cashing travelers' checks has risen to seven percent in some countries.

- ## Cash Advances in Lieu of ATMs

Few countries are without ATMs—Tibet comes to mind—but even in this single remote instance cash advances can be obtained inside Tibetan banks. Some countries will only allow dribbles to be withdrawn from ATMs, such as Indonesia. But go inside an Indonesian bank and get a whopping cash advance of up to $2500, for a disbursement fee of three dollars.

Most foreign banks charge nothing for a cash advance on a debit card, not even the equivalent of an ATM fee. Thus obtaining a cash advance inside a bank is often cheaper than using an ATM. However, a few banks charge a cash withdrawal fee of up to three percent. For example, banks in Phnom Penh, Cambodia advance U.S. dollars, the preferred local currency, for one percent, while the same bank charges two percent in Siem Reap, Cambodia, at the site of Angkor Wat. In the far western boondocks of Kashgar, China, and in Tibet, which have no ATMs, the withdrawal fee was three percent.

- **Cash Advance Traps**

The only countries where we've had difficulty obtaining local funds on a credit or debit card (excluding Serbia during the U.S. embargo) were Brazil and Ethiopia. Brazilian ATMs claimed to be part of the international Cirrus and Plus systems but they weren't. When in Brazil skip the ATM machine and go directly to the bank manager to arrange a cash advance. Anyone of lesser status is a complete waste of time. A further difficulty in Brazil is a credit limit of $200 for each daily transaction, imposed to discourage the kidnapping of those who too readily flash plastic.

Several countries in Africa, such as Ethiopia, had no ATMs; one was finally installed at the Hilton in Addis Ababa. The best way to get around in Ethiopia (and to avoid the official low exchange rate in Venezuela) was to carry a sheaf of greenbacks, the amount necessary to pay for the time spent in either country. Before going to Africa research ATM availability in detail, for every country on the itinerary.

CHAPTER TWENTY
Staying Healthy When Traveling Abroad

It's so beautifully arranged on the plate - you know someone's fingers have been all over it. Julia Childs

Health abroad is a complicated subject easily resolved with little expense and large common sense.

Potable Water

The tap water in most countries isn't potable, except in most of the United States, Europe, Australia, Singapore, New Zealand, much of Malaysia and parts of South Africa. Potable water in Europe excludes southern Italy where containers must be filled at natural springs alongside the locals, or purchased. When in doubt buy water. It's usually inexpensive compared to the wages of upchucking and lying low for a week or so until able to again face the world.

Install a water filtration system in any RV, camper van, camping car or whatever it's called where acquired, removing the bad stuff including giardia and bleach. We've used a filter-equipped (.01 microns) RV to deal with cholera areas in Mexico and Central American. Add bleach or iodine to the water tank and revel in safe water with no taste of iodine or chlorine. Finally Mary can drink the water in Wyoming and South Dakota. The only adulterant a .01-micron filtration system can't remove is salt. On *Grendel I* a water maker made perfectly pure water from saltwater. It's easier and cheaper to buy water.

Those lacking a sophisticated filtration, reverse osmosis or water-maker system can always buy bottled water to drink and to wash vegetables. It may seem expensive in some countries but an alternative is hepatitis A, which may impose six weeks of agony, a singularly unpleasant experience.

Eating Out

Food is an important part of a balanced diet. Fran Lebowitz

Sidewalk vendors may be safer than restaurants. At street-side kiosks food preparation can be watched with an eagle eye, as opposed to dining at Maxim's where food is slapped together in absolute secrecy. In Turkey and Malaysia the diner is invited into the kitchen, encouraged to point at which dish looks good and it instantly appears on a plate. But the best bet is to buy from local markets or supermarkets and fix it personally. This assumes cooking skills have progressed beyond an ability to open cans; oh, yes, and that nutrition is a known subject, detailed in the last chapters.

Beyond carefully choosing restaurants beware of knives used to cut the fruit for sale in exotic locations. The knives are often rinsed in filthy water or not washed at all, harboring bacteria climbing over the backs of each other to attack the digestive tract. Mary has gotten sick in this fashion, in the boondocks of Costa Rica.

Skeeters

The world's most dangerous predators aren't the gangs of New York, hippos or humans. They're Skeeters carrying anything from malaria to dengue fever, both common in the tropics. Before traveling between the Tropics of Cancer and Capricorn in Africa, Central, South America and Asia, consult a travel doctor, the Centers for Disease Control or IAMAT, the International Association for Medical Advice to Travelers. Or check with all three for currently recommended preventatives. Eons ago the Chinese discovered a natural wormwood derivative for the complete prevention of malaria and are tardily sharing it with the world. The FDA may approve it in twenty years or so.

The most effective preventative against malaria, dengue fever and other mosquito-borne diseases is a combination of insect repellant and clothing. I prefer herbal repellants such as Repel's lemon eucalyptus; love the smell. Mary hates the smell, instead depending on deet-laden repellants, which I dislike. Use whatever works to avoid malaria and dengue fever. Both can be extremely debilitating.

Proper Clothing Protects

The other excellent preventative is nylon clothing with long sleeves and long pants sold by Columbia, North Face and other brands available at REI and similar stores, all made in China. Those headed to China or Southeast Asia can find fifteen-dollar shirts or pants that cost between thirty-five and seventy-five dollars in the States. Nylon is easily washed by hand, durable and dries in a few hours, even in countries with one hundred percent humidity. We take four outfits each wherever we travel, becoming instantly recognizable from a distance. Most people hide their mirth well, diplomatically, though behind palsied hands.

Nylon is cool. Though worn with long sleeves and long pants it's no warmer than shorts and T-shirts, which provide neither sun nor insect protection. Those opting for fashion and clothes of brevity in lands of warmth and one hundred percent humidity should carry vats of insect repellant and 50 SPF sunscreen. We try not to forget sunscreen near the poles where the sun's intensity may be hidden by chill and breeze.

• Hand Laundry

Hand launderers will find cotton difficult to dry in countries with high humidity. Denim, which is elephant-weight cotton, is as slow to dry as the ocean. Plus who can wring it worth a darn?

Inexpensive laundries are available in most of the world outside Europe and Japan where you must resort to hand laundry or pay dry-cleaners' prices. In France it cost twenty dollars to do two loads, way back in 1995. In 2006 Malta it cost $22 for a single load, down to $18 in Corsica. Thus hand-wash may be you, the same as it was us. Use the Steinbeck method described in *Travels with Charlie.* Toss the laundry into a bucket half-filled with water in the shower or bathroom of the RV. The jouncing from driving down the road will wash clothes cleaner than a Maytag.

CHAPTER TWENTY ONE
The Dratted Problem of Healthcare Abroad, Isn't

The single major pitfall of traveling the world is the relative unavailability of American health insurance at a reasonable price. Insurance companies are captives to medical costs, which vary little within a geographical area. There's no real competition within the medical profession or among health insurance companies, particularly in foreign countries. The good news is that American health insurance is unnecessary for most people who choose to RV the world.

Proper Chow and Working Out

> *Vegetables are a must on a diet. I suggest carrot cake, zucchini bread, and pumpkin pie.* Jim Davis, *Garfield*

Of course the best health insurance is illness prevention, achieved by a modicum of discipline, healthy diet and regular exercise—the things we like least. Those who only covet a healthy lifestyle instead of actually eating the food pyramid and exercising will always need comprehensive health insurance. The number of diabetics and those hopelessly obese is increasing in direct proportion to the fattening of America and worldwide.

Way back in 2002 we were completely taken aback when landing in Hawaii after months in China and Southeast Asia. The indigenous Hawaiians are big people but the non-indigenous were no better. Then we found the same percentage of fatties on the mainland. It was a shock after svelte Asians.

• The American Unwellness Epidemic

Obesity is the number two cause of preventable death in the United States, after smoking. According to the CDC we can't blame it on bad genes. Being overweight is caused by lack of activity, which is laziness, poor diet (further laziness) and overeating, which is compulsiveness. Studies have found that a lower intake of food, at least in rats, lengthens their average lifespan by forty percent. Still, the advice to eat less appears to apply to human and nonhuman alike.

Nutritionists suggest we serve smaller portions, jettison the TV, walk or bike instead of driving and don't make the kids clean up their plates—as if most of us could actually pull this off, except the very last part. The solution is to RV the world. Back home with hectic lives we're often too busy or tired to follow good advice, instead spending a fortune on health insurance and dying early. As anonymous said, *Eat right, exercise regularly and die anyway.*

When Mary was diagnosed with hereditary high cholesterol her internist said, *we're not meant to shop at Safeway. We evolved as hunters and gatherers, not as consumers of saturated fat.* She can do nothing about her cholesterol except take dubious drugs and exercise regularly. Her level of exercise and diet is in the top one percent of the population. She can skip the drugs because her good cholesterol is sufficiently high to cancel out the bad cholesterol, a result of exercise and diet.

Handling Health Care Abroad

To preserve the sloth of the American majority we've fabricated the most expensive health care system in the world, spending far more per capita than European countries with socialized medicine. We *crave* health insurance because our most common and serious diseases are traceable to lifestyle—smoking, excessive alcohol consumption, inactivity and the gobbling of fat. The other causes of premature death are relatively minor, such as auto accidents.

Most obtain health insurance through employers as a *benefit* for which employers and employees pay dearly. We pay out the wazoo because doctors and health specialists are the most highly compensated in the world. Meanwhile we're among the least conscious about the basics of nutrition.

Mary's doctor charged $187 for the nine-minute recital, over twenty dollars a minute. In no other country on earth would the charge have been more than a fifth this amount. Perhaps the pronouncement on Safeway, hunters and gatherers was worth the additional $150. It could be worth far more than $150 for those whose eating and exercise habits, as a result of this advice, executed an about face.

- ## Unhealthy Travelers' Solutions

When we were working, back in the misty fogs of time, health insurance cost almost nothing, about twenty dollars a month. Without an employer there's no reasonably priced market or leverage to obtain health insurance. Family health insurance through other than an employer may cost $800 a month and up, sometimes way up. We had no health insurance for fifteen years after early retirement. At the lower figure of $800 a month we saved over $200,000, factoring in modest interest earnings.

I qualify for Veteran's Administration health-care, scheduling a V.A. physical every year or so when briefly in the States. But I'm better served by periodic trips through Bangkok. More later about the excellent and inexpensive health care available in Bangkok and worldwide. Mary pays cash for medical expenses, a yearly amount outside the United States that's the tiniest fraction of what she'd have to pay for health insurance.

Health insurance and care in all countries outside the United States is relatively inexpensive and in most countries, of equal quality. No U.S. health insurance policy covers care outside the country. At best it may provide reimbursement. Those unable to pursue a healthy diet and regular exercise will spend more for health insurance than the cost of as-needed health care outside the United States. They should either reconsider fulltime international travel, increase the travel budget by several hundred dollars a month to pay for health care reimbursement or pay up to $800 a month for medical insurance, periodically adding ten percent to costs seemingly governed by yearly hyper-inflation.

Poor health insurance with large deductibles was historically available for $1.25 a day. Trip insurance will fly the insured home in case of a medical emergency. For $139 Traveler's Emergency Network in 2009 would provide evacuation and other health services abroad for those up to age 59, the price of which will likely increase yearly. See www.tenweb.com and www.alltripinsurance.com. Research alternatives at sites easily found on the Internet, such as full medical coverage for seven percent of the some tour costs. Unfortunately, health plans unilaterally alter benefits and prices almost monthly. Those RVing the world must perform their own research for health insurance and alternatives.

The Quality of Health Care Abroad

In case of a medical emergency the United States is one of the last places I'd opt to be evacuated to. Why pay exorbitant U.S. health care prices to obtain mediocre health care? I'd rather fly to Bangkok, New Zealand or a dozen other locations with reasonable health care costs and excellent quality care. A visit to a Kiwi doctor cost fourteen dollars in 2001. Hospitalization in New Zealand doesn't cost multi-hundreds of dollars a day and care quality is equal to that in the States where doctors and hospitals charge five to a hundred times as much.

Many Americans combine a Southeast Asia tour with medical tourism, fixing up medical needs at Bumrungrad Hospital in Bangkok, a luxurious experience where a private room, board, doctors, tests and meds cost less than $250 a day, prices between one fifth and one twentieth of stateside prices. A hospital admittance form in the States couldn't be signed for $250. Pay for the flight to Bangkok or Auckland and back, plus all medical costs, for a fraction of medical treatment costs in the United States.

- ## Bangkok's Bumrungrad Hospital

Bangkok's Bumrungrad Hospital doesn't operate out of a rice paddy. It's one of the top hospitals in the world with a standard of care substantially above that of most European and American hospitals. It enjoys International accreditation by the U.S.-based Joint Commission on International Accreditation. In 2009 the simplest private room cost $120 a night, boasting a contemporary couch and coffee table, hotel-like toiletries in the bathroom, Internet plug-in for a laptop, plus cable TV with CNN, BBC and other English-language stations. The in-house restaurants included fancy Japanese, succulent Thai, scrumptious-looking Italian and French Au Bon Pain, or order a Big Mac at McDonalds. Except for the last choice these restaurants offer the best food available in any hospital anywhere. No wonder Americans and Europeans are the hospital's happiest and most loyal customers, and many patients come from the wealthy sheikdoms of the Middle East.

- ## My Bumrungrad Experiences

Upon first arrival at Bumrungrad's entrance valets were busy parking cars. I walked gingerly past stainless steel columns and a Starbucks, into the two-story vaulted reception area that looked like a Five-Star Hotel. A smiling Thai woman *wai-ed*, bowing with hands folded, and asked, *Do you have an appointment today? I'm here to help you.* Very unhospital-like. This is the Land of Smiles, the usual and inimitable Thai hospitality in perfect English.

I blinked. This was a hospital? It was like none I'd ever seen. I'd heard about Bumrungrad but harboring a First World bias I had to see it to believe it. By 2005 four hundred thousand tourists from 154 countries fixed up their yearly medical needs at Bumrungrad Hospital, avoiding terrible U.S. hospital bills and European queues. But the very best part was the attitude and the caring, as if I were an actual human being instead of an insurance statistic. When was the last time a hospital seemingly cared about anything other than insurance coverage? It could be that how a hospital, physician or nurse makes the patient feel has some relationship to ultimate health. If there's any effect whatsoever then Bumrungrad is the world's best, bar none.

My lovely greeter led the way to the proper floor where I was handed to a pair of equally congenial Thais for initial registration. In minutes I was given to a smiling Thai girl who accompanied me to an initial examination for a routine physical, which was anything but the routine I'd experienced for umpteen years in American hospitals.

When a Stateside friend learned I was getting my annual physical examinations at Bumrungrad Hospital, he wrote me the following email in 2007:

I'm glad that you are checking into Bumrungrad. You'll get a much better physical than you might get here. Very few doctors in my area even give physicals anymore. Instead, you tell them what you think you have, they deny it and then prescribe a very potent drug for whatever it is you don't have. And it's getting worse. The new Medicaid scheme introduced by the Bush Administration is supposed to pay for prescription drugs provided that you can find a provider. When you go looking for one, you discover that it involves joining the provider's HMO, going to their doctors, giving up your old doctors, and subscribing to three magazines you don't want. The entire program is being run by the insurance and drug companies. The Medicare Office of the Federal Government is not involved. So far, the whole thing is a rude bust, especially for the poor it is supposed to help.

A friendly Thai took me every step of the way, from blood and other tests through EKG, X-ray and advanced ultra-sound for an upper GI analysis. Less than two hours after I'd walked into the lobby I was meeting with my primary-care physician to review the results of a fifteen page computer print-out and lab analysis, handsomely bound for leisurely perusal. Total cost, including a teeth cleaning, $125. It was hard to believe Bumrungrad was under American management

Chuck Impersonal American Healthcare

When feeling surly, queasy or due for an annual physical, take a break like I do and fly to Bangkok or any of the world's premier hospitals in Malaysia, Singapore or India. Bumrungrad's world-magnet hospital will graduate anyone from a bad run into the pink of health, inexpensively in the style of a Five Star Hotel. Fly to Bangkok for less than a thousand dollars from Europe or the United States. Hong Kong based Cathay Pacific Airlines offers thirty-day roundtrip excursions from the U.S. to anywhere it flies, including Bangkok, for $999. Similar or cheaper fares are available from Europe, especially through London Bucket Shops. Google *Bangkok Airfare* and be overwhelmed with inexpensive fares.

For more information on Bumrungrad Hospital see Bumrungrad's multi-lingual interactive website, www.Bumrungrad.com. Appointments can be made by email at appointment@bumrungrad.com, or information obtained on any clinic or procedure including costs at info@bumrungrad.com. The hospital promptly responds to queries on procedures and costs and its website contains voluminous information.

Top level Blue Cross health insurance in Thailand costs about $1000 a year, less than $100 a month, covering most medical costs with little deductible. But at Bumrungrad Hospital any First-Worlder can afford world-class health care for practically pocket change.

• Our Actual Medical Costs Abroad

During the first dozen years of international travel Mary and I spent an aggregate of perhaps $1000 for medical and dental care, religiously obtaining teeth cleanings every six months, dermatological screenings because of excessive exposure to the sun in our youths and other preventative measures. We spent less for medical care in twelve years than the cost of U.S. health insurance for three months.

Our foreign medical consultations have been few, but fruitful. Mary lifted weights for years. Until diagnosed by a genial Greek doctor on Crete she didn't realize that painful joints meant she had carpal tunnel syndrome. The office visit cost $25 and included as many follow-up visits as she wished. The exercises he prescribed completely fixed the problem and she followed them for years. She's stopped lifting weights except when we pause for a few weeks, rent an apartment and she joins a health club. It's difficult to permanently conquer bad habits.

- ## Easy to Find English-Speaking Doctors Overseas

How do travelers find English-speaking doctors abroad? It's easy anywhere in the world and particularly simple for members of IAMAT, the International Association for Medical Advice for Travelers, located at 417 Center Street in Lewiston, NY 14092. Benefits include a world directory of English-speaking doctors plus inoculation information and health suggestions for every country it's possible to visit. Don't leave home without it. Call IAMAT at (716) 754-4883 or check out the IAMAT website at http://iamat.org. The site has links to the Centers for Disease Control and Prevention and the World Health Organization plus charts showing immunizations recommended for every country. Membership is free, though a donation is requested and richly deserved.

- ## Quality and Inexpensive Medical Care Abroad

We set up an emergency fund for medical problems that might occur abroad. In most countries the size of an emergency medical fund can be relatively small. Medical care almost everywhere outside the States is inexpensive. The Centers for Disease Control and Prevention offers an International Traveler's Hotline, (404) 332-4559, with information on current health risks, needed immunizations and precautions for food and water in sixteen world regions. Excellent software is available to diagnose any ache or pain.

We've had teeth cleaned poorly in Spain, excellently in Israel, both well and pathetically in Australia, adequately in Mexico—though a leaky instrument squirted water up my nose—perfunctorily in Chile and in many other places with no adverse consequences, usually with passable competence. All were inexpensive, averaging ten dollars a visit. We've also received excellent dermatological examinations in Australia, Mexico and Europe, plus Bumrungrad in Bangkok, all for a fraction of what they'd cost in the States.

Pharmaceuticals Abroad

Health-related savings are available by buying generic drugs, or drugs from Canada or Mexico. Whoa, buy drugs from a foreign country? Isn't that un-American? Truly, but the companies that manufacture drugs in the United States manufacture identical drugs all over the world. Those who don't trust them outside the States have little reason to trust them inside.

Prescription drugs from Canada cost about half of what the same companies charge in the United States. Drugs in Mexico are even cheaper though duplicates of those manufactured in the States. Out of sincere altruism pharmaceutical companies dispute the quality of Mexican drugs, denigrating their own foreign operations. U.S. Customs will confiscate foreign-bought drugs, if it stumbles across them.

- ## Prescription Drugs Vary by Country

Prescription drugs are a particular government's opinion that adults are unable to make personal decisions without the intervention of Big Brother. Traveling the world opens the eyes to the truth about prescription drugs. All countries have drugs available only by prescription. However, every country's listing is similar to no other country. A prescription drug is what the government has decided can't be bought by an adult unless a doctor first scribbles its okay. Then fork over big bucks to pharmacists who, some hours later, will hand over what every *adult* should be able to buy over the counter. The identical drug in a neighboring country is likely sold over the counter. Half the drugs sold only by prescription in the United States can be bought over the counter in other countries, while such as vitamins are prescription only in many European countries.

If all drugs were sold over the counter without a prescription doctor's fees would drop precipitously, pharmacists would be unemployed and the ultimate cost of many drugs, by excluding the cost of a doctor's visit, would drop by ninety percent. Instead governments treat adult citizens as children, requiring a prescription to feel better or improve health. Without prescriptions some adults would act like children, buying drugs on a whim, without research or for the pleasure of abusing themselves, but many do so anyway and always will. The drug companies run glossy, multi-page ads in expensive magazines urging everyone to ask their doctors to prescribe expensive drugs. Not surprisingly doctors do exactly as asked. After all we're paying them big bucks. Only responsible adults suffer from the government fiat of *prescription* drugs.

- ## Generic Drugs

I always buy generic drugs when they're available though Mary is more reluctant, depending on the drug. Drug companies operate a perfectly legal scam through the Food and Drug Administration, extending the protected date on patented drugs by a perfunctory notification to the FDA that they're *refining* the identical drug. This automatically delays the ability of competing companies to market generic drugs.

Everyone knows generic drugs cost far less than patented drugs and are almost always chemically indistinguishable, though the fillers may vary which may in turn alter the effectiveness. Still, I prefer to buy generic, Canadian or Mexican drugs or drugs in any country of temporary residency—over the Internet or in person. Do an end run around the government, monopolistic drug companies, pharmacists and doctors, whenever and wherever possible.

CHAPTER TWENTY TWO
RVing the World Requires Hanging onto Health

The only way to keep your health is to eat what you don't want, drink what you don't like, and do what you'd rather not. Mark Twain

A medical revolution is not the purpose of this book though anyone could save a packet of money on food *and* greatly improve health by avoiding junk food, expediting a more enjoyable travel experience.

The best money-saver for long-term travel is good health. Eating nutritiously, pursuing a balanced diet and exercising faithfully to keep in shape cancels most health worries. The food we like to eat determines how we feel. The same as we wouldn't burn kerosene in a brand new Hummer we shouldn't cram junk into the only body available. We can buy a new Hummer but we're stuck with one body for which parts are neither readily available nor reasonably priced.

Health in Five Easy Pieces

The traditional food pyramid of five daily veggies, four fruits, a few carbohydrates, some protein—preferably non-animal—and a tiny dab of fat abides as the bible of nutrition. We violate it at our peril, which many do without a thought. If we seriously gave a hoot and worked at a proper diet with regular exercise we'd get rid of most medical expenses and health problems. Instead we jeopardize health with eating plans such as the Atkins diet. Anyone would lose weight eating mostly red meat but in the long run it destroys health, the same as it did for Dr. Atkins. Still people prefer the Atkins diet and Tommy Smothers' advice, *Red meat is not bad for you. Now blue-green meat, that's bad for you!*

• Cut Down on Meat; Slather on Veg

It's easy to eat healthily, reading the old pyramid chart starting with lots of fresh fruits and veggies. Help, people say; they can't stand veggies the same as when they were children and neither could any close relative they've ever had. They're from cattle country, Colorado or Texas, and need a steak at every meal.

Cancel the steaks, though a monthly treat of a million-calorie bacon-cheeseburger is not beyond the pale for those who eat five servings of vegetables and four servings of fruit the other twenty-nine or thirty days a month.

Yuck; how can anyone eat that many vegetables? It's easy. Get the vegetable requirement in one meal, which for Mary and me is lunch. We've grown to love veggies raw, chopped up with a teaspoon of olive oil, which is pure fat with no cholesterol, or crumbles of feta or blue cheese, which is pure fat with an abundance of cholesterol, and a handful of Brazil nuts or your preference. We're partial to a few cloves of chopped garlic, which adds an enormous amount of flavor. Whatever the druthers veggies can easily be made tasty, especially with a favorite bread on the side. Olive oil is good for health and veggies may become someone else's favorite dish. Probably not, though we've become hooked and suffer withdrawal if we miss a day. Buying nutritious food saves a mint and promotes longevity for those who exercise regularly, barring common genetic defects.

• Nutrition Internationally

Traveling internationally promotes a healthy lifestyle because it's easy to find lots of interesting fruits and veggies. Local fruits around the world are usually excellent and because most must be peeled, are safe to eat abroad. Vegetables, unfortunately, require more care because only cucumbers and carrots are routinely peeled. Other vegetables should be washed in bleach, vinegar or iodine water and thoroughly rinsed. This regimen is easily followed for those with a camper bus, van or RV.

• Exercise and Travel

Getting a broad range of exercise is easy abroad, just walking around and gawking. Besides gawking we've followed a strict exercise regimen for years. After several minutes of floor exercises to strengthen abs and back muscles we run two or three miles every day, unless it's raining. These runs have let us explore immediate surroundings, first thing every morning.

I have to run early when I'm still asleep and didn't know any better. But the runs have always revealed interesting locales. We've run with reindeer in Finland, kangaroos in Australia, left way behind by the fast little devils, above fabulous fiords in Norway, past snarling Tasmanian Devils in Tasmania, through little Mexican, Portuguese and Spanish towns, dodging barking dogs, along the Moroccan coastline, through Turkish ruins, on Greek beaches and in dozens of other countries with hundreds of other interesting sights. We've never been bothered by the locals though we've been stared at and became relatively competent at fending off dogs.

• Education and Regular Exercise

Interestingly, health through regular exercise is directly proportionate to formal education. A 2002 report by the CDC found that the percentage of those who engage in vigorous activities for at least twenty minutes, three or more times a week, broke down by educational attainment like this: Master's or doctorate degree, 33.7%; Bachelor's, 30.8%; Associate of Arts, 23.1%; high school graduate 14%; with some high school or less, 7.9%. The better educated the healthier so never stop learning! Unfortunately, most people's idea of exercise is the same as Phyllis Diller's: *a good brisk sit.* As observed by Joey Adams, *If it weren't for the fact that the TV set and the refrigerator are so far apart, some of us wouldn't get any exercise at all.*

• Restaurants and other Dangerous Activities

Eating healthily means seldom eating out; most restaurant food everywhere is high in fat and salt, low on vegetables and fruit. To put restaurant food in perspective most nutritionists figure women age nineteen to fifty need 2200 calories a day; men need 2900. Neither should eat over thirty percent of their calories from fat. Ten percent would be much healthier.

A pound of cheese fries made with one-third pound of cheese, sprinkled with four crumbly slices of bacon, ranch dip on the side, swaggers with 3010 calories, 140% of a woman's daily caloric needs and over a hundred percent needed by men. A woman downing cheese fries would triple her maximum healthy fat intake. The maximum daily fat allowance is three times the healthy consumption of fat, multiplying healthy fat consumption nine-fold.

A 1560-calorie slice of cheesecake from The Cheesecake Factory would constitute over half a man's daily quota of calories and over two thirds of a woman's. A large McDonald's shake represents almost half a woman's daily caloric allotment. These lovely dishes are crammed with fat globules aching to glom onto gut, arteries and thighs—heart attacks and strokes in waiting.

Fast food *restaurants* have recently introduced salads; without the high-in-saturated-fat dressings they'd be decent fodder. But one packet of the dressing constitutes more than the daily-recommended intake of saturated fat, far more than doubling the calories of a naked salad.

True, eating out is less for satisfaction of hunger than for a change of scene and cuisine. The only thing known with certainty is that most restaurant food is high in fat, sodium and often unpalatable. Most restaurant food is a heart attack on a plate—Thailand may an exception. The health hazard and expense of restaurants are two reasons to avoid them. I prefer Mary's cooking and she would almost never rather eat out. Good for her.

Those Exciting Grocery Labels

We could do worse than read grocery store labels, and we do worse. Eating properly conserves our most valuable asset; not the travel kitty but the bod. Unless we last long enough to spend a bulging travel account the treasure will be a boon only to our newly orphaned children. Eat right, stay healthy and spend the kids' inheritance, exactly like we're doing.

Healthy grocery shopping requires reading labels and actually understanding them. How many grams of fat are recommended daily? How many grams of carbohydrates? Aren't measurements in grams un-American anyway? Sure they are. Grams are a measurement used by every country in the world except the good ole U. S. of A. Pounds of fat are more what we adore.

• One Gram of Fat = ___ Calories

Few people have a clue how many calories are in a single gram of fat: there are nine. Grocery labels are meaningless without knowing this number. The daily healthy fat quota for a woman is twenty-four grams and the maximum is seventy-two grams. Beware of misleading labels. They use the maximum fat intake as the norm, often fudging on the math.

A single ounce of butter—pure fat—is twenty-eight grams, more than a woman's healthy daily consumption of fat and near the maximum healthy quota for a man. The maximum daily fat for a woman would be two and a half ounces of butter and a man's would be three ounces. We may average more than three ounces of cheese a day, particularly for pizza aficionados, though cheese is pure fat. We also eat more than three ounces of fat in other dairy products. *Got milk?* means *Got fat?*—except for those drinking skim milk.

• Add Total Fat Consumed

Add the dairy fat we eat to the fat content of meat consumed every day. A Big Mac has thirty-four grams of fat, more than a man or woman's daily healthy intake, while a Whopper will deliver thirty-nine grams of fat. These numbers exclude the French fries in the Big Mac or Whopper Meal, which triple fat calories. Most restaurant meals, especially fast food, exceed the daily healthy allotment of fat many times and the maximum by hundreds of percentage points. However, I confess a weakness for the occasional hot fudge sundae at McDonald's or KFC, a treat when returning from the few undeveloped regions where fast food joints don't yet exist. In Thailand and Vietnam McDonald's or KFC hot fudge sundaes were only fifty cents, now rapidly approaching a dollar. I truly admire Kinsey Millhouse who's able to eat fast food every chance she gets.

But she will likely never expire from the saturated fats fictionally clogging her hearteries.

- ## Not Our Fault

We know our fattening is entirely the food's fault, not ours, as opined by Kathleen Parker in the *Orlando Sentinel* in July 2002. Thus a New York attorney sued McDonald's, Burger King, Wendy's and KFC for forcing his fifty-six-year-old client to eat their yucky food, which resulted in diabetes, obesity, high blood pressure and high cholesterol culminating in two heart attacks. Dang! Big Mac jumped into the poor guy's hand four times a week for decades and practically killed him, ignoring heredity, a career as a potato on a couch and whatever else the gourmet client ate elsewhere. Such a lawsuit is tantamount to saying, as pointed out by Ms. Parker:

I am a really stupid person who has no clue about the world in which I live. It is simply not possible to live in this country and not know that fast food restaurants serve fattening foods. The information is everywhere, very likely including the live, three-dimensional human being standing in line in front of you.

Blame the lawyer, blame the client, blame the culture—we're Americans who have a constitutional right to eat as much fat as we can stomach, as often as humanly possible. Love those hot fudge sundaes.

Mea Culpa

If Mary didn't cook I'd probably eat junk and fast food to excess, in lock-step with my fellow Americans. To enjoy eating healthily requires a cook on the premises. Mary collected cookbooks her entire professional life but like the rest of us, had little or no time to cook and concoct marvelous recipes, which are additionally healthy. When we retired early Mary photocopied the best recipes from her favorite cookbooks, of which she'd accumulated multi-dozens. She put the recipes on index cards and fit a few hundred into one small card box. We've been eating off those recipes for more than sixteen years and haven't touched half. It's more romantic to live fast, love hard, die young and leave a beautiful memory, even if the memory is that retained by ungrateful heirs.

Frozen meals and prepared foods cost several times what we'd pay for the raw ingredients, plus the raw stuff is better for health. We know all this but we're too busy to worry about it, otherwise we wouldn't have time to supervise TV for a national average of three hours a day.

Eating habits are extremely difficult to change. If it weren't for the health angle I wouldn't have mentioned food at all and will now gracefully retire from the subject, because this is the end of the book.

CONCLUSION

We've been traveling for sixteen years and have lived in 147 countries, so far. Perhaps we have another dozen years of physical fitness to see the rest of the 191 countries represented in the United Nations. After many years of travel we've visited barely two-thirds! We still have a few countries left to see in Africa, much of the Arctic including Greenland, the diverse islands of the South Pacific and the bulk of Russia left to explore

To those who've are planning a life outside of work, such as RVing the world, hearty congratulations are in order. We can do anything we set our minds to; we just can't do everything. Keep in touch and we'll leave the lights on, hoping to see readers somewhere down the road, RVing the world.

Made in the USA
Lexington, KY
06 December 2011